ALL THE WAY TO BANTRY BAY
—and other Irish Journeys

ALL THE WAY TO BANTRY BAY

—and other Irish Journeys

by

BENEDICT KIELY

LONDON
VICTOR GOLLANCZ LTD
1978

First published January 1978
Second impression September 1978

Printedi n Great Britain at
The Camelot Press Ltd, Southampton

Dedication

For Brian and Mary and Gary and Catherine,
my English connections in the flat land by the
Ouse.

Acknowledgments

To Douglas Gageby, editor of *The Irish Times*, to Brian Fallon, the literary editor, and to Fergus Linehan, arts editor, Rosemarie Doyle and Shiela Rogers of the editorial staff. To Betty Healy, editor for the Irish Tourist Board (Bord Fáilte) of *Ireland of the Welcomes*: and for the invaluable aid of Tim Magennis of that same organisation. To my fellow-travellers: Séan J. White, Anthony O'Riordan, John Ryan, Patrick Gallagher and David Hanly.

B. K.

CONTENTS

LIST OF ILLUSTRATIONS

Following page 96

Omagh Town on the Strule (*courtesy The Ulster Herald*)

The author at Carleton's cottage with Annie McKenna (*Photo Roy Bedell, courtesy Radio Telefis Eireann*)

Seamus Heaney (*photo Nancy Crampton, courtesy Faber & Faber*)

Patrick Kavanagh (1950) by John Ryan (*courtesy John Ryan*)

The Big Stone at Crolly (*courtesy James Hemmings of Crolly and the Derry Journal*)

Errigal, the Cock o' the North, Co. Donegal (*courtesy Irish Tourist Board: Bord Fáilte*)

Coolbanagher Church Emo, Portlaoise (*photo Michael Scully, courtesy Irish Tourist Board: Bord Fáilte*)

The Spanish Arch, old Galway (*courtesy Irish Tourist Board: Bord Fáilte*)

Galway City today (*courtesy Irish Tourist Board: Bord Fáilte*)

Lough Gill, Co. Sligo (*courtesy Irish Tourist Board: Bord Fáilte*)

In the Clare Glens near Nenagh, Co. Tipperary (*photo Douglas Duggan, courtesy The Irish Press*)

The Main Guard, Clonmel, Co. Tipperary (*courtesy Irish Tourist Board: Bord Fáilte*)

The Suir and Kilsheelan Bridge (*courtesy Mary M. Thornton, Garden House, Newtown Anner and the Clonmel Nationalist*)

Rock of Cashel, Co. Tipperary (*courtesy Irish Tourist Board: Bord Fáilte*)

Following page 176

The Virgin Mary's Rock, West Cork

On the Healy Pass, Co. Cork (*courtesy Irish Tourist Board: Bord Fáilte*)

Puxley Hall beside site of Dunboy Castle, Castletownbere, Co. Cork (*courtesy Irish Tourist Board: Bord Fáilte*)

Rathmelton on Lough Swilly

Coomhola: the valley of a million sheep (*courtesy Irish Tourist Board: Bord Fáilte*)

FOREWORD

These journeys or revisits begin in the North in the spring of 1969 before the horrors began in that part of Ireland. So that I looked on some other aspects of Ulster than those we read about, with deepening gloom, in the newspapers day after day.

The seeds of evil were there as we all know and then knew; but there was nothing that would not have been, and has not been, made infinitely worse by the actions of fanatics, madmen or plain, blunt criminals, on one side or the other.

The only solutions were in reason and neighbourly decency and, fortunately, there are many people who still believe in them. Something, sometime, may come of that.

But this is not a book about the Ulster problem, nor the Irish problem, nor any problem. It is about revisits, if not to past scenes of delight, at least to some Irish places that have always pleased me.

B. K.

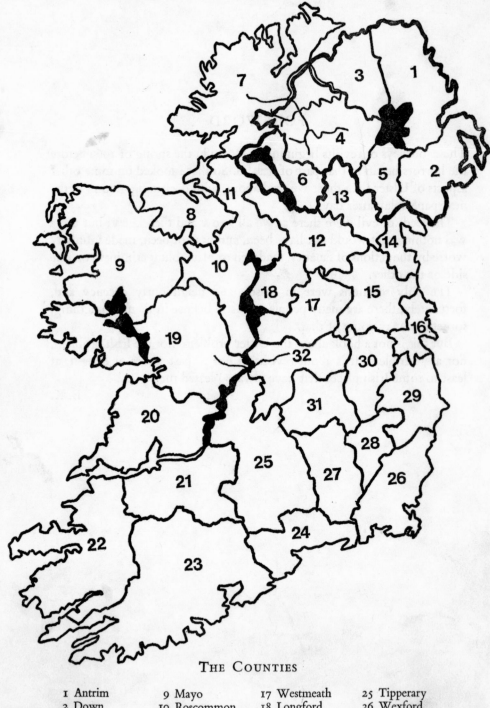

The Counties

1 Antrim	9 Mayo	17 Westmeath	25 Tipperary
2 Down	10 Roscommon	18 Longford	26 Wexford
3 Derry	11 Leitrim	19 Galway	27 Kilkenny
4 Tyrone	12 Cavan	20 Clare	28 Carlow
5 Armagh	13 Monaghan	21 Limerick	29 Wicklow
6 Fermanagh	14 Louth	22 Kerry	30 Kildare
7 Donegal	15 Meath	23 Cork	31 Laoighis
8 Sligo	16 Dublin	24 Waterford	32 Offaly

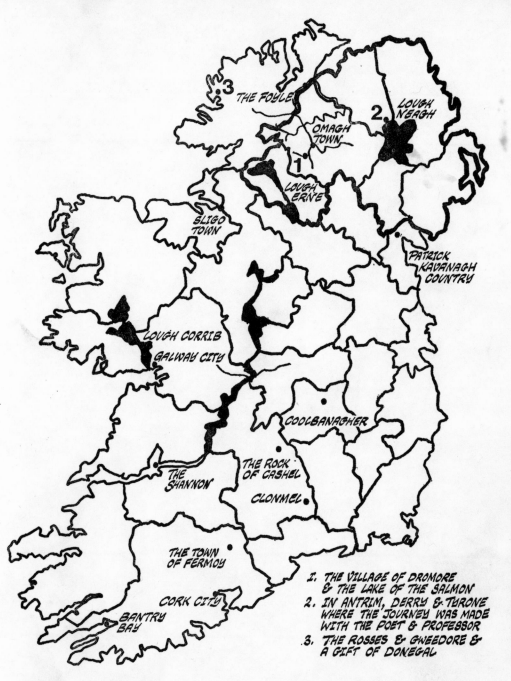

THE FOYLE

OMAGH TOWN

LOUGH NEAGH

2.

1

LOUGH ERNE

SLIGO TOWN

PATRICK KAVANAGH COUNTRY

LOUGH CORRIB

GALWAY CITY

COOLBANAGHER

THE SHANNON

THE ROCK OF CASHEL

CLONMEL

THE TOWN OF FERMOY

1. THE VILLAGE OF DROMORE & THE LAKE OF THE SALMON
2. IN ANTRIM, DERRY & TYRONE WHERE THE JOURNEY WAS MADE WITH THE POET & PROFESSOR
3. THE ROSSES & GWEEDORE & A GIFT OF DONEGAL

CORK CITY

BANTRY BAY

APPROXIMATE INDICATION OF PLACES MENTIONED IN THE BOOK

I

TO THE LAKE OF THE SALMON

EVERY MAN WAS RELEVANT

The little Ulster town below there in the hollow is compact, all of a piece, a neat unity of about 600 people. Morning smoke hovers over the roofs. The air is very still, and sunny.

In the rookery by the priest's house higher up the ridge the rooks keep up an extraordinary conversation. If you listen for a space of time to a parliament of rooks it becomes apparent that they have something to talk about. There is a pattern of voice and note, treble and bass and everything in between, that is comically, or alarmingly, human.

I am standing in an old graveyard where unclipped unkempt grass has, over the seasons, been beaten down into a solid mass, shiny and yellow, that seems to rise and fall like the waves of the sea. Old headstones rise up out of it, jagged rocks out of water. A few dogs doing their morning rounds sneak over the grass or flex themselves in the sunshine. The fragment of a toy machine-gun, left behind by some child, lies in a hollow of the yellow shining sea. These toys are so well made nowadays that for a moment it looks alarmingly real. Children come up here to play at war in the middle of this ancient peace.

There is very little left of the ruins of an old parish church. The first reference to this parish is in 1521 when, as a priest and historian who is a friend of mine has written: "The parish priest was Father Felim McSorley. By that time the Omagh branch of the ruling O'Neill house of Ulster controlled this district. And we are told in the Irish annals that they hanged here in Dromore, in 1528, two of their royal cousins—Henry O'Neill of Castletown at Fintona and his son, Cormac."

A cousinly trick to be at, i'faith.

But the power of the O'Neills passed at the battle of Kinsale, and at the Ulster Plantation (1610–11) in came the Mervyn family who lasted until the middle of the eighteenth century when they declined and were succeeded by the Lords Belmore. Which reminds me that the first time I ever had a haircut in a barber's saloon, as they were then called, the only other customer at that moment was the then Earl of Belmore: a big man with big feet and a straw boater and a striped blazer. The haircut cost me, or my father, fourpence which was then the juvenile rate. But I saw the earl give the barber a £5 note and take no change. He had the reputation for being generous.

But my clerical historical friend has this also to say: "Today perhaps the east gable and window of the old ruins here are about all that survive of the 14th–15th-century church of the days of the O'Neills." And there it is, woebegone and desolate, below me; and the headstone on which I lean, while nothing as old as the fragment of the old church, has also its respectable antiquity. It says that it was erected by Mathew McEleer of Classan in memory of his wife, Mary, who departed this life March 29th, A.D. 1829. Aged 89 years.

Which means that she was born five years before the Scots and some of the Irish were out with Bonnie Charlie. She was carried up this road to be buried just 90 years before I was carried up it to be baptised in the church over the ridge beyond the priest's house and the haranguing rooks.

Rest your soul, Mary McEleer, and the souls of all who lie under the shiny yellow waves of neglected grass.

My friend, John Hewitt the poet, will forgive me if here in this old graveyard in the morning I steal a few lines from his poem "Townland of Peace" and shout them out to the rooks. There is nobody else to hear me at the moment: the dogs have moved on. But who knows if rooks may not understand, as readily as dogs do, what men say.

One day during the Hitler war John went walking by the southern shore of Lough Neagh where his people came from.

> Once walking in the country of my kindred
> up the steep road to where the tower-topped mound
> still hoards their bones, that showery August day
> I walked clean out of Europe into peace:
> for every man I met was relevant,
> gathering fruit or shouting to his horse,
> sawing his timber, measuring his well.
> The little appletrees with crooked arms
> that almost touched the bright grass with
>   the weight
> of their clenched fruit, the dappled calves that
>   browsed
> under the melting sunlight of the orchard,
> the white hens slouching round the rusty
>   trough,

the neat-leafed damsons with the smoky
  beads
the rain had failed to polish, and the farms
back from the road but loud with dog and
  can
and voices moving, spelt no shape of change,
belonging to a world and to an age
that has forgotten all its violence,
save when a spade rasps on a
  rusty scabbard.

That was Ulster at peace—almost 40 years ago.

In the main street of the village a man says to me: "I mind the time your father left here to go to Omagh. It would be about 1920, not too long after you were born, so you can't remember much about this place. It wasn't until the 1920s that the Munster and Leinster bank came up into these parts. Before that it was all the Ulster bank. We had one grand old tyrant of a manager here, a staunch Free Mason, buried with all his regalia. When a client came into him he might say: 'First things first, sir, take off your hat'."

PEARSE AND THE COUNTRY PARSON

Patrick Pearse came up this steep road from the little town: to his left the old ruin and the graveyard, to his right the priest's house and the talkative rookery. He crossed the ridge to the parish church, was welcomed by the parish priest and spoke to the people. Not from the altar rails, though, as he was asked. He seems to have been rather diffident. He stood a little down into the body of the church and spoke very quietly. Nobody, among those who were there and are still with us, seems to have much recollection of what he said. It was only when, seven years or so afterwards, the 1916 Rising happened and Pearse and the others died by the firing squad that people remembered he had passed that way.

But in the days of Father Mathew, the celebrated temperance reformer, there was a rare ecumenical meeting in that church. Granted, the subject was not doctrine but booze, or rather anti-booze, Ireland sober is Ireland free and all that jazz. Yet it still must have been a momentous occasion. Father Monaghan, the Roman Catholic curate of the time (the 1830s), invited the Presbyterian minister, a Mr Dill, to speak in the Catholic church at a great temperance demonstration with a visit by Father

Mathew, who came from the far province of Munster. The Church of Ireland rector, a Mr St George, was also invited but declined. The church-by-law-established took a distant view of both papist and dissenter. Consider the attitude even of that friend of liberty, Jonathan Swift. And the 1830s, too, was the worst period of the Tithe War which may have caused Mr St George to have a snuffle in his nose. Or it may have been that he just liked his book and his bottle.

The Rev. Mr Dill, in 1888, wrote about it in his *Autobiography of a Country Parson*:

Although some of my people objected to my acceptance of Fr Monaghan's invitation, my own mind told me that I shouldn't allow bigotry to prevent me helping in a good cause, even in a Romish house of worship. Before the celebration of Mass, Fr Monaghan, with the nicest consideration, took me into the vestry, requesting me to stay there until after mass when he would come for me.

In due time he made his appearance and conducted me to the altar, where were seated a number of priests and others. There couldn't have been fewer than three thousand, all standing, and so closely packed together in that immense building that when one moved, the whole mass moved. I was introduced by Fr Mathew to the audience who gave me a most enthusiastic reception. I was cheered to the echo: hats and caps were thrown up, without any danger of their falling to the ground or being trampled upon.

What a careful Presbyterian he was, keeping an eye out to see that nobody ruined a hat or a cap! What a splendid scene in a church, as novel to him, he said, as to everybody else: a Presbyterian minister addressing a Roman Catholic congregation from the altar!

True for him, nor has it happened often since. What cause or crisis or calamity could bring Ian Paisley to the pulpit in the pro-cathedral in Dublin? There could always be, of course, the atom bomb or/and the ineluctable day of wrath. But on the day on which Paisley leads the Roman Catholic Pioneer Total Abstinence Association on a rally to Croke Park in Dublin then I'll know that Ireland is at last united—and the publicans may organise their own civil-rights movement.

This great white house stands square and solid on a Tyrone hillslope that is marked with daffodils, and to the right-hand side of a road that leads from Dromore to the village of Drumquin. In the sunshine of a pet of an April day it is as brightly white as the best of washing powders are supposed to make fabrics. The priest-historian at the wheel of the car says: "A most interesting lady lives in that house. A *Cumann na Mban* girl, a revolutionary, in the days when Pearse talked in the church back there in Dromore. We'll say good-day as we pass."

Which we do, and are courteously welcomed. A fine house, a spacious sitting-room, a lady with a decided Scottish accent talking about her recent trip to Derry to join the civil-rights marches (this is 1969); talking about John Hume and Ivan Cooper; about the thorn bushes at the Long Tower Church in Derry sacred to the name of St Colmcille and close to the walls of Derry sacred to the names of the Rev. Mr Walker and the Apprentice Boys who closed the Ferry Gate against the soldiers of James Stuart. The jostling mixum-gatherum of Irish history is all around us, but what country isn't in a similar state and, God above, think of what America has gatherumed and mixumed in a short two centuries.

She talks about books and music and about her family. Family photographs are all around us, a large number of them of young people in graduation robes in Irish or Scottish universities. The link with Scotland is very strong. It is a house that we leave with reluctance, solid and square and set on that Tyrone hillslope as if it and the hillslope and the world would last forever. It has that air of security and cultivation and peace: a house and a place that have been well cared-for and for a long time. A great house for a graduate or for anybody to come home to.

Our road goes on around Dooish mountain. Up there in a sheltered corner there's a house built in the 1930s by a returned-American couple: my aunt who was also my godmother and her husband. They spent most of their lives in Philadelphia and returned in the end to settle in Ireland. They lie in peace now, and God be good to them, in Langfield churchyard not far from Drumquin. When they came back from the States they could have had their choice of landed properties in the flat land near the big town: Omagh. But it was their ambition or nostalgia to wish to build on the very site where the man had been born and reared.

They did so. The house was built. The builder had gone to school with the man who employed him, for old time's sake. Music built the towers of Troy and a good deal of merriment and malt whiskey went into the building, up there on the mountain where the fields meet the moor, of as neat a fragment—apart from central heating—of the American home as you could possibly imagine. I wonder who lives up there now. Do they realise anything of the passion and pride that conquered the wet Irish mountain and brought two worlds quite happily together?

"Does it prove," I say to my companion, "that, in spite of Thomas Wolfe, a man can go home again?"

"It proves," he says, "that a returned exile who lives, as they used to say in the Gaeltacht, *eadar dha shaoghal*, between two worlds, can draw those two worlds together. But just for a moment of fantasy. He was born here and here he had his first vision of happiness—and his last."

So, as we go on, I quote the Reverend Marshall of Sixmilecross:

> *Sure I know that just a stranger*
> *Sees no beauty there at all,*
> *Sure I know him and forgive him*
> *That his rapture is but small,*
> *For the song my heart is singing*
> *Strangers never heard it sung,*
> *And the secret of Dunmullen*
> *You must find it when you're young.*

Our road turns south into high moorland dotted with small farms and neat houses—and on towards the border of County Fermanagh. As guide and navigator I go half-blindfold, depending on a memory that has not been polished-up since 1937. Or was it 1936 when I last came up this road to fish, high on the mountain, in the lost glimmering lake of the salmon? Did salmon ever get up there to spawn along the lake's gravelly fringes? Or was it just one mystical salmon that gave the place its name, Loch a'bhradain, some salmon of wisdom that came from the Atlantic by way of the many-islanded Erne? For we are over the watershed now and away from the influence of the Foyle.

This corner of the road I remember: a steep right-angled bend at a bumpy bridge. The road is surfaced now as it wasn't then, because I recall the way the loose stones shot from under my bicycle wheels when the brakes gave, and how the man, leading the horse and cart up the hill, let go the horse and crossed himself—the faith being strong in these mountains—as I shot past like a rocket between himself and the hedge. It was not precisely a Proustian moment, but the memory is still vivid. Apart from the surfacing the road hasn't changed much.

"Further along here," I say, "there should be a small schoolhouse on the left."

"You've an elephant's own memory," he says, "there it is."

There it is, indeed, but closed and abandoned, windows shuttered forever, the pupils who would have gone there travelling now by bus to bigger places. The teacher here that I remember was a tall red-headed laughing girl, a Kavanagh from the green mountains of Pomeroy in East Tyrone. She later became a Loreto nun.

"And here to the right there should be a boreen."

There is. But just at this moment something goes wrong. We drive a few yards and see, just in time, that it isn't possible to drive any further. The house is visible over there to the left where I remember it. But either my memory is unstrung or the house is abandoned. For no traffic but cattle or kneebooted men could follow that track. Being neither, we yet bravely leave the car and go forward, floundering, sinking in black earth, we climb one fence and then another and come to the street before the house where the mystery is made plain. For there stands a huge motor-car, and a new motorway opens out to the public highway, and the old cart-track abandoned. One should have remembered that in almost 50 years the automobile would have conquered even this quiet corner of Tyrone-Fermanagh as it has conquered everywhere from Bomacatall to Bali. As has also the television. This house at the moment has two sets. Otherwise things are much as they were. A canary chirps in a cage. But scarcely the same canary. The kettle is on the hob. The welcome is as warm as ever.

Once a man lived in this house who was tall, musical, a great lilter. It was said of him that once he lilted all night for the dancers in a country house when the fiddler failed to turn up. He was also a wonder with his hands and could take a bit of a stick and carve it into a usable table-knife or a whistle as good as you'd buy in a music shop. Music drew music to it. Three brothers, pipers and fiddlers, used constantly to frequent the house and, with them, all the young people who wanted to dance. It was the showband country of the time. Now his son stands before me—as fine a man as his father. I ask him about the three brothers.

"Two dead. Peter's alive but bedridden. But he'd play the fiddle if you asked him.'

The three of us cross the fields behind the house, down a rocky bushy slope that I remember as a great place for hedgehogs, across a stream that had crayfish, up a hill that's as near to perpendicular as makes no difference to ageing knees. There across the moorland is the Lake of the Salmon, more secret now than ever, for new dark forestry lines the far shore and the lake has been made a protected reservoir for two or three neighbouring small towns.

We look down on the townlands of Meenmossa, Marrock and Garrison Glebe. Pillars of smoke from the burning of furze and scutch-grass stand in a dozen places all over the wild slanting hills. Over there is the glint of the Erne and the smoke, not of furze-burning, but of the chimneys of the town of Ederney in County Fermanagh. The smoke of the village of Drumquin, in the County Tyrone, we can't see, since it's hidden from us by the very hills above Drumquin that Felix Kearney of Clanabogan wrote about in his ballad:

> Drumquin you're not a city
> But you're all the world to me,
> Your lot I'll never pity
> Should you never larger be;
> For I love you as I loved you
> When on schooldays I did run
> On my homeward journey through you
> To the hills above Drumquin.

Our host tells us: "I was over the mountain in Drumquin last on Ascension Thursday. And damned but if I ever saw so many drunk men in my life. Three-by-three and arm-in-arm and staggering back and forward across the street from one pub to the next. So I spoke my thoughts to a man I know there and he said quite casually: 'Surely. Isn't it a holy day of obligation?' "

Then, as if embarrassed by his own irreverence, this modest man of mountainy places points across the valley to where the sunlight semaphores on some white object. "That's Gortnasole," he says, "where James and Bridget McVey put up a marble calvary in 1957 on the site of a homestead from which they say a McVey was evicted by the then landlord in the days of the land war. They're a famous family around here. James and Bridget made a fortune in England and they put up the crucifix to the honour and glory of God in abiding gratitude for his manifold blessings. That's what the writing says.

"We'll cross over and see it," he says. "As we go up to it you'll see two of the tidiest farmhouses in Ireland. But we'll have to be wary crossing James Cassidy's street. There's a gobbling turkey-cock there that would eat an ostrich."

A PAISLEY PARADE

The Swinging Bars in Omagh town, where I was reared, is a place where three roads meet or the road splits into three—all depending on which way you're heading. Nobody seems to know how the place got its curious name. It was the right place for the civil-rights marchers (in the spring of 1969) to begin their marching, for it is, more or less, still the town's end even though suburbia has in the last twenty years spread far over hill and dale. The courthouse towards which they were marching for the meeting and speeches is a fine eighteenth-century, Doric-fronted building and high on a hill it is the crown and top of the town—except for the soaring, limping, imitation-Gothic spires of the Roman Catholic church. The town has about 15,000 people not counting the British soldiers—a lot of them these days—in the barracks.

There is more to the Swinging Bars than merely being the town's end. In the angle between two of the three branching or contributory roads, one of the two going to Mountfield and Cookstown, the other to Carrickmore, there stands a house. In my time in the town it was inhabited by a Doctor Brien O'Brien who was, I believe, of the family of that William Smith O'Brien whose statue stands in O'Connell Street in Dublin for being, perhaps, the most gentlemanly rebel who ever rebelled against the British crown and who was sentenced to death (commuted to transportation) for his part in the effort of the Young Ireland movement to rise in revolution in 1848.

That house was also the house in which Alice Milligan, the poetess, whom I had the privilege of knowing in her last years in the early '40s in the old rectory in Mountfield village, spent at least portion of her childhood, and the garden around it would have been the garden she was remembering when she wrote her celebrated poem about the Fenians, the revolutionaries of 1867:

> To hear of a night in March,
> And loyal folk waiting
> To see a great army of men
> Come devastating ——
>
> An army of papists grim,
> With a green flag o'er them,
> Red coats and black police
> Flying before them.
>
> But God (who our nurse declared
> Guards British dominions)
> Sent down a deep fall of snow
> And scattered the Fenians. . . .
>
> But one little rebel there,
> Watching all with laughter,
> Thought 'when the Fenians come
> I'll rise and go after.'

"Ah well," Mr Paisley might say, "wouldn't that be the right place for the civil-rights rebels to put forward whichever foot they put forward."

But along the route of that march there was, as we all know, a blockade or boom of Paisleyites. We all saw the picture in the newspapers: Union Jacks on broomsticks; and hard faces, not of Omagh townspeople but of rural people from the small, bitter, unchangeable townlands. To the left of the picture there's a building, the name above the wide windows legible: J. B. Anderson. It's a big furniture and drapery store that once had as an employee Ian Paisley's father who came from one of those secretive townlands and who took religion very seriously and later went east to found a tabernacle, I'm told, and to ordain his eloquent son.

It's a long march, indeed, but not in miles, from the place where the poetess as a girl played in the garden to the house where the preacher's father worked.

Is it that a while on the American academic circuit has set me seeing symbols everywhere? To think that when, in sixth grade in the Christian Brothers in that town, I first read *Moby Dick*, I thought it was a story about a one-legged man chasing a white whale.

This and other matters absorb my priest-historian friend and myself as he drives out of his gateway and past the squabbling rookery, and we head towards the border, and Clones in the County Monaghan for a meeting of the Clogher Historical Society.

Here, where the road splits left for Fintona and right for Trillick and Enniskillen, there is, for those who know the history of the place, a shadow over the fields. An evil thing happened here on one of the dark days or nights of 1920 when the men from the blind bitter townlands came in to take the town and teach the Fenians. They could find only three young men who may or may not have had anything to do with the IRA of the period but who were, at any rate, brutally murdered at this dividing of the road. The Dromore murders, as they are still called, became part of the black folklore of the countryside and in the days of my boyhood it was commonly said that any man who had hand, act or part in what happened on that unfortunate night would never die in his bed. Two tragic accidental deaths of the time were pointed to in proof. One was quite freakish.

The victim was walking home by night through a low-lying part of Omagh town close to where two rivers, the Drumragh and the Camowen, meet to form a third, the Strule. The road was under a foot of water which had lifted the iron cover of a manhole. When the flood subsided the corpse was found stuck in the manhole.

Another man was, because of his reputation, the object of the scientific curiosity of some of the townspeople. He has since died in his bed. Was the legend thus proved to be a lie? Or was he simply not here on the night of the murders?

About this sombre matter I find that I wrote down in April, 1969, these guilelessly optimistic words:

One can only find comfort—if there is any comfort to be found—in the hope that such unhappy things belong not to the present or the future in this country but to a black past, the sort of past that William Carleton, the novelist, who came from these parts, meant when, in his unfinished autobiography, he wrote about the Clogher valley of South Tyrone in the years after the rebellion of 1798. He was born in 1794.

One night in mid-winter the house of Carleton's father was raided by the Orange yeomanry who said there was a gun concealed therein. They called his father a liar. They called his mother a liar. They jabbed his sister in the side with a bayonet because the bed in which she lay might conceal a gun; and, when she screamed with pain, one of the yeomen, more humane than the others, called the man who used the bayonet a cowardly scoundrel. In the end they discovered that the cause of the trouble was a toy gun given to one of the Carleton children by Sam Nelson, a neighbouring Protestant, a good-natured slob of a man. Sam's brother was one of the raiding yeomen. The Carletons were Catholics.[1]

Long afterwards Carleton commented:

Merciful God! In what a frightful condition was the country at that time. I speak now of the north of Ireland. It was then, indeed, the seat of Orange ascendancy and irresponsible power. To find a justice of the peace not an Orangeman would have been an impossibility. The grand jury room was little less than an Orange lodge. There was then no law *against* an Orangeman, and no law *for* a Papist.

Carleton died in 1869 and would have written all that sometime in the previous ten years.

In 1969 a hopeful man said to me: "For the old-fashioned bigot, Orange or Green, the writing is on the wall."

But another man, an Omagh cynic, said: "The old-fashioned bigot can't or won't read."

ON ACROSS THE BORDER

"And here," says my friend, "is the house you were born in. You may be interested to know that the townland name is given wrongly in the baptismal register."

"A simple plaque," says I modestly, "should set that right. Nothing elaborate. Limestone quarried near the spot. That sort of thing."

Back in Dromore the people had said: "You left there as an infant. You'd remember nothing about it."

"But I was back for a visit at the age of ten when John McPeake lived in the house."

"You've a memory, anyway."

Memory lives precariously on what the eyes have seen and the ears heard. On taste, too. See Proust. Also, I suppose, on smell and touch. There was an orchard here to the right hand where, at the age of ten, I tossed apples from the trees, and ate them. Now there are only a few crippled mossy trees. That was more than 40 years ago and nine years after the murders.

My memory is of one house, not of two stuck together. Was it always that way? Both are empty and nobody here to enlighten us.

What the ears have heard repeated over the years is more durable. That gable window, now, was broken by a bullet the night the IRA raided the mail-train at Dromore Road station, the width of a meadow away from the house. The house dog, Gyp, whom I was too young ever to know, disappeared that night to return a week later, whimpering and terrified and glad to be home. It was suspected that the raiders had muzzled and kidnapped the dog in case he'd betray them by barking.

"And wasn't there a lake somewhere hereabouts where I heard my elder brother say he used to fish with Mr Beatty, the station-master? Wasn't it visible from the train going west to the sea at Bundoran?"

"Galbally Lake. Old swords were found there once. The name means the place of the foreigners. And Gallogley's a common name hereabouts. The gallowglasses. The foreign warriors. The MacDonalds of the Isles."

The elder brother told me that in Easter Week, 1916, when we didn't have the instant enlightenment of television and when rumour, painted all over with tongues, as the man said, was running wild on the roads, a travelling woman called Nan the Rat stepped over this threshold and told my father and mother that the rebels had entered Strabane with fixed bayonets. My brother was then nine. He remembers feeling sorry for the rebels who couldn't afford good new bayonets and had to used fixed ones, tied up with string or stuck together with glue. He wasn't too clear as to what a bayonet was. In Belfast and the Bogside today the nine-year-olds are wiser in the ways of the world.

The road definitely rises with us. That high ridge, to the right, with the television booster-mast is Broughter mountain.

Up on top of Broughter, as we both know, there's a windblown peace and the air vibrating with skylarks, and a view of the long waters of the Erne, and the shining white cone of Errigal mountain on the edge of the open Atlantic, and the hills of Quilcha where the Shannon rises from a mysterious enchanted pool, and the bare head of Ben Bulben that stayed to the end in the vision of Yeats. Errigal is a roughened version of the Latin word, *oraculum*, a praying-place. The saints went to pray to the tops of the mountains.

In our mythology, Diarmuid the handsome who eloped round Ireland with red-headed Grainne, pursued by Finn, the enraged and two-timed master of heroes, died on the side of Ben Bulben from a wound inflicted by an angry and magical boar. He might have lived had not Finn allowed the life-giving water to trickle through the fingers of his cupped hands and go to waste in the ground. In the civil war of 1922 young men were shot dead on that same mountain. In 1970 five men in a BBC van on its way up to that television booster were blown to bits on Broughter mountain. From which you can see Ben Bulben.

Our landscape is still so peaceful and beautiful and unspoiled in so many places that it is often easy to think that we live in peace.

We are crossing the Barr of Fintona: which means the high place near the little town of Fintona. "I wish," says my friend, "that all the schools here would at least give the children enough Irish to let them know what the placenames mean. You'd be amazed at the number of people who think this place was called after some pub."

We go on towards Tempo, Maguiresbridge, Lisnaskea. The first and the last time I travelled this road was in 1936 and I was going to the funeral of a schoolfriend. The dead who died when they were young with you are a different sort of people. Is it simply that the things, good and bad, that have happened to you since, have not happened to them and that when you think of them you are young again in a melancholy sort of way?

There were four of us, knocking about together and all in our sixteenth year: TT, FF, LLL, and myself. Those, in truth, were their initials. TT was gentle, slow moving, tall, one of those young fellows with such long legs and such big feet that on the football field they actually get in their own way. He was swept to the hospital from his lodgings one night and was dead before morning from peritonitis. In incomprehension we followed his coffin to somewhere near here, in the hills above Tempo. The old parish priest preached a brief, moving panegyric but it wasn't half grand enough for the three intellectuals from the big town. So as the writer of the three I was delegated by the other two to report on the funeral for our local nationalist paper, *The Ulster Herald*, and to substitute a fitting panegyric for the parish priest's pitiful effort. It was the only sermon of mine that was ever published and I have since often wondered did the old priest read it and, if so, did he think he was going crazy.

Two things that escapade taught me about newspapers.

Grandly I had written of: "The Guerdon of Eternal Life". *There* was a phrase, by the sacred name of Cyrano de Bergerac, who also wrote behind a mask and gave burning words to another man, a phrase, indeed, to sweep the stars away from the blue threshold. It was misprinted as Querdon: which is a good word, mind you, in its own way.

Also: when with great temerity I brought my masterpiece to the editor's office—he was Anthony Mulvey, a gentleman, a fine journalist, an Irish nationalist member of the Westminster parliament—I was sent further seeking him to the office of Mr Parkes, the editor of the local unionist paper: *The Tyrone Constitution*. There I found the two of them drinking tea in perfect amity.

What, thinks I in my learned wrath, is this Bacon and Bungay out of somewhere in Thackeray? Being young and foolish I was unaware that journalists, regardless of politics, have frequently learned to live and work together in which, perhaps, they manage to set a good example.

We cross that blighted Border which the unfortunate British army have since been trying to pinpoint or something by blowing holes in the roads, a great imperial annoyance to neighbouring shopkeepers and small farmers. They who ruled the seven seas now blow up bridges at Crossmaglen and lesser places little marked on maps.

We come to the town of Clones and to *Cumann Seanchais Chlochair*, the Clogher Historical Society: Clogher is a diocese and also the name of one of the five small towns of the Clogher valley in South Tyrone.

Marcus Burke, a lawyer and historian, is down from Dublin to give a diverting talk on the early days of the Gaelic Athletic Association at the beginning of the century, when athletics were used by the Irish Republican Brotherhood as a cover for revolution: the Carbonari were in among the hurlers and the footballers. Diverting: because Burke (who has written a good book on John O'Leary, the Fenian revolutionary who inspired Yeats the poet) takes a lot of the matter for his lecture from the files of the

Royal Irish Constabulary, the upholders at the time of British law and order. In those files every man who kicked a ball or swung a hurling-stick was noted down as some class of subversive.

It reminds one crazily of Gogol's *Dead Souls*. All those harassed constables taking notes and notes, at sermons, sports-meetings, everywhere. Divil a bit wonder the sons and grandsons of RIC men were so literate as to do almost as much for our literature as the sons and grandsons of Protestant rectors.

Nowadays in the age of McLuhan and the new media the Royal Ulster Constabulary and the Special Air Services of the British army may (Bondwise) have tape-recorders in the heels of their boots or in places even more secret. No future there for literature.

2

THE ELK AND THE PONDEROSA

THE LONGEST WALL IN IRELAND

The estate wall that seems to line all the roads around Antrim town must be the longest structure of its kind in Ireland, and a good second in these islands to Hadrian's Wall and, in the wide world, to the Great Wall of China—that is, if the Great Wall is still there, or ever was.

But even long walls built by lords, to keep themselves in and the tenantry and/or peasantry out, must nowadays give way before motor-roads; and the new widened road from Belfast to Derry, or the other way about, is just now crashing through a corner of the Massareene meadows and woods, outraging the bluebells which came late this year and had clearly determined to hang on as long as they could. Let us hope that his lordship has been duly compensated, unlike the decent woman near Reading, in Berkshire, who lived in Rose Cottage, the view from the latticed windows of which hadn't altered in three and a half centuries until the makers of the M4 motorway made their mark noisily on the land, 50 yards from her door.

Get the cars quickly from here to there, or there to here, and the hell with rose-trellised cottages and bluebell woods.

In Antrim town where, in 1798, the tyrant stood and tore our ranks with ball, the merchants of the place have made with each other, for every Wednesday, an amicable gentlemanly arrangement. This Wednesday you close. Next Wednesday I close. That way somebody has a free Wednesday every fortnight, and a chance to stay in bed in the morning instead of a free half-day every week. That half-day was never much use to anybody.

Meditating on this arrangement, and wondering is it widely spread throughout the towns of Ireland, the poet and myself look at the books—all four of them—in the window of a closed shop. The professor who is a native of Manhattan has crossed the street to the post-office, which is open, to send a cablegram to his native village where nothing ever seems to close except the pubs on a Sunday morning.

One of the books in the window is called *In Green Pastures*, and by all outward appearances, for there are times when you can judge a book by the cover, it's the sort of book that a good Protestant girl would get as a prize at Sunday school. Startlingly, it lies in the window side-by-side with Norman Mailer's *The American Dream*. The cablegram the professor is sending would almost breathe, in passing, its aerial angelic breath on Norman Mailer if he happened, at this moment, to be in the El Quixote, a good Spanish place on 23rd Street. But then the time is different there and in Manhattan it's both too late in the morning and too early in the morning for the El Quixote to be open. For over there now it is the heavenly lull when even barmen may sleep. When a Broadway barman says goodnight . . . because of the muggers and rapists the babies may nowadays go home earlier.

At any rate, on a sunny morning in Antrim town, Norman Mailer rests in a shop-window between the Sunday schoolgirl's prize, *In Green Pastures*, and *The Schoolgirl's Pocketbook*—a tantalising sort of a title. For what would a schoolgirl wish to find, and constantly refer to, in her pocketbook? Did anyone ever find out what Katy did at school? Smoke pot? Or what Katy did next?

But the shop is closed and we will never know what is in that pocketbook.

It gladdens my heart to see that the fourth book in the window is as near as anything could be to being a local classic: Alexander Irvine's *My Lady of the Chimney Corner*. Let's hope that it's being read in Antrim town and all over the north-eastern corner of Ireland for we still have a lot to learn from Alexander Irvine's gentle, sentimental, pawkily (it's the only adverb but a bloody awful one) humorous memories of his father, Jamie, who was a shoemaker and who, in the days just before the great starvation of 1847, married a Papist called not Brigid McGinn but Anna Gilmore.

Once upon a time this little book was what you might call a bestseller in the North—or somewhere—and to be found in the hole in the wall behind many a hearth. For I see that my own copy of it, dated 1916, was the twelfth impression since the book was published in 1913 in London. So that it was circulating well during momentous years.

Irvine's mother was a quiet wise lady who ruled her world and helped her neighbours from her seat in the chimney corner. Because of the blackness of our hearts or the thickness of our heads the book is still, alas, very much a tract for the times. Jamie Irvine and Anna Gilmore contracted what is oddly called a mixed marriage: as if there were, all other things being unequal and natural, any other sort. But neither in Jamie, the Protestant, nor Anna, the Papist, was there any fanaticism or bigotry. Love drew them together. Religion could not hold them apart. All through the book Irvine makes the point that the way in which they managed to live in harmony could have been a shining example to their countrymen. It still could be.

Their parents object to the wedding. The priest won't marry them. The vicar does.

"Sufferin' will be your portion in this life," the girl's mother says, "an' in the world t' come separation from your man." Catholics and Protestants, you see, go to a different eternity.

They are natives of Belfast. After the wedding they walk out of the city and stop at the first place where four roads meet. He is inclined for Dublin. She opts to go back to Belfast. So Jamie stands his staff on end and lets it fall fair, and it points towards Antrim town. On the road between Moira and Antrim they come on Willy Withers the stone-breaker, as cynically wise as stone-breakers always were supposed to be. He doesn't think much of the choice of destination made by Jamie's staff.

"Antrim's a purty good place for pigs an' sich to live in. Ye see pigs is naither Fenian[1] nor Orangemen. I get along purty well m'self bekase I sit on both sides ov th' fence at th' same time. I wear a green ribbon on Pathrick's Day an' an Orange cockade on th' Twelfth of July...."

Their first child is two years of age in 1847, and they lose a child to the hunger. Jamie goes to the fields to steal the milk from a farmer's cattle and is captured by the farmer but, when he pleads his case, the farmer walks with him to his house and the milk is given to the ailing child.

"Turning to Jamie, the farmer says: 'Yer a Protestant'."

" 'Aye.' "

" 'An' I'm a Fenian, but we're in th' face of bigger things'."

In the chimney corner, as she grows older, Jamie's wife has her eloquent moments. With a rapid left and haymaking right she deals with both the warring creeds: "God isn't a printed book t' be carried around b' a man in fine clothes, nor a gold cross t' be dangling at the watch chain of a priest."

When Sam, "the tall imperious precentor of the Mill Row meeting-house", talks to her about a disputed text, the fourteenth of John, she says: "If there's anything this foul world needs more than another it's undisputed text."

She has also her own views about the long wall I was talking about a while ago: "Everything aroun' Antrim is just a demesne full o' pheasants an' rabbits for them quality t' shoot an' we get thransported if we get a meal whin we're hungry."

In that matter times have changed for the better. But the long wall of fear and hatred that divided the people of the lady in the chimney corner still stands as strong as ever.

A SURFEIT OF LAMPREY

At the bridge over the big river at the eel weir the poet's country begins. This is Toomebridge where Rody McCorley went to die in 1798 and, if you're at all interested, it should be as easy to think of the name of the poet who is with me as it is to find the river on the map.[2]

There are people, who haven't given much thought to the matter, who would say that a man would want to be a strange sort of poet to write good poetry about eels. For to a lot of people the eel, even at his silver-bellied stage, is not the most poetic of fish; at his yellow-bellied stage he is matter for nightmares. But then to a lot of people the eel—smoked or fried or jellied—isn't even the most enticing of foods, and the sight of a tank, as big as a fair-sized room and packed with eels by the hundred, all swarming over and under and around each other, would be most unsettling.

The poet, the professor from Manhattan and myself lean on the bridge above the eel weir and give a little thought to the matter that in Elizabethan times, and later, the best people were given to dying from a surfeit of lamprey. The lamprey, either the river or sea variety, is an odd fish indeed, and does not seem to be highly regarded nowadays. Why, at this very eel weir, didn't I see a man take a lamprey, not a very big one, from a tank of wriggling writhing eels and toss it aside. To it, where it lay writhing, ran the dog and sniffed and backed away with a disgusted look on his face. What didn't please a Toomebridge dog in these fastidious times was good enough, or bad enough, to eat and be killed by, for the gluttonous courtiers of Gloriana.

Bad as the male lamprey may be, the female of the species is assuredly more deadly, and to her own kind, for it takes four or five males to bring to her faceless face (look a river lamprey straight in the eyes, which aren't exactly there, and you'll see what I mean) the blissful smile of motherhood; and the whole team of fathers die as a result of their exertions.

But Tosh Mullan, who studied the ways of nature and shared the delights of boyhood with me on the river-banks round Omagh, had found a use for the lamprey (amper eels we called them) that not even the most devious Elizabethan would have dreamed of. He captured a big one, a real brute, in the Camowen River. Not wishing to throw it back, eat it or bury it, he carried it about with him for use as a weapon of offence and, on

B

occasion, defence, until the odour of decaying reptile proved too much even for his dearest friends and he ceased to be invited to the best houses. The day of his disarmament was momentous and the heaven's breath smelled the more wooingly for it.

What's left of Rody McCorley, the rebel of 1798, or, rather, of his memorial after some local Orange enthusiasts blew him up, is over there across the water, a little pile of rubble to the rear of the RUC barracks. It wasn't the world's greatest work of art but, God knows, it was causing no offence—no more than Rody did in his brief life in which he merely managed to get himself betrayed and hanged. Were the polis all asleep the time the charge was set right bang up against their back gate?

That was some years ago, and why talk today of such a trivial thing? For since Rody's memorial took to the air and the dust, what I've heard described, with calm but savage irony, as the Irish gelignite tradition has gone far even beyond the limits of lunacy. Will holy Ireland ever, or should she ever, forget the story of the young girl who went shopping for her trousseau and brought her sister along with her, and met with gelignite upon the way, and the bride-to-be lost both legs and one arm and one eye? Her sister merely lost both legs. John O'Leary, the great Fenian who inspired Yeats the poet, said that there were things a man might not do, not even to save his country. He probably meant something mildly dishonourable, like telling lies. We know so much more nowadays. Stop, said the Belfast surgeon who saw the mangled bodies, stop in the name of God. The Bann river flows here, north forever out of the great lough, the tanks at the eel weirs are filled, are raised and emptied and lowered again. Life such as it is goes on; goes on, too, for the mangled sisters. We hope that the man who planted the bomb will remember them even to the day of his own dissolution. Who was he? Who knows? Does it matter? Our society on these islands did it: fools and knaves in office and, inevitably, madmen on the streets.

Most of us know our Rody McCorley from Ethna Carbery's[3] song:

> Oh, see the fleetfoot host of men
> Who come with faces wan
> From farmstead and from fisher's cot
> Along the banks of Bann.

It doesn't really tell us a lot about Rody except that he went to die at the bridge of Toome—on which we three now stand. But some of us know Rody from the more informative older ballad that tells us a lot about the locality and about who and what Rody McCorley was. You'll find the words in Colm O'Lochlainn's second book of street ballads and I'm proud to say that it was myself had the privilege of bringing the words to that veteran scholar:

> Come tender-hearted Christians, all attention to me pay
> Till I relate these verses great, these verses two or threy,
> Concerning of a noble youth who was cut off in his bloom,
> And died upon the gallows tree near to the Bridge of Toome.

The words have been printed only in one other place, as far as I know, and that's in *Songs of Irish Rebellion*, a collection with commentary by the Swiss scholar, Professor Zimmermann, who had them from that great authority, Donal O'Sullivan, who had them from F. J. Bigger, the archaeologist and the relation of Joe Bigger, Parnellite and parliamentarian, who once, it is said, replied to a haughty noble lord, who asked him if he were a pork merchant, by admitting that he was and that, moreover and furthermore, he knew a pig when he saw one.

I had the words of the old ballad from a man here in Toomebridge on the day, twenty years ago or so, when Rody's memorial was unveiled by Father Eamonn Devlin, and curiously enough it was a priest called Devlin who stood by Rody when he went to the scaffold 179 years ago:

> They called upon priest Devlin,
> The priest he came with speed . . .

Well, perhaps, it's not so curious. Devlin is a great name in these parts. The wife of the poet who stands with the professor and myself on the bridge of Toome is a Devlin whose father's place is right beside the ancient high cross of Ardboe on the Tyrone side of the lough.

Just at the moment it isn't the season for the eels to be in the big tank, but I've promised the man who is the master of the weirs that I'll be glad to be back when the eels are in residence, to renew old friendships, of course, because eels are an image of eternity, and to see the old weirs that stand further downriver on the way to Coleraine. Meanwhile I can walk a little apart from weir-master and poet and professor to meditate on the way in which the poet, standing here on the border of his own country, has looked on the eels and seen in their comings and goings a reflection, in the lough, of the lives of men. By tradition, enamelled in the words of

Thomas Moore, Lough Neagh is a place for reflections and shadowy
images:

> *On Lough Neagh's banks as the fisherman strays,*
> *In the clear cool eve declining,*
> *He sees the round towers of other days*
> *In the waves beneath him shining . . .*

Seamus Heaney's poems that make up "A Lough Neagh Sequence" are
to be found in his second book of poems: *Door Into the Dark*. They have
also been published separately by Phoenix Pamphlet Poets and dedicated
to the fishermen of the lough-shore, the long-line fishermen. From
Francis Day's *The Fishes of Great Britain and Ireland*, published in London
in the 1880s, he takes, for the booklet, two fascinating quotations. In the
first of them, and in the mysterious movement of the eels, there is a quite
frightening image of all life and, for all we know, of eternity:

> At an early period in the summer it is an interesting sight (at the Cutts
> near Coleraine, on the lower Bann) to mark the thousands of young
> eels then ascending the stream. Hay ropes are suspended over rocky
> parts to aid them in overcoming such obstructions. At these places the
> river is black with the multitudes of young eels, about three or four
> inches long, all acting under that mysterious impulse that prompts them
> to push their course onwards to the lake.

The poet's eels are not simply eels. John Clare's harried and slaughtered
badger was not just a badger.

The sequence moves from the myths of the lake, the virtue of the water
that will harden wood into stone, the legend of the town sunk beneath its
water—those round-towers of other days; the fable that the vast cavity or
crater holding that water is "a scar left by the Isle of Man" when some
Titan tossed his two hands full of Irish earth against a foe and formed a
new island. From those myths and legends on to the doom of the eels
hooked on baited lines that can be all of ten miles long, or to a more
modern but less dignified doom at the weirs where 500 stone of eels can
be lifted out in one go. From the fate of the eels on to the fatalism of
the men who fish for them and never learn to swim:

> *The lough will claim a victim every year.*

In one poem "Beyond Sargasso", a poem that has the glistening
muscular unity of the eel's body, the poet brings the eel from the utmost

deeps to the belly of the lake. By pointed lamplight in the lough-shore fields the fishermen pluck the worms, "innocent ventilators of the ground", for bait. Then with the gulls above them, an umbrella of "responsive acolytes", the fishermen conceal in the worms the murderous bouquet "of small hooks coiled in the stern". The whole process is somewhere outside time:

> *And when did this begin?*
> *This morning, last year, when the lough first spawned?*
> *The crews will answer, 'Once the season's in'.*

Quoting again from Francis Day: "Aristotle thought they [the eels] sprang from mud . . . while Helmont gives the following curious recipe: 'Cut up two turfs covered with May dew, and lay one upon the other, the grassy sides inwards, and then expose them to the heat of the sun; in a few hours there will spring up an infinite quantity of eels'. Horse-hair from the tail of a stallion was asserted to be a never-failing source of young eels."

Which of us hasn't in childhood tried that experiment: steeping a hair from a horse's tail in water overnight and hoping it would turn into an eel? Once, in the morning, my research was rewarded with the sight of an elver, nimble in a baking-bowl of water where I had sunk the hair from the horse's tail and it was sometime before I found out that there was a practical joker, or an atheist, in the vicinity.

What were once the speculations of wise men, groping for meanings, remain as the fantasies of children which, in turn, shadow forth images of the life of the grown man. The little boy is told that unless his hair is fine-combed the lice will coagulate and make a rope and drag him down to the water. Years afterwards the grown man watches by night the mysterious movement of eels over wet grass, as Francis Day watched them on the hay ropes at the Cutts near Coleraine, and sees there the inexorable continuity of life:

> *To stand*
> *In one place as the field flowed*
> *Past, a jellied road,*
> *To watch the eels crossing land.*
>
> *Rewound his world's live girdle.*
> *Phosphorescent, sinewed slime*
> *Continued at his feet. Time*
> *Confirmed the horrid cable.*

On the Bann meadows, which are marshes in wet weather and lie to the right of the road to Glenshane Pass and beyond the Bridge of Toome, the poet says he spent a part of his boyhood counting cattle. His father kept cattle on that rich but treacherous fattening ground: "Some got lost. They just drowned themselves."

"Between Sheridan Square and the Battery," says the Manhattan professor, "there are a lot of lost women."

Delightful images! There is also a Battery on the Tyrone shore of Lough Neagh. How happy to be abroad on a summer's morning with a poet and a professor!

The tall stack of a brick kiln sticks up like a sore thumb from the flat dark-green land.

Over the telephone table of the hallway in the poet's home in Belfast there's a reproduction of Goya's two bloodied, battling gipsies, clubbing each other with infernal gusto, both well-embedded in the quagmire that will swallow them: a delightful image, we cheerfully decide, of the corner of Ireland that we, at the moment, move in. Or of all Ireland down the ages: great hatred, little room. Yet Ireland all around us on the lough shore on this lovely June morning, is a clean, well-lighted place. It is Ireland "sliding under a clear sea-depth of sunlight" as the returning exile sees it in the opening pages of Francis MacManus' novel *Watergate*: "Thin smoke coiled upward slowly like stirred chalk ooze above trees petrified in the stillness; the hedges were ridges of brilliant white hawthorn; along a road a cart drifted, moving at an imperceptible gait that would lodge it finally in some deeper sundrowned valley, among limewashed lost houses."

But is it all as clean and clear and well lighted as that? MacManus' returning exile looked out on a Munster valley that may have had its memories of bloody ambush and reprisal, famine deaths, tithe wars, maimed cattle, landlords shot with good aim and better reason. We, here and now, are on the road that leads to Burntollet Bridge and bigotry, brutality and bludgeons. What maggots are all the time chewing down there in the darkness?

To the left of the road there's a pub called the Elk Bar because there in the Bann meadows somebody once dug up the bones of an ancient Irish elk. The name is as it should be. If the Gaelic poet, Cathal Buidhe MacGiolla Gunna, who lamented in a magnificent poem[4] the death from thirst of a long-necked yellow bittern that he saw stretched by the side of the road, had passed this way he must certainly have been moved to write a poem about that elk. Did the great animal, like the lost cows, sink and drown himself in the soft ground, dying not of thirst but of overmuch moisture?

High up in the bare Sperrins in Glenshane Pass there's a roadside pub called, after television, the Ponderosa. Now, no harm to the man who owns it and no harm to that harmless family of ponderous bovine cowboys that we saw on that television series, but the name seems a little odd on an Ulster roadside. How about Hugh's Hideout? For over the ridge there in Glanconkyne, with its multiple mythologies, the great O'Neill found refuge for a while after the disaster of Kinsale, and it's fitting that he should be remembered even by frivolous travellers when they stop to raise a glass.

But when we stop to speak our criticism to the man of the house and to drink to the memory of Hugh in hiding—as men once drank to the king over the water—we are quenched by a ready wit. When he opened the pub two names were suggested to him by friends and he picked the one that seemed to him the more suitable. The other suggestion had been Castelgandolfo.

But all that is miles ahead on our road and we are still in the poet's meadows where the river Bann, sleek, deep and brimming-full, comes out of the great lake.

The school the poet should have gone to as a boy was eaten by an aerodrome. He was born hereabouts 30 or so years ago, just before the bombs dropped on Pearl Harbor and sent the US airforce to Lough Neagh's banks. So the school, Anahorish school, changed its location to make straight the way for the big bombers, and changed its shape from that of the old-style school-house to that of a covey of Nissen huts. The huts, too, have now gone and somebody has built on the place where they were an American-style bungalow.

Anahorish school is now a new building a short distance away and the scholars come to school by bus. Will all this easy travel affect the minds of children? For every country-reared man knows that anything he ever learned, of good or bad, was learned not in a classroom but while idling along the road from school. It used to be said of a man of partial education that he never went to school but merely met the scholars coming home. Must we say of him henceforth that he was simply knocked down by the school bus?

Seamus Heaney here at Anahorish tells me that Robert Frost was the first poet who really talked to him: a strong voice from north of Boston talking across an ocean to a young Irish poet by the great lake that is north of Bannfoot. But we agree here and now that it is John Clare, who also means a lot to Heaney, who has painted the best picture of country boys going to school long before buses were heard of:

The schoolboys still their morning rambles take
To neighbouring village school with playing speed,
Loitering with pastime's leisure till they quake,
Oft looking-up the wild-geese droves to heed,
Watching the letters which their journeys make;
Or plucking haws on which the fieldfares feed.
And hips, and sloes! And on each shallow lake
Making glib slides, where they like shadows go
Till some fresh pastimes in their minds awake.
Then off they start anew and hasty blow
Their numb and clumpsing fingers till they glow;
Then races with their shadows wildly run
That stride huge giants o'er the shining snow
In the pale splendour of the winter sun.

One Protestant boy went to Anahorish school. All he had to do to go home was to walk a few steps and hop over a gate. Safe on the other side of the gate he'd drum his chest with his fists, King-Kong style, and shout: "Ah cud bate every Fenian in Anahorish school." Since this was a daily performance no serious enmity could have been involved, reprisals were never taken and the Anahorish experiment in integrated education could have been judged a success.

Four Protestant boys sat with me in my class at the Christian Brothers in Omagh, and we were all the best of friends, and no fighting references were made to Fenians, nor was there any defiant shouting of that in-elegant rhyme that tells how Protestant Dick went up the stick to fetch a load of hay and let a fart behind the cart and blew the hay away. Little Protestant boys have rhymes equally elegant about the nature and practices of the Church of Rome. Of course we were ultra-civilised schoolboys, townies in a garrison town where every cornerboy had seen the Taj Mahal, or said he had or even thought he had; and we were also, in that class, at secondary level. One of the four was the son of a local big farmer. One was a Canadian. One was from Cornwall. The fourth was a townsman and is now a Protestant rector. Once, years afterwards, when I was going through the motions of giving a lecture in the town in which he is rector, he was there to introduce me and to say in gentlemanly jest that while he had read one of my books I had never listened to one of his sermons.

But isn't it an odd sad thing that a Protestant going to a Catholic school should, so long after everything, be still a matter for comment?

Few Catholics that I ever heard of went to Protestant schools at that time—or since. Although from the day of my confirmation by Dr Bernard O'Kane, then Bishop of Derry, I do recall one odd spectacle. Up the middle aisle on that day stepped two girls with flaming golden hair. They wore white dresses with crimson sashes. Behind them walked their mother, as beautiful and damned nearly as young-looking as her daughters. For style and appearance you never saw the like of that parade. A few of us, even at that age and in spite of our being far advanced in contemplative prayer, had also eyes in our heads. Our thoughts as we watched those women were, I fear, very far from the Paraclete.

This *tableau vivant*, in flaming gold and white and crimson, posed itself apart from everybody else at a corner of the altar-rails. Catechism was asked, and answered to the satisfaction of his lordship. Then the two young beauties were struck on the cheeks and confirmed. Later we found out that all this was not just a vision, or a fashion display put on by the parish priest to brighten our lives. Those radiant sisters, for geographical reasons, went to a Protestant school and so had to be dealt with specially and separately to ensure that their doctrine was sound. The Holy Ghost had a special interest, it seemed, in the Smiths, which wasn't their name, of Altamuskin, which wasn't their place; and so had we—distracted, love-smitten, enthralled embryos of Omagh men.

THE TROUT IN THE RIVER ROE

The public-house at the cross on the road from Toomebridge to Castle-dawson is being thatched. Further on along that road there was a man who once upon a time kept an unlicensed bull. The poet wrote a poem about that bull and called the bull and the poem: "The Outlaw".

> *His knobbled forelegs straddling her flank,*
> *He rammed life home, impassive as a tank. . . .*

Then "in his own time" the law-breaking giver of life "resumed the dark, the straw". A poem to set a man wondering whether the Castle-dawson bull didn't actually know that his love-making was unlicensed, unblessed; and wondering, too, about other laws, licences and blessings.

Have you ever looked, as I did twenty years ago or so, at the big bulls, terrifying as trumpeting elephants, in the model farm attached to Mitchels-town creamery in the County Cork? Chained giants, led literally by the nose, contributors to the process of artificial insemination and—if you study them sympathetically—most irritably aware that life has played a trick on them. For them, cloistered involuntarily and without vows, no blazing hearth shall burn nor busy housewife ply her evening care nor would the children know their sire from the Brown Bull of Cooley. The outlaw of Lough Neagh (celebrated in song by Seamus Heaney as J. J. Callanan celebrated the outlaw of Lough Lene) had a much happier sex life.

The poet also wrote a poem about the man who is thatching the pub at the crossroads. He sees the thatcher as musician, a fiddler testing the strings:

> *Next the bundled rods: hazel and willow*
> *Were flicked for weight, twisted in case they'd snap.*
> *It seemed he spent the morning warming up. . . .*

He sees him as artist: writer, poet, story-teller:

> *For pinning down his world, handful by handful.*

He sees him in the end of all as a magician, turning old straw to new gold:

> *And left them gaping at his Midas touch.*

There's a whole rural culture, as old as measurement, in that poem; and an ancient magic.

But it so happens that on this blessed day of our visit we are not to have the pleasure of meeting the thatcher: half the roof is still in sere and . . . not yellow but weary brown, the other half is new and golden. The tools of the trade are all there assembled but the thatcher has had to go elsewhere on other business. The woman of the house has a welcome for the poet and his two companions. Why wouldn't she? When he was a boy, a neighbour's child, hadn't he day after day carried the milk to the pub from the farm he was reared in? A rare thing, when you think of it, for a poet to be at: carrying the juice of the cow to the house where men at their pleasure knock back the juice of the barley.

In the absence of the thatcher we talk a lot about thatching, about wheat straw and rye straw and the growing of wheat just for the sake of the straw, about the combine-harvester that ruins all straw as far as the purposes of the thatcher are concerned, about a ton of wheat straw that was once destroyed by rats, about the rarity of thatchers today and about the good thatchers who are still at work in this or that part of the country. On along the road the thatch has been taken away and replaced by slates on the poet's old home: new people, new ways. Some trees too, that were dear to him in his boyhood have been cut down. The felling of trees, a sharp reminder of mortality, must certainly be one of the seven or even one of the three things that are most mournful. On the slopes of Slievenamon at Kilcash in Tipperary the Gaelic poet lamented:

> *What shall we do for timber,*
> *The last of the woods is down?*
> *Kilcash and the house of its glory*
> *And the bell of the house are gone . . .*

Equally the English poet lamented on the flat banks of the river Ouse:

> *The poplars are fell'd, farewell to the shade,*
> *And the whispering sound of the cool colonnade!*

Beyond Castledawson, on the road to the house on the hill where the poet's people now live, we give a lift to a neighbour woman walking home from the town: on along narrowing roads to her house with a clump of bushes to one side of it and hidden in the bushes a fine specimen of a windlass well:

> *As a child they could not keep me from wells*
> *And old pumps with buckets and windlasses.*
> *I loved the dark drop, the trapped sky, the smells*
> *Of waterweed, fungus and dank moss.*

He calls the poem "Personal Helicon". He remembers a bottomless well in a brickyard, and a shallow one that "fructified like an aquarium" under a drystone wall; and a scaresome well where "out of ferns and tall foxgloves a rat slapped across my reflection".

The grown man cannot so easily go on all fours: Narcissus staring into the mirror of the water. But the poet sublimates, and rhymes to see himself, "to set the darkness echoing". He digs with the pen as, before his time, his father and grandfather had dug with spade, or sliced with slean or loy. Weedgrown well, farm implement, are transformed into living images. But the new house on the hill has all the windy freedom of the cattle fairs that his father and his father's people followed and much preferred to any close grappling and wrestling with the mulch earth. The great cattle fairs, like the saga of the Brown Bull, are gone into the past:

And watched you sadden when the fairs were stopped.
No room for dealers if the farmers shopped
Like housewives at an auction ring. Your stick
Was parked behind the door and stands there still.

We are at the house, where the stick is parked, in time for a late breakfast. Welcome and content are all about the place. The Lough Shore
country spreads out that way, the Sperrins are over there, and Slemish
behind us—where Patrick the slave-boy herded sheep—or so it was once
said. Our man from Manhattan relaxes, the Irish in him uppermost and at
home, and forgets skyscraping buildings built as much to defy God and to
frighten men as to accommodate men; and forgets the swarming restless
people and the odour of gasoline and the world's accumulating garbage.

I viewed the groves and valleys along its rugged side,
Likewise the Stoney Battery where the timber rides the tide,
And the moorcock he kept crowing the pleasure of that day
All along the moss and heather on wild Slieve Gallen brae.

On a fine day it's a hard thing to pass without stopping over a bridge over
a mountain river. This day it is quite impossible, considering the easy
mood of the morning's journey, and the pleasant late breakfast, to pass
this bridge over the Roe (the Red River) which comes down from the
Sperrins and goes out to the sea by Limavady—or Dog's Leap. Some
water-sprite or nymph, damned nearly visible, is there to delay us and, for
long sunny hours, to set three grown men playing Narcissus by the
Roe's clear pools. "Three Chinese philosophers," says the professor,
"looked for so long at three golden carp in a pool that the question arose:
which were the fish and which the philosophers?"

Like gods on the bridge we study that particular corner of the world of
trout: who seems frisky, who lethargic, who talks to whom, who stays
over in a corner under a bush and sulks by himself. Seamus Heaney and
John Montague, too, have done their poet's duty by the trout in northern
streams. But the lines we piece together as we lean on the bridge come not
from an Ulster hillside but from an imagined English garden where
Thomas Hood walked out and met with Shakespeare's fairies, "those
pretty children of our childhood " he called them. His long poem, "The
Plea of the Midsummer Fairies", makes an odd and interesting contrast
with what happened to Brian Merriman,[5] the Gaelic poet, in the midnight
court of the queen of the fairies in the bawdy wilderness of Munster, all

the more odd and interesting because Hood had a savagery in him, wilder than Merriman, when he wrote, say, of Miss Kilmansegg who was married for and murdered for, and by the means of, her golden artificial leg. But I'm not on a bridge over the Roe to give a lecture. What I meant to say was that Hood had a good eye for fish moving in and on the water:

> And ever at a wish
> They rose obsequious till the wave grew thin
> As glass upon their backs, and then dived in,
> Quenching their ardent scales in watery gloom,
> Whilst others with fresh hues rowed forth to win
> My changeable regard. . . .

At Cookstown that day, by way of a change from the peace of the Sperrin valleys, there's a motor-cycle race roaring through at intervals, raising some interest and a lot of noise. But if that were the only noise the North hears we mightn't complain. Last June three soldiers were blown to bits up among the larks and the sheep and the heather of Glenshane Pass. Death and destruction creep out like a fungus from the narrow bitter little streets; and it seems to me that by the high cross of Ardboe on the Lough Shore might be as good a place as any to pray for wisdom and justice and the peace that should go with them. But the thought of all the greed and stupidity in high places making for hatred in the streets would destroy the peace of heaven more effectively than the revving of a million motorbikes. The lough, a sunny mirror now before us, may claim a victim every year, but old hatreds and misgovernment between them add up to the makings of an all-devouring monster.

In the old graveyard and close to the coin-riddled, bare-branched wishing-tree there's another footnote to the story of the name of O'Neill. Captain Lewis Gordon O'Neill died at the Cape of Good Hope in 1808. He was 27 years of age. Six years later his brother, another British officer, died at Bombay at the age of 30. They lie together here and with them their mother, a native of nearby Killygowlan. She died in 1818 at the age of 66. It's one of those gravestones that set a man making up stories or fragments of a chapter for a novel.

The poet's wife's people, Devlins, a good name, as I said, live along here: "down by the lake where the wild tree fringes its sides". A lovely place for a poet, or anyone, to come courting in. Across a grainfield from the graveyard an Ardboe couple, who spent most of their life in America, have returned, "the long vexations past", and restored the homeplace.

Green grainfield, brightly-painted house, infinite blue lake beyond . . . but the professor is pursued by a vision of the towers of Manhattan. The poet and myself who "have travelled much in Concord" know uneasily that that name could not readily be given at the moment to any of the tormented corners of our tragic north-east.

> *Now I stood in amazement to view the harbour*
> *Where the purling streams they do gently flow,*
> *Where the trout and salmon were nimbly sporting,*
> *Which brings more order to you, old Ardboe.*
> *Now I've travelled Roosia and a part of Proosia,*
> *I have travelled Spain and all along the Rhine,*
> *But in all my rakings and undertakings*
> *Ardboe your equal I could never find.*

Those lines I owe, as I do the earlier lines about Slieve Gallen, visible just there a little west of north, to Davy Hammond of the BBC, a prince among balladmen both for scholarship and performance; and a great man to be out with. Had he been with the poet, the professor and myself, this journey from Belfast to Ardboe might even have taken us through part of Proosia, if not Roosia itself. Yet who, having seen the Roe, would bother about the Rhine?

3

THE STAR OVER CASSIDY'S HILL

EMOTION OF GREEN LEAVES

Carrickmacross in County Monaghan would have been the market town of Patrick Kavanagh, the poet, when he was a young fellow—and of his people. So it would have been of Carrick he was thinking when he wrote in love about meeting his mother by accident at the end of a fair-day when the bargains had been made, and about walking with her through shops and by stalls: "free in the oriental streets of thought". He could frequently see eastern visions in the haze over the fields. Elsewhere in his poems the air is "drugged with Egypt".

Tarry Flynn's mother (in Kavanagh's novel *Tarry Flynn*) held that a man always learns in a fair. Addressing Charlie Trainor on the subject of Tarry and also in the presence of Tarry, a trick that mothers have, she said that there was nothing for Tarry when he went to the fair but "the face in a book" and she complimented the cunning Charlie: "No fear of you reading a book."

The gulf between the novel about Tarry and Kavanagh's poem about his mother on market-day in Carrick should warn all of us about treating the novel too unwarily as autobiography.

It would have been a good road on a dry mild day to walk home from the market, for on that stretch from Carrick to Kednaminsha and Mucker and Inniskeen on the river Fane, the Monaghan countryside is at its best: rolling hills, rich valleys, noble trees. You feel that when he wrote of the place he may have exaggerated the greyness, the stoniness of the soil of his black hills that never saw the sun rising:

Eternally they look north towards Armagh.

Travelling that road now in a bus with a party from the People's College in Dublin I think back to when I first saw the face of Patrick Kavanagh. That was towards the end of 1936 or the beginning of 1937 and the place was the front page of the *Irish Press*. A feature writer, Peadar O Comhraidhe, who was to become a notable figure among editors I was to know, cycled west from Dundalk to meet the poet whose book, *A Ploughman and Other Poems*, had just been published. The poet, hand outstretched, quoting poetry, came to meet him on the threshold of the farmhouse.

DIGRESSION: It occurs to me that fewer copies of that newspaper or any Dublin newspaper would be read nowadays in the sorting-room in Omagh Post-Office where I first looked on Kavanagh's picture.

When in the 1930s I was for a brief period a sorting clerk and tele-graphist (SC & T), a rank now I'm told, as extinct as the dodo, the arrangement was that the Post-Office would take on two tyros at the same time: one Protestant and one Catholic. A pathetic arrangement, indeed, but it represented the British effort to be fair in the face of the unfortunate circumstances in that backyard of the disunited kingdom.

Older postal officials prided themselves on telling the young ones that the organisation was fairly and justly run from London. One of them said to me: "Because I am a postal official I am, of necessity, a socialist." But one of those older officials who is now in retirement tells me that all *that* has been changed since then, as part of the big overall Stormont campaign that managed to bring bigotry and job-grabbing into a town where previously they had not been too noticeable.

It would be interesting to know how the Orange lodges managed to corrupt another great British institution: the impeccable unassailable Post-Office.

Back now to happier things and green places, to fill our minds as Tarry Flynn did with "the emotion of green leaves" to meditate as Father Mat (in one of Kavanagh's poems) and as the glib curate on the bicycle never would or could do, on the "undying difference in the corner of a field". Back to Drumcatton into which the sun went down when the new moon hung "by its little finger" on the telegraph wire; and to the vision of Cassiopeia "over Cassidy's hanging hill", to the poet's outlying possessions in Shancoduff, to Drummeril and Candle Fort and the Long Garden; and to where we were a while ago at the door of the house in which Patrick Kavanagh was born. To Peadar O Comhraidhe he came quoting Yeats:

> For to articulate sweet sounds together
> Is to work harder than all these, and yet
> Be thought an idler by the noisy set
> Of bankers, schoolmasters and clergymen
> The martyrs call the world.

Very apt indeed, I thought, and on the strength of that story in the newspaper in 1936 or 1937 I procured me a copy of Kavanagh's slender book and was able to quote it to myself with great spiritual satisfaction the best part of a year later. For in the Jesuit novitiate in Emo Park (to which I graduated from King George's Post-Office, and into which, it must be said, only Catholics were admitted—a clear case of discrimination) in that novitiate, I say, there was a long corridor with a window open at each end, and a draught that in winter would skin St Simeon Stylites. Remembering Kavanagh's book I'd recite in between the paterandaves and the spiritual exercises, the examens of conscience and compositions of place, these telling lines:

> There's a wind blowing
> Cold through the corridors,
> A ghost-wind,
> The flapping of defeated wings,
> A hell fantasy
> From meadows damned
> To eternal April.

Perhaps for the first time in my life I felt that a poet had been speaking personally for me and, years later, when I came to know the poet, we made jokes about that moment of recognition, and I knew that the wind that blew cold through the Jesuit corridor was the same wind that Paddy Maguire in the long poem, "The Great Hunger", felt blowing through Brannagan's Gap on its way from Siberia.

The wind's over Brannagan's, now that means rain.

So here we are in the poet's village of Inniskeen: neat new houses, the old school, the one-sided street of the village, the church on the hill, the churchyard where the poet lies among his people. By the slow lovely river an old ruined church almost smothered in long grass. Beyond the river the disused railway track, a smaller cluster of houses, and the road to Dundalk.

Inniskeen, a lovely name! The haphazard translating of placenames back from the name now commonly used into what we imagine may have been the original Irish is always a tricky occupation. Who would think now, I say to myself, as I look at the signpost in the middle of Inniskeen that the original of Crossmaglen, if translated straight into English, would end up prosaically as Flynn's Cross: and no mention of any glen? But I am quite prepared on this sunny day to accept the argument of a young man on the bridge over the Fane who says that Inniskeen does actually mean: The Quiet Island. It doesn't mean anything of the sort, but to talk of a quiet island is perfectly to describe the place; and on top of that, the Fane does in the vicinity make a small island, a dreaming birth-place for quietness, reeds and long grass and bushes and trailing river-weeds and trees overhanging the still water.

In this sunny quietness I should remember for comicality how on one Holy Thursday long ago the poet, who rests over there on the hillside, and myself met in Eason's bookshop in Dublin. He was on his way back from a visit to Inniskeen. He was worried, he said, at the way in which the boom in smuggling was breeding spivvery among the young fellows along the border between Inniskeen and Crossmaglen which is in County Armagh in the Six Counties. Then he brooded for a while: "But begod I suppose it was never any different. Crossmaglen was always, as you know, famous for dealers in windbroken horses."

We talked of the plight of the innocent youth in the ballad, a teetotaller, who learned a bitter lesson at the fair:

> I was a bold teetotaller
> For nine long years or more,
> The neighbours they respected me
> An' dacent clothes I wore.
> My kinsmen they looked up to me,
> Till one unlucky day,
> Just like a child, I was beguiled
> By whiskey in my tay. . . .
> It wasn't the lads from Shercock,
> Nor the boys from Ballybay,
> But the dalin' men from Crossmaglen
> Put whiskey in me tay.

"There were the Guelphs and the Ghibellines of Crossmaglen," the poet said, "and any one of them would trade in his grandmother for a packet of Woodbines."

The Guelphs and the Ghibellines were not (precisely) the families he mentioned.

Coming up in the train from Dundalk that day he had been talking about such things with a fine, well-set-up, well-dressed class of a gentleman. He listened with great attention to the poet who enlarged on the mercantile abilities of the two families. Then the gentleman slapped the poet on the knee, and roared laughing and said: "Paddy Kavanagh, you never said a truer word. I know it well. I'm one of the Guelphs myself."

In the warm green peace of the quiet island I hear the great laugh of Kavanagh that day on the street outside the bookshop: "He was proud of every rascality I mentioned. You never said a truer word, he said. I'm one of the Guelphs myself."

GOGARTY RUINED IT

The prose book in which he described his youth and boyhood here by the bridge over the Fane he called *The Green Fool*. Crossing O'Connell Bridge, over the Liffey, with him one evening of east wind in the 1940s I asked him had he made any money at all out of *The Green Fool*. With that roar of a laugh that defied both the east wind and the sour recollection, he said: "Not a hoorin' penny. Gogarty ruined it."

For in one of the essays or sketches or stories or chapters that make up that book (first published in 1938) Kavanagh told how he walked from Inniskeen to Dublin, a long 60 miles, to call on some of the literary people, and how he knocked on the door of Oliver St John Gogarty, fashionable surgeon, poet, wit, jester to Yeats and George Moore, friend for a brief while of James Joyce and afterwards to appear in Joyce's *Ulysses* as "stately, plump Buck Mulligan".

When Gogarty's door was opened to Kavanagh: "I mistook Gogarty's white-robed maid for his wife—or his mistress. I expected every poet to have a spare wife."

It seems now and it should have seemed then a harmless remark, particularly since Kavanagh was actually laughing at his own ingenuousness; yet Gogarty objected and took his objection to the law, and the book was withdrawn and Gogarty awarded one hundred in damages. The Dublin joke was that Gogarty was even witty about the business, saying that what he really resented was the implication that he had only one mistress. Nevertheless, he went to law and ruined the book, and *The Green Fool* became a rare thing, something to hide if you had one or steal if you hadn't, until 33 years later (in 1972) it was splendidly reprinted in London by Martin Brian & O'Keeffe.

It is as honest and unaffected and happy and humorous a book as any young poet ever wrote about himself. Michael Joseph, the book's first publishers, were aware that they were on to something good, to the extent of saying that they considered *The Green Fool* one of the best books that had, up to that date, appeared under their imprint. They saw that the picture of a life faraway from mechanised industry, modern finance and urbanisation, of a community retaining its own conventions, beliefs and superstitions would "fascinate the anthropologist". English reviewers then seemed to feel, and for a long time had felt, that way about a lot of Irish novels. But anthropologists have now come to view with fascination the ways of mechanised computerised man and of urbanisation. Professor Saintsbury considered that Ibsen was a provincial, while Professor Saintsbury would have made a worthy character in another Ibsen play, say: *Ghosts of Academe*.

But Michael Joseph did also see that the real value of the book was in its vision of life dawning on a percipient, healthy, sensitive young animal of a man who was also a poet. Everybody and everything in this book is alive even to the ghost of Sonny who hanged himself by using a sack of oats for a scaffold and who, to make a bad job worse, slithered down, rather than jumped off, the sack. He left a shadow on the wall and nothing on the floor, a fair symbol for a poor soul who swithered so sadly over his suicide.

The poet's life here begins with the blackbird who is also a poet, but a destructive one and an enemy to old thatch, foraging for red worms in the ancestral roof and picking holes through which the spitting rain follows to startle the sleeping faces of children in their beds. Little hills, all tilled and tame, rise up around the house and are, later on, when he tills them himself, to become those black hills that have never seen the sun rising, that "eternally look north towards Armagh" and a view that went back to St Patrick and the druids; and in the evening faraway thunder went shouting about the hills of Down. He was conscious of the past of the place and of the Gaelic poets who had lived there, and he called one of his poems after Art McCooey, the poet, who in the eighteenth century had wrought in the fields a few miles from where Kavanagh was born.

But when he walked as a young fellow all the way to the Gaelic west of Ireland he decided, on the strength of one brief visit and against all received opinion, that there was no culture in Connemara as compared with Monaghan, "where the spirits of the old poets haunted the poplars". It was the sort of sweeping judgement he could deliver on some contemporary, half-in-fun, whole-in-earnest, and with a deplorable assurance masking his real uncertainty: "He has no brains. He's a bollocks." In much the same way he claimed that in his boyhood his father's house had the only clock in the townland.

He and his people, as he elected to see them, were as Yeats said about the animals in Milton's Paradise and about the peasants in the novels of William Carleton: "half-emerged only from the earth and its brooding".

Which is a nice way of saying that they were arse-deep in the dunged clay. They were ordinary country people: each family holding a spite against at least two others; feeling not at all heart-broken when the rain flattened a neighbour's stooks; talking mostly about going to mass and saying the rosary and making money. At the gamble, the pitch-and-toss school, on a sunny evening: "Beauty, beauty was everywhere, but it was money we were after."

He exaggerated, and knew he did, the little meannesses for comic effect and also, that the poet could stand out more distinctly on the skyline, like one of those haunted poplars. The poetry began in the clay, with the eels in the mud in the drain:

As I crossed the wooden bridge I wondered
As I looked into the drain
If ever a summer morning should find me
Shovelling up eels again.

The poetry went out to "Baghdads of dreamland", to moments "innocent with revelation" as when he was hired out as an agricultural labourer in Ballytrain in the county Louth: "Many years afterwards, when I was older and farther from angelhood, I told of that beatific wonder to clods and disillusioned lovers. I asked them if they didn't see something beyond the hills of Glasdrummond. They laughed and said I was mad."

But his big feet were still settled on the clay, and the ecstasy came back always to human laughter. He remembered with delight his mother's father: "Oul' Quinn liked me because I had big bones, a big voice and could eat fat bacon. He liked a person who could eat fat bacon. He didn't like delicate people and fell out with one of his sons because he had married for love a puny girl. He was an unconscious disciple of Nietzsche. I must have been eleven years old at that time." Did Kavanagh ever, I wonder, read in that most learned professor, Thomas O'Rahilly, that: "One of the ways in which divination was practised in pagan Ireland is described by Cormac in a well-known article in his Glossary. The *fili* chewed (cocna) a piece of the raw flesh of a pig, dog, or cat, and then chanted an incantation over it, and offered it to the gods whom he invoked. He then slept, and in his sleep the knowledge that he sought was revealed to him." There may have been ancient wisdom in Oul' Quinn's fat bacon.

So, on this sunny day there are three of us leaning on the low stone parapet of a bridge and looking down into the waters of the Fane at sand and gravel, trailing weeds, one lugubrious trout, and a motor-tyre that will never more grip the road as its manufacturers, for sure, said it would. No matter could be more out of place than a motor-tyre in a trout stream in a poet's village. Around the ancient ruin on the right bank of the stream the mad grass and rank bottom-land weeds are as high as the adam's apple. The motor-tyre lies like a hoop thrown with bad aim at a charity bazaar.

Three children come towards the bridge from the larger part of the village which, with the church and the churchyard and the poet's grave, are to the south of the river. Two boys, one girl. They see the strangers but pretend not to see them. Children can be as secretive as a Kerryman in a witness box. One boy says to the girl: "Ask no questions."

The children played in the poet's garden of the golden apples, between a railway and a road:

> In the thirsty hedge old boots were flying sandals
> By which we travelled through the childhood skies,
> Old buckets rusty-holed with half-hung handles
> Were drums to play when old men married wives.

That dead tyre in the river could as easily be a magic circle of African ebony or malachite. What the hell colour is malachite? It is given to few young people as it once was to Martin McGowan and myself to find a cavalry sabre below Donnelly's bridge in the Camowen river near Omagh town. Yet the imagination can make a sabre out of a twisted stick.

The three children sink into the long grass. It's clear to anyone with a brain in his head that they're on the way to the coral island: that sunny green triangle down there by the edge of the water. In time, out they come, not secretively now, but with laughter and shouts into the sunshine. As far as they are concerned the three strangers on the bridge are a whole green tunnel of jungle grass away from them. One of the boys has accumulated a long branch with which he pokes in the water as industriously as if he were being well-paid by the minute. Nothing surfaces.

Behind us on the bridge a motor-car goes by, in no great hurry, towards Dundalk. Another, either to be perverse or to pay respect to the law of divine compensation, goes the other way towards Carrickmacross. Carrick was his market town as I've said before, and it always comes as a surprise to find that Inniskeen is so close to Dundalk where in a big hotel there's a room called the Kavanagh room which is used for dances and other functions. Now that I've written that down I realise that dancing also has to be some class of a function. David did it, too, before the Ark and Salome before Herod and Fred Astaire before most of us were born.

That very day we have met at the door of that dancing-room two young men, long-haired as only poets and Carolean cavaliers were ever supposed to be, and carrying drums and things. When one of my friends asked one of the two why the room was so-called, the decent boy honestly admitted that he hadn't a bloody notion. There never was, you see, a Paddy Kavanagh showband.

Dundalk, of course, is closer now to Inniskeen than it was when he was born. Sixty-nine years ago the roads were rougher and cars slower, if at all, and ten miles was still a distance. He covered it on foot, simply walking or, more actively, driving cattle to the fair. In *The Green Fool* the mother advises him: "If there's running to be done, let someone else do it." A wise maxim that, to hold onto in more ways of life than the driving of cattle to a fair. We are so urbanised and motorised nowadays that it may be necessary to point out that no beast, homesick for its fields and byre and feeling instinctively that the road ahead led to the slaughter-house, ever walked a straight road to the fair. So that every drover needed a nimble lad, or two, who could run to guard open gates or leap stone walls into cabbage gardens. Hence the mother's cautious advice.

He covered the road to Dundalk on bicycle and on horseback: at Drumnay crossroads the bicycle was a stirring symbol, particularly when a female girl was in the saddle. Then there was the train that came from Carrick, going round half the world and on to Dundalk. One New Year he told me how, suitcase in hand, he set off from Dublin to go home for Christmas: a few drinks with friends in Dublin, a few with people met for the first time or met again in Amiens Street station, a few more in Dundalk, then on by train to Black Horse Halt—closer to his home than Inniskeen station.

"At the last hill I ran like a carthorse pulling a load and knowing it was the last hill between him and home."

He would have been running back to the music of his father's melodeon on a Christmas morning in "the gay garden that was childhood's". The melodeon called across the wild bogs to Lennons and Callans; and the six-year-old boy pulling on his trousers knew that something away out of the ordinary had happened: Christ was born.

> *Cassiopeia was over*
> *Cassidy's hanging hill,*
> *I looked and three whin bushes rode across*
> *The horizon—the Three Wise Kings.*

The toiling horse could be for him an image of the plight of man. Paddy Maguire in the long poem "The Great Hunger" saw the days slipping by in this place, and the drills slipping by, and "trembled his head away and ran free from the world's halter". When the poet himself, as an aspiring young farmer, was fool enough to buy an animal that would kick any plough to the moon it was apt that the animal should be a female, or mare, skittish as the nymphs that Maguire saw on the grassbanks of lanes on a Sunday "stretch-legged and lingering, staring". The mare kicked the poet into poetry that AE (George Russell), the mystic, printed:

> I turn the lea-green down
> Gaily now,
> And paint the meadows brown
> With my plough.

Kavanagh saw the joke and while the neighbours, rejoicing in a neighbour's downfall with a sort of crossroads malice of which at times he displayed his fair share, laughed at him for his bad bargain, he laughed back at the mare. "As I dragged the mare after me over the whitening spring road, I was feeling humbled. My genius has been of a ridiculous turn. I sensed the joke and laughed back into the mare's face."

He came home here for the last time, by hearse from Dublin: by the road he walked when he first set off for Dublin to knock on AE's door, and on Gogarty's door, too, for all the good that did him. Never did a poet get a poorer welcome on another poet's threshold.

On a wet day when he was young his mother and himself had got lost in that bewitched maze of roads around the village of Louth, and wandered haplessly around and around until they had the sense to give the donkey his head. He led them safely home, for the ass is a blessed animal and immune to the delusions and witcheries of the other world. It is well known that the Good People have the mastery over that maze of roads: twice I was lost there myself, and once with a whole busload of people.

STONES ACROSS THE STREAM

So the three of us leave the bridge over the Fane and walk through the village to the poet's grave.

A man who went to school with him leans against a low wall and says, oddly enough, and echoing the old Dublin-British-army jingle that the poet once parodied: "He was a quare one."

If ever you go to Dublin town
In a hundred years or so
Inquire for me in Baggot Street
And what I was like to know.
O he was a queer one
Fol dol the di do,
He was a queer one
I tell you.

In *The Green Fool* one of the sisters says to him: "The next thing is the people will be calling you the bard." As far back as the dolmens the bards have been quare fellows.

The accent and intonation of the man by the wall are exactly those of the dead poet. The effect is uncanny.

On the far side of the road a car coming from Dunleer or Castlebellingham, or the moon, pulls up and a group of people gather around it. A woman in the car calls to us: "Is Billy there?"

"No ma'am."

"Are any of ye Duffy?"

"No ma'am, none of us has the luck and honour to be a Duffy."

One of the group joins us, a decent wee man. He says: "They didn't give him a great grave at all. Nothing, now, like that."

He shows us a huge square monument conforming to no style known between here and Easter Island, stones stained with age, that some death-defying lunatic built to himself and his family.

On gravestones all around us are placenames that we have hitherto known only from his talk and his poems: Drumcatton, Drummerill, Donaghmoyne, Shancoduff. In the Yeats country in Sligo you can wonder which came first: the places that made the poet and loaned him their names, or the poetry that used the places as euphony and symbol. Names can have their own poetry, as we all know. They can also have a new ring and timbre when they have passed through poetry.

The poet's grave is very simple: a small cross, large flat stones from the stream laid level with the earth, a few words of his own: "There were stepping-stones across the stream. Part of my life is there, the best part." The simplicity, the stones, the repeating of those words, was I'm told the idea of his brother, Peter: nor could any devoted brother pay a better tribute than to choose such a translucent memory, lay the stones in Monaghan earth above the sleeping man, and let him talk there forever to all who come to his grave.

Are the three children still below there, taking the sun on the coral island?

The Fane is one of three small rivers that come unobtrusively to the Irish Sea between Drogheda and Dundalk. The other two are the Dee and the Glyde. Where you cross them on the main Dublin–Belfast road, drainage has reduced them to the dull uniformity of canals, but inland they still have their moments of natural beauty and the Fane, where it flows through Patrick Kavanagh's Inniskeen is very restful to look at.

He had, as any decent man should have, a high opinion of his own river: "The river Fane ran through our parish on its way to the Irish sea. It was a clear swift-flowing stream. Anglers came long journeys to dream and smoke tobacco on its banks.

"These anglers said the Fane was as good a trout stream as there was in Ireland. I shouldn't say so—the trout in its waters took after the people of Inniskeen in being hard to catch."

But the salmon in their season ran westwards in that water, fat and sleepy "like well-thriving pigs" and Patrick, the youthful bard, was out with the best of them with gaff and torchlight to search and kill. God look down on the salmon in a parish where even the sleepers on the railway-line weren't safe. For think of those shadowy figures who move regularly across the fields of the townland of Mucker and the pages of his novel *Tarry Flynn*, bearing railway-sleepers away with them: for what purpose is never stated.

Railway-sleepers don't make good fuel. Built into the walls of lean-to sheds or henhouses, or stopping gaps in fences, they would be painfully noticeable if the law came looking for them. The matter has long interested me and it grieves me that I never remembered to ask the poet what the looters did with the looted timber. In retrospect, too, it gives me a nervous bit of a shudder to think that I actually travelled a few times on a track whose stability had been so sadly sapped by ghostly thieves who faded into the dusk of the hedges around Drumnay crossroads, or under the height of Rocksavage.

The railway was, otherwise, useful to the poet as a symbolic contrast: it related to order of a sort, to something planned by man and, in a haphazard way, to time. The river, draining out of the lovely Lough Muckno at the back of Castleblayney and idling on towards the eastern sea, was the world unspoiled but also the world marked by history. It was the future, too. It was infinity.

There's a good ballad, and I don't know if he knew it, about Lough Muckno and the maid of Lord Blayney's demesne:

When the foes all surround me in battle
And I'm in the midst of all pain,
To you I'll be true, lovely Mary,
Fair maid of Lord Blayney's demesne.

It's odd that I can't remember if we ever talked about that ballad, because one day in a small room in a newspaper office in which we once worked together, he came to me with some verses that it seemed he had just written out in pencil on a sheet of paper, and said: "Would this sing to the tune of 'The Dawning of the Day'?"

We raised our voices together in a Monaghan-Tyrone cacophony and, by the grace of God, nobody was listening. It remains with me as a delicate memory that I must have been the first person after the poet to see and hear these words:

On Raglan road on an autumn day I met her first and knew
That her dark hair would weave a snare that I might one day rue.

In the woods by Lough Muckno the young man, strolling, espied a young maiden, and sweetly her voice did complain that her love had gone over the ocean from the maid of Lord Blayney's demense. On Raglan road in Dublin the poet saw the danger yet he "walked along the enchanted way". The theme is ubiquitous, and eternal.

Of those three unobtrusive rivers the Dee has its large place, larger than the river itself, in our mythology. Ardee, as we all know, is the ford of Ferdiad where Cuchullain fought to the heroic head-hunting end with his friend in the war over the brown bull of Cooley. If the river Glyde has literary or mythological associations I don't know of them. It seems unfair that alone of the three it should be devoid of a history. It is a beautiful stream where it goes under the direct road from Ardee to Dundalk but drained and, I suspect, polluted, it is a dismal dyke as seen from the main road from Ardee to Carrick.

The Fane came into our literary history in the early nineteenth century with William Carleton who spent a while in the valley when he was tramping from his father's cottage in South Tyrone to Dublin, to make his fortune as he hoped—God look to his wit. He had read in Smollett's translation of Le Sage how Gil Blas had also set out hopefully from Santillane to Salamanca.

Not far from Carrickmacross is the site of Wildgoose Lodge where in 1817 the local Whiteboys, agrarian revolutionaries, burned out and massacred the family of a strong farmer called Lynch. It's a complicated story which I've written about elsewhere[1] but it gives a special odd feeling to this part of the country. Carleton passed the road not long after the fatal events and saw the bodies of Paddy Devaun and his fellow-conspirators dangling in corruption from gibbets. Years afterwards he was to write his blood-red story of "Wildgoose Lodge" in the *Traits and Stories of the Irish Peasantry* and later still, and as an old man, to remember the business in his unfinished autobiography. Here and now I quote both from myself and William Carleton:

Near the parish of Killaney in County Louth, William Carleton walked suddenly into a terrible townland of death where decaying bodies swung on roadside gallows, poisoning the wind and the sunshine. He was then living with, or on, his former schoolfellow, Edward McArdle, parish priest of Killaney, who hadn't a book in his possession, who couldn't provide his guest with anything to read. So the guest killed his time walking out over the autumn roads, filling his healthy lungs with the crisp air that blew over the flat land of Louth.

At a crossroads in a village he came upon a gallows, a few idle soldiers guarding the frightful thing and gossiping casually and in the "slight but agreeable breeze ... something like a tar-sack swinging backwards and forwards". Long ropes of slime shone in the light, and dangled from the bottom of the thing that swung in the air. In the pitched sack the sergeant told him was the body of a man called Paddy Devaun.

Altogether there were 24 dead bodies hanging from gibbets in that district and, in the warmth of an unusual autumn, the bodies went the way of all flesh, the pitch melted, the sacks burst, and the mixture of pitch and putrefaction trailed in slimy ropes right down to the ground. Women fainted at the sight. The flies gathered and fed and went away in buzzing swarms, and the people of Louth let the fruit lie rotting in the apple orchards.

Within a hundred yards of the gibbet on which Paddy Devaun was hanging, his mother walked in and out of her own door, busied herself about ordinary household duties, looked up now and again at the hideous thing and said: "God be merciful to the soul of my poor marthyr."

The blind and oppressed struck out savagely in the darkness and wounded only themselves. The lords of this green land were well content, as Arthur Young noticed, to imprison, and transport or hang. They felt at ease about it all and went drinking and hunting and gambling to their hearts' content.

So a century and a half later we stand in peace on the bridge over the Fane in Inniskeen, and also in the warmth of an unusual autumn. Not a long walk away men are shot dead on the streets of Newry, and the bewildered remnants of an imperial army are digging holes in the roads over there by Flynn's Cross or Crossmaglen. Join the army and see the world, the recruiting posters used to say from the barrack walls in Omagh when I was young. Join the army now and walk the Falls in Belfast or the Bogside in Derry, and dig holes and blow up little rural bridges on the north-west—no, the north-east, and last frontier. The strategy of containment? But who contains what and with which and to whom, and where or why?

Here in the Fane valley, Kavanagh the poet, who was born in 1904, thought a lot about William Carleton, the novelist, who died in 1869. I have often thought that Carleton whom I never met—he had passed on exactly 50 years before my time—and Kavanagh whom I knew well, had a great deal in common, were similar psychological types, as the jargon goes. They were simple impulsive men, not unmarked by rural crossroads cunning, knowing and feeling with the people, touched by the breath of God that we call genius, able to step back at will into a sunlit land of childhood. On the upper floor of the old schoolhouse at Inniskeen Patrick Kavanagh went to country dances. The building is now a joint Carleton-Kavanagh museum. That quiet, islanded village, lost between two main roads, has also the grave of the poet, a man who could be rough and difficult at times (and which of us can't?) but who never lost the gentleness of heart that he had here as a child:

> Child, remember this high dunce
> Had laughter in his heart and eyes,
> A million echoes distant thence,
> Ere Dublin taught him to be wise.

4

A GIFT OF DONEGAL

THE ROCKY ROAD TO DOOCHARY

It was no harm at all that my fellow traveller and myself were chatting so much as we drove through the town of Ballybofey that we missed the corner and the turn for the great central city of Doochary and swept on instead towards Donegal town.

Chatting and singing, I fear, we were although our last stop for food and refreshment for ourselves and fodder for our horse had been as far behind as Ardee, a town immortalised by Tom Kinsella and the Turfman.[1] But turning out of the rich green valley of the Strule and the Mourne, and safely passing the frontier post, barriers, barbed wire, and soldiers and all, at Strabane and Lifford, and then slowly ascending, with the lovely river Finn below us on the left, into the heart of Donegal, nostalgia or something overtook us. So we sang.

Remembering Rannafast and the days of our innocence when the blood was strong and the heart Gaelic we sang about the *Cruacha Glas na hEireann*, the green hills of Ireland, and about being down in the middle of the glen *trathnóna beag areir* (late last evening) and about *mheall sí le na glorthái mé*—how she deceived me with her soft talk. We talked of the genius of the brothers O Grianna of Rannafast, Seamus and Seosamh and Sean Ban, writers of stories and songs, and of Hudí Pháidi Hudí Devaney, the singer, and of the lovely man he was and the winsome way he had of singing. We talked of Father Larry Murray, that wandering scholar who founded the Gaelic college on the Rannafast peninsula under the iron rule that the student who spoke a word of English took the first train to the east from the station by the Big Stone of Crolly; and how he once broke a ceiling-board over a fellow's head because he heard him say: Jesus Christ.

But did he hit him with the board because he was taking the holy name in vain or because he didn't say: *Iosa Chriost*?

Choking with that nostalgia, or whatever, I even began to quote the translations of my youth and this, now, is my sly way of getting four lines of them printed, and riddle me the original of this and you're a good man:

I cried last night at the little door in the distance,
And I cried again on the love of my heart, my joy,
Till her mother came and told me over the threshold
She had slipped away in the night with the brownhaired boy.

Then we were well out of Ballybofey and on the road not to Doochary but to Donegal town. It was a mistake well worth making. For there ahead of us in the winter evening, and beyond a small still lake, were the dark shapes of the Bluestack mountains, and the sun dropping, a crimson host into a gigantic chalice, into the cup of Barnesmore Gap. Many sunsets had we seen in West Donegal but never anything to equal that. We stood on the roadside and watched until the crimson faded and there was nothing around us but shadows. That was on a Christmas Eve.

This now—our navigational error corrected—is the road to Doochary, and Doochary in one way is a sort of the centre of Donegal; and in another way like Farranfore in Kerry, like Kilfree or Manulla in Connacht, it is the centre of nowhere.

During the war when dead bodies from broken ships came drifting in on the coast, a body was washed up bearing papers that showed that the man when alive had been a true believer and a follower of Muhammad— the prophet, not the boy who boxes. So before he was laid to rest there was considerable discussion about which way the body should lie in relation to the points of the compass. One savant pointed this way and another that way, and maps were consulted, and lines drawn from Donegal to the putative neighbourhood of Mecca. Until one aged counsellor took the pipe out of the gob and coughed once and spat thrice and said: "Face him to Doochary and he'll rest in peace."

So leaving Ballybofey we face to Doochary (Dubhcharaidh), and ahead of us, all deep sable and shining steel in the winter dusk, is the heart-breaking lonely beauty, the awesome stillness of Lough Finn. Cattle calling on the way to the byres only emphasise the stillness. McMenamin's bar, so high on the side of Glenmore with the River Finn deep down in the shadows, will be a place to return to on some bright day in summer. From Fintown a lonely house with a black wall of mountain behind stays in the mind's eye and, you might say, travels the road with us: one of those houses, glimpsed in passing, that you can imagine living in—and happily.

Ahead in the west the clouds are dragonish, and a dozen other odd shapes as well. There's one like the head of a girl with long hair blown horizontally behind her. The last red breath of the sun has faded from the cold heather. The Christmas candles are alight in the windows of the roadside houses and of the houses back there on the slopes of the hills. Joseph and Mary and the child may pass this lonely road on the way to burning Egypt, this side of Mecca. The road ahead goes on to the Glenties, the road to the right to Doochary and Dungloe.

> *The purple mountains guard her, the valleys fold her in.*
> *In dreams I see her walking with angels, cleansed from sin.*
> *Is heaven so high and saintly*
> *That she can hear, though faintly,*
> *One word of all my mourning on her grave beside Loch Finn?*

I quote from memory, because time and time's thieves, the bad borrowers of books, whose patron saint was Colmcille, a Donegalman, have made away with my copy of *The Four Winds of Erin*, and even with my copy of the anthology, *They Sang for Ireland*, which old Seamus MacManus, the storyteller, put together to honour his first wife, Ethna Carbery and her friend Alice Milligan.

Ethna Carbery is buried in the village of Frosses, down there along the straight wet road to Glenties and she may have had a prophetic moment when she wrote those lines. When I was a boy with never a crack in my heart it was important to me that I owned a copy of her book *The Four Winds of Erin*:

> *Sheila Ni Gara it is lonesome where you bide*
> *With the plover circling over and the sagans spreading wide,*
> *With an empty sea before you and behind a wailing world*
> *Where the sword lieth rusty and the banner blue is furled.*

With a patriotism simple and naïve for the brutal times we live in, the poetess, who died young and innocent and 70 years ago, talks to Mother Erin under the name of Sheila Ni Gara, as good a name as any, and asks why, of all the four winds, she loves the best "the black black wind from the northern hills". The bold Sheila, her face to the ocean and her back to the bogs, replies that it is a kind wind and a true, that it rustled oft through Aileach's halls and stirred the hair of Hugh:

> *Then blow wind and snow wind, what matters storm to me*
> *Now I know the faery sleep must break and set the sleepers free?*

The Grianan of Aileach is the great circular stone edifice, the best part of 2,000 years of age, 900 feet up on a hilltop in north-east Donegal and

just over the border from the tortured city of Derry. Hugh is the great
O'Neill who fought as long as he could against the armies of the first
Elizabeth. The hopeful legend is that he and his warriors rest asleep under
Aileach hill for the day of awakening when they'll burst forth to liberate
Ireland. *La ar bith feasta*, as the cynics would say out west there on the
rocks of the Rosses and Gweedore to which we are bound—Any day
henceforth! Mañana!

Ethna Carbery wrote a fine song about Moorlough Mary, a rural
beauty from near the town of Strabane in north-west Tyrone. It's not the
old country ballad now that Paddy Tunney, from Castlecaldwell on the
Erne shore, sings as only Paddy Tunney can sing a ballad, with no god-
dammed messing about with guitars, but with a voice as lonely and
triumphant as the voice of a bird, with a love of the music and the words
and what they mean:

> *The first time ever I saw Moorlough Mary*
> *It was in the market of sweet Strabane.*
> *Her smiling glances did so entrance me,*
> *The hearts of young men she did trepann.*

Try as I may on this road to Doochary I can only recall from Ethna
Carbery's song some lines about the corn lying low in a golden rout and
about the golden shafts of the sun coming out. Where the hell is my book
and who was the blackguard who borrowed it?

But the day 42 years ago when I cycled all the 60 miles from Omagh to
Frosses to see her grave, I could remember and sing (sort of!) those words,
and also the song she wrote about Rody McCorley which everybody
knows, and the savage ballad she wrote about Brian Boy Magee—which
not so many know. That ancient savagery of the massacre of the native
Irish at Islandmagee in the seventeenth century might, naturally, be better
forgotten, apart from the academic consideration of how wicked the
gentle, good-mannered, long-skirted, bun-haired, young ladies of the
turn of the century could be:

> *I will go to Phelim O'Neill*
> *With my sorrowful tale, and crave*
> *A hard bright blade of Spain*
> *In the ranks of his soldiers brave.*
> *And God grant me strength to wield*
> *The shining avenger well,*
> *When the Gael shall sweep his foe*
> *Through the yawning gates of hell.*

C

The short-skirted, no-skirted, wild-haired maenads of today could be no more vivid. Up guards and at 'em with your hatpins and no mistake about it.

The west, as the man said, yet glimmers with some streaks of day, now spurs the lated traveller, and so on. Doochary, golden immortal city of the Aztecs, is just behind us, twenty houses or so clustered in a valley by a fine trout river in the very heart of the Donegal highlands. In summertime it can be beautiful and lazy and blessedly detached from tourism: the tourists go searching for the seashore which is a good ways away yet, over the next concentration of mountains.

There's a portion of Doochary that looks oddly like a fragment of an Edwardian suburb that somebody mislaid. Or was it only the enchantment of the Donegal dusk that made me see or think or feel like that? The road twists up westwards out of the deep valley. Then suddenly against the last Atlantic light there rises up the behemoth back of Arranmore island. A great view must always come as a surprise. That is why Paul Valéry said that everywhere they showed him great views and always it was the same view. A great view must be your own discovery, your personal vision, even if it is only "the undying difference in the corner of a field". You can't be told to expect it, or that it was there before you saw it.

Nor can you live with it always and expect to be surprised by it every morning. If you try to, or if it is your lot to do so, then it may become as valuable but as unexciting as a good and faithful wife: it's there all the time like the brother of the prodigal son. Although, as in the case of the good and faithful wife, there are always moods that can startle, colours that change, cloud-patterns whose outlines wriggle like eels. The great view, the vision, is something instantaneous, almost stolen:

> But ever and anon a trumpet sounds
> From the hid battlements of eternity,
> The shaken mists a space unsettle, then
> Round the half-glimpsed turrets slowly wash again.

What I mean is that out there is the long black back of Arranmore, and the sun drowning itself in crimson and smoky purple, and some Christmas eve you must go and see it for yourself. West in Donegal the sun, even in winter, dies slowly and splendidly.

As in the case of the town of Clogher in the county Tyrone, it was said of the village of Frosses that the people on one side of the street never spoke to the people on the other. This was because both the town and the village were all to the one side and across the street were the church and the churchyard. To go to eternity meant that you crossed, or were carried across, the street. But the population explosion or urban expansion or something has affected even such tiny places and the jest is not now as exact as it once was.

In the churchyard in Frosses a Celtic cross marks the grave of Ethna Carbery whose real name was Anna Johnston MacManus who was the first wife of Seamus MacManus, who wrote "A Lad of the O'Friels" and other homely tales of old Donegal. In Irish and in English in 1902 Seamus wrote her epitaph. She died young. Quoting again from memory here's some of it: "In her country's cause and for her country's language, bravely she taught and nobly she sang. At God's footstool her bright soul now pleads for the dawning of the glorious day of the Gael."

When Seamus died in New York at the age of 80 or thereabouts he was brought home to be buried in the churchyard at Frosses, over there beyond that wall of wintry black mountain. Now there was living on the hillside above Frosses an old man who had shared a boyhood's friendship with Seamus, and the friendship had endured over the years because Seamus, although he could be haughty and irascible, had the heart of a man who valued friendship, old houses and fields and twists of the road he had walked barefoot, old stone walls and hedges and trout streams and still mountain lakes.

Seamus and the old man of Frosses had spent a lot of their lives talking together and swapping stories, and naturally there were always people to say that Seamus never wrote one blessed page that he was supposed to have written but that he cogged it all from the friend of his boyhood. There are always people who say things like that. For instance, in Bela-shanny town you may still find a few to say that Allingham's Irish poems were all done by an oul fella who from Assaroe outwards would pull an oar, or a lugsail set or haul a net from the Point to Mullaghmore. Similar remarks have been made about fragments of Yeats and Colum and, I daresay, about Dante, Goethe, Banjo Patterson and about Nasir-I-Khusran, a Persian who died in 1061 and who wrote many odes of a religious and moralising character. And it's well known that the men who wrote the Bible have had all their hard work ascribed (as the professors say) to another and a single and/or triple author.

Anyway: it was a sight to see, they say, the old man who had stayed in Frosses all his life and his friend who had gone away but who came back every year: tall, a great head of white hair, green zipper jacket, a fine figure of a man. They'd talk all day and it is to be assumed that in those talks Seamus renewed his soul. To return to boyhood is a sort of a sacrament or at least it used to be.

On the day of the funeral the old man of Frosses was heart-broken. Dressed in his best he sat from dawn on the side of the street where the living people live. He waited for the funeral to come from Dublin or Shannon or Cobh or wherever it came to after New York. There was a long wait, and when it did come there were a million motors and in the motors bigwigs and tall hats and dignitaries of church and state, and all looking as important as bejesus, and most of them, for a cert, had never known Seamus nor ever read a word he had written. They crowded the street that divides the living and the dead. Nobody paid any attention to the old man. By the time he had hobbled across the street and through the crowd the grave was closed and his friend gone to where they could no longer swap stories unless, perhaps, the greatest story of all happens to be true.

WHERE THE THRUSH ATE THE ROBIN

On this Christmas eve in Teach Osta na Rosann, the Rosses hotel, in the town of Dungloe, or Clochan Liath, a man at a microphone is singing about Mexico. He sings not in Irish but in English although we are in the heart of the Donegal Gaeltacht. "South of the border," he sings, "down Mexico way."

Once I was nearly there, in Mexico I mean, but a sense of modesty inculcated into me, as the octogenarian said at the annual dinner, by the Christian Brothers, restrained me on this side of Tijuana. For an Oregonian student of mine told me that the local ladies were so lively that they stripteased and more on the very bar counters. A class of carry-on that might easily come between a man and his beer. Tijuana brass, you might call it. Mexican beer, now that I think of it, is much superior to those inducers of the trotting disorder that they produce (brewing can have nothing to do with it) in the US.

"That's where I fell in love," he sings to the guests and the folk from Glasgow for the Christmas, "when stars above came out to play."

In Teach Osta na Rosann in holy Ireland there is nothing on the counter but elbows and drinks and the conventional cherries and olives and oranges and lemons.

"It was siesta," he sings, "and we were so gay."

My friend and myself are halfways out the door. The last light is dying far out towards America. The sun that lends that light will shortly warm Tijuana, if it needs to be warmed. Paddy the Cope's pier is a black forearm on the steady water. Later I will tell you who Paddy the Cope was and will be forever.

"Did you hear," my friend says, "what I heard?"

"Siesta," says I.

"The singer was influenced either by a slip of the tongue or by an imperfect understanding of the language and/or customs of the Spanish people," says my companion. He is a grey-headed man with a sense of style.

"Bill O'Donovan tells me," I say, "that he heard a better one from a street-ballad singer who was wrestling with the Rose of Mooncoin. What he should have sung was: 'Where the thrush and the robin their sweet notes entwine, on the banks of the Suir that flows down by Mooncoin'. What he did sing was: 'Where the thrush ate the robin and two balls of twine'. He could have been half-brother to the balladman who sang of the wild colonial boy that: 'He robbed the rich, he robbed the poor, he murdered John Devoy'."

So laughing and being merry together like brothers akin, guesting awhile in the rooms of a beautiful inn, and having had for the moment our ration of cold Atlantic air, we step back into Teach Osta na Rosann. A beautiful modern inn it is, too. In the imagination of the barefooted boy who was to become the Moses that came down from the mountains of Cleendra to save the people of Templecrone from the pharaohs of gombeen men, such a palace as this would have seemed like one of the heavenly mansions, or one of the halls of the king in the story that Mici Pháidi in Rann na Feirsde used to tell about the boy from Burtonport who married the King of Spain's daughter.

Now what under God, you ask me, am I talking about and where, under heaven, is Cleendra, and what was Moses doing in these parts?

Cleendra is over there in winter darkness on this side of Croghey which is a wild headland with an outline to match Arranmore island. On Croghey the road, high on the cliff-edge, does in one place turn green, giving you a surface more fitted for the feet of goats than for the wheels of automobiles. No harm to the tourist trade which has done a power of good in these parts, but it might be no harm if the road remained that way, if only to show that there's one place in Ireland where the automobile is not the master.

That's the way I'd feel in the evening rush and the stench of petrol in most of the cities, Peking being the most notable exception, of the world we live in. There are no privately-owned automobiles in Peking. But if I were living on the cliff-edge of Croghey and had a sick person in the house who had to get to hospital, I'd think and feel otherwise.

From Cleendra, the best part of a century ago, came a barefooted boy called Patrick Gallagher. The house he was born in is still standing. We remember him as Paddy the Cope or, at least, we should so remember him. For I had the consternation the other day of talking to three young Irish people who had never heard of him and didn't know what Cope meant. As I frequently say: "You Irish fascinate me."

He was born in 1871. He was called Paddy Pat Bawn because he was Patrick, the son of fair-headed Patrick. The young people from this rocky place of small fields, high drystone walls, went at an early age and barefoot and to keep body and soul together, to hire out to strong farmers in the rich lands along the Strule and Mourne and Foyle in Tyrone and Derry and East Donegal. As a boy he went with them and, later, to the potato-fields and the coalmines of Scotland. He married a girl from his own place and, with her and her careful housekeeping, discovered through the Scottish co-operative societies what co-operativism offered to poor people.

Back at home in Donegal for the birth of their first child they bought a small farm. AE the poet and painter and mystic who was also, under Sir Horace Plunkett, an organiser for the co-operative movement in Ireland, came to speak in Dungloe and inspired Paddy and his neighbours in Cleendra to set up their own co-operative society which, afterwards, moved its headquarters to Dungloe and became in 1906 the Templecrone Co-operative Society. By a simple abbreviation Patrick Gallagher became Paddy the Cope.

The work prospered in spite of fierce opposition from the local merchants who saw it as a threat to their profits and their usurious power over the poor who lived, on perpetual interest (*gaimbin*), through the merchants' books. Hence, gombeen man. Today, six years after Paddy's death, the Cope continues to flourish, employs 75 people, does an annual trade worth half a million pounds, has its own shopping centre and knit-wear factory in Dungloe.

My Story by Paddy the Cope was first published by Jonathan Cape in 1939. In paperback it is now available from the Templecrone Co-Operative Society, Dungloe, Co. Donegal.

When Paddy the Cope was running once for membership of the Donegal County Council he was opposed by a merchant prince of the town of Dungloe—in which we now are. In oratory which some Dungloe people still say was disgorged like a rope and was loud enough to silence a compressor (the streets of the town were being dug-up at the time), the merchant said: "Who is this Moses who descends upon us from the mountains of Cleendra to lead the people of the Rosses to the promised land?"

That was a good question.

My own first meeting with Moses was sometime in the 1940s when the life-work that earned him his name was behind him and when he had written the life-story that later Michael Powell, a great director, and a gentleman and a friend of mine—two interchangeable terms—hoped to turn into a movie. The pity was that, for lack of money, the movie was never made. Powell had made *Edge of the World*, a sensitive study of the decay and dying of a community on the fringe of the Hebrides. He had the feeling for that simple life, for those most desolate stony places. The Hebrides in a way are closer to West Donegal than is the rich valley of the Strule and Mourne: they have the same style. Powell could have got onto the screen the epic quality of the struggle that Paddy Pat Bawn and the Cleendra people, and the people of all the Rosses here from Gweedore to Gweebarra and back inland there in the darkness to Doochary, made to improve their way of life. They won, too, and that makes the story all the better in the telling.

This was what Moses was like to look at and to listen to.

He was a stout butt of a man dressed stiffly in a good dark suit and with one of those hard, white, detachable shirt-collars with rounded corners on it and no points: the dress, say, of a respectable small farmer or shop-keeper of about 40 years ago. The face was red rather than tanned with wind and weather and the head bald, but the complexion was young and the eyes as bright and lively as if he were a very good-humoured sixteen. The colour of those eyes I can't remember but I only saw their like once elsewhere and that was in the head of John F. Kennedy: they were boyish but shrewd, hard.

Moses talked just as my father talked, that is with a definite Donegal accent. He talked about the great people he had known, a lot about that odd trinity who godheaded the co-operative movement in Ireland: the poet, AE; the gentleman and Unionist converted to the cause of the people, Sir Horace Plunkett; the Jesuit priest, Father Tom Finlay. He talked about my own part of the country, the valley of the Strule, the Mourne and the Foyle, where as a barefooted boy he had hired out to labour for a pittance for the hard-fisted farmers. He was good to listen to: old-fashioned and even naïve if you were foolish enough to think so. But unless you were very foolish you pretty soon realised that he was playing at being naïve, that he enjoyed laughing at and exaggerating the mistakes he said he had made.

He talked a lot about Scotland where he had worked in the potato-fields and the coalpits, but above all he talked about his dead wife or, as he put it, about "coortin' Sally". Once he loaned me a great mass of typescript that had not been included in the book, that was enough to make another book, and it was all fragments of a simple love-story. This block of a man, as tough and hard as the western rocks he was reared on and the Scottish fields and mines he had worked in, who for the sake of his own people had fought the greed and tyranny of the gombeen men or merchant princes, had really all the time wanted to tell the world how much Sally meant to him.

But even in those later affluent days he was never one to put a penny astray. He had been reared in a world where every penny counted. Right up to the end when he set off from Dungloe to cover the 200 miles or so to Dublin he travelled in no limousine or chauffeured car as the merest executive does today. But he took a lift in a lorry to Strabane and the train from Strabane to Dublin. It got him there. He talked to people on the way. He was always in touch. He remembered the days when he had travelled barefoot.

He was good to talk to and to listen to. He liked his whiskey and never that I knew of bought a friend a half-glass (small one) when a glass (large one) would do as well or better. But he never in his life lost a day's work over whiskey. That was the only pledge that he ever took against drink and he took it in no association, pin-wearing or anonymous, but to himself one day in Letterkenny when he was on his way back to the Scottish mines: and he kept it.

The only time he ever had a hangover was on a morning in Derry jail where the machinations of the merchant princes had landed him. He and the two sympathetic constables who conducted him from Dungloe to Derry started drinking on the train, continued in a pub in Derry until the publican told them they'd better finish up and go or the jail would be closed. He was released two days later not because of the hangover but because Father Tom Finlay, who had been fishing in Doochary, rushed up to Dublin and told the lord-lieutenant that Paddy Pat Bawn had been wrongfully arrested, mistried and imprisoned. Never was Jesuit intrigue at a court so rapidly successful.

Oh God, that Michael Powell had only filmed that story. Or the story about the time Paddy went over to Manchester and London to show and sell the textile work of the co-operative. He was dressed in a tight suit spun for him by Sally, and a cap, and a collar to his shirt because he was

crossing the sea to another country and had to look his most respectable.
He had a cooked hen (never a chicken) with him for provender, and he
thought of the migratory labourers on the Glasgow boat who mightn't
have a hen at all. On the advice of an English hall-porter he brought a
dark suit to make him look like a commercial traveller, and a hat that the
hatter hammered this way and that so as to fit it to his customer's cannon-
ball head. But next day the hat had sprung back to its original shape and
it fell off his head on the steps of a big store and by accident he put his
foot through it. When he told the story to a Donegal woman in London
he didn't mention the hard fate of the hat. He knew that no vow of
secrecy could keep her from telling the tale to everybody in Donegal, from
Buncrana to Ballyshannon.

Or the story about how he and his fellow-miners in a place in Scotland
lived for a season on fresh salmon, poached—out of the river. "I never saw
a [water] bailiff while I was there. It was a very nice place and the people
were very kind."

Or the story . . .

But I digress.

He was born a century ago and on a Christmas night. That merchant
prince might more aptly have talked of the Messiah. He was born into an
Irish-speaking world of poverty, small farms, rocks, stone-walled tiny
fields, fishermen who had only currachs to fish from; of chronic
emigration and migratory labour. The capital city was not Dublin but
Glasgow, or New York or Boston or Chicago. To this day West Donegal
has less to do with Dublin than many people imagine. The tyrants of that
world were those shopkeepers in whose debt the people lived perpetually,
never even knowing precisely what they owed, afraid to ask for an
account in case they'd be refused credit in the future.

But in Scotland Paddy had seen for himself how co-operative societies
worked for the benefit of the consumer. Sally and he had saved their first
money through the Pumperstown co-operative. Then from Plunkett and
Russell and Finlay and others in Dublin Paddy got the idea that what was
good for Pumperstown would be better still for Cleendra. The rest is
history, and very lively too, for usurers do not like to lose their usufruct,
and the forces of money and·respectability ganged-up against the red
revolutionary, Paddy Pat Bawn. When Finlay the Jesuit (whom I had the
privilege of listening to in his last days in a convalescent home in Dublin)[2]
came here to Dungloe to lecture, the merchants put it about that he was an
Orange priest—something never heard of before or since. That vision of
an Orange Ignatian does, at least, show that the gombeen men shared
with the people they ruled and robbed a rich Celtic imagination.

It was a privilege, too, to have known Paddy the Cope, and to have relished his wry wisdom. He came from a careful but humorous people. Once, in his mining-days, when he got back from Ireland to his butties in the Scottish lodging-house he had nothing better on him for a toast than a half-bottle of whiskey. There was only one glass in the house. He wrote long afterwards: "When you have only one glass you can make a wee lock of whiskey go a long way if you hold on to the bottle."

Sitting here in the light and heat and comfort of the crowded lounge in Teach Osta na Rosann I am shaken by the contrast between the scene before me and the cold bare hillside that would have been here in the days of the boyhood of Paddy the Cope. In those days a polite lady in London decided, against the advice of her friends who feared she would never come back alive, to travel all the way to Donegal to see what was going on there.

Quite close to my greyheaded friend and myself three polite ladies (late middle-aged) from London are settling down to enjoy a Donegal Christmas. They have no relatives hereabouts. If they did they'd have Glasgow, not southern English, accents. They have spent summer holidays here. They love the place and the people. So they make up this little party, all old friends you see, and come again for Christmas. They have no worries in the world about getting back alive to London.

The name of the London lady who was so courageous so long ago (1887) was Dinah Mary Craik who wrote about John Halifax, Gentleman, the poor boy who, in Victorian times and according to the impeccable maxims of Samuel Smiles, was so good that he made good. The boy from Cleendra made good for his people and for himself because he was tough as a rope and I doubt if he ever had any of the waxen virtue of John Halifax.

Dinah Mary Craik passed along this way on the road below this hotel which, to be Hibernian-bullish about it, wasn't here then. She tells us that she once heard a "rustic" who helped a crippled girl out of a London omnibus say that a handful of help was worth a cartload of pity. When she got back safely to London she—to put a "similar idea into the heads and hearts of English people"—wrote about her trip to Ireland a book called *An Unknown Country*. There was no tourist promotion in those days.

Her unknown country was a land of black hovering desolation, of fever and famine, and it staggered her to think that it was only a few hours journey away from the great, populous, central city of the world. "England would be mad indeed," she wrote, "to close her eyes to the black cloud which overhangs Ireland, and the social upheaval now convulsing her from end to end." How often could that not have been written about the two countries?

In the year of Dinah's journey Lord George Hill who was a big land-owner in these parts compiled a biteen of a book called *Facts From Gweedore*. He had 23,000 acres there, with 700 tenants paying rent out of a total of 3,000, and he may have had, as he professed to have, good intentions. Not many Gweedore men would have agreed with him, then or since. In among the facts there was this odd bit of verse:

Although each holding wouldn't feed an ass,
It went by the name of the cow's grass;
For Shane had two, Teague two and a half,
Manus five-eighths and Margery a calf;
Each portion was only the breadth of a staff.

Odd medieval fragment to come back into the mind and this bright scene before us, and the three chattering ladies beside us, happy to be away from London, unaware that the ghost of Dinah Mary Craik is passing there on the road below. All along the crowded shore of the Rosses and Gweedore the dogs will be barking from house to house. *Bionn na madaidh a'tafann*, as the people say, the dogs do be continually barking. The dogs in the Rosses always seemed to me to go in more for communication than dogs did elsewhere in Ireland.

At the far corner of the great square hotel-lounge, people are dancing to music and singing as they dance. The Christmas candles will be burning in every window all along the coast. The accents around us are various: Donegal, Glasgow, London, refined Dublin, and now and again Irish. Then the door opens and Lord George Hill comes in with Dinah Mary Craik on his arm, and followed by John Halifax, gentleman, and Paddy the Cope.

"No more brandy," my good friend says. "We have miles to go before we sleep and a visit to pay in the little town of Kinncasslagh."

"She smiled," we sing, "as she whispered banana."

We say farewell to the lovely ladies from London where Rhodo-dendrons grow. They, the ladies, have become noticeably younger and more lovely over the last hour. We go on our way through the dark towards Gweedore.

From the picture on the wall of the bar in Kinncasslagh Napoleon Bonaparte stares sombrely out at a fair and representative selection of the people of the district. Outside, the wintry air is quiet for Christmas and there is no roar of the sea from the rocks that intricately fortify the little harbour nor from the long red strand of Mullachdearg, just behind the house, where I and others once spent happy and idle days—under the name of learning Irish. The bar is beautiful with those mirrors, lettered in black and gold, in praise of beers and whiskeys no longer to be found. The Corsican is reflected in several of them. He doesn't look very pleased. But it isn't Kinncasslagh that's the cause of sorrow to him.

He's cheesed, and with good reason, at the predicament he finds himself in. He's on the deck of the *Bellerophon* in a reproduction of that painting by Sir William Orchardson, RA. If you're about my age you'll know it well. Bibby's (soap) calendars long ago made the scene as familiar to people in these islands as that incident from the boyhood of Raleigh, or the story of the little Cavalier boy, all plush and ringlets, being interrogated by the Roundheads: "When did you last see your father?"

Napoleon is in the foreground, hands behind the back to balance the prone brow oppressive with its mind, and all that. He's staring straight at the three of us, my travelling companion, a daughter of the house and myself, where we sit in a corner by the fire. He looks as if he had just swallowed a raw egg and forgotten to smell it in time and can't find the Courvoisier. Behind him and somewhat apart stand seven officers of His Majesty's fleet, seven long-nosed, malevolent-looking gentlemen. Their expressions say: "Egad, sir, we have you now and this time you won't get away." They have all the appearance of lords of the sea and land who'd flog a stableful of tenants and hang a dozen rebels and mutineers just to work up an appetite for the roast beef. By men with such sweet faces was Britain's power built up from Brighton to Burma. The fearful thing is that Sir William Orchardson, whoever in hell he was, looked back on them with an admiring eye and could do no better for them. In spite of him the truth came out.

A little boy in long tight white pants is leaning over a bulwark, calling to someone on a lower deck and displaying in all innocence the most darling bottom: the homely touch, the playing-fields of Eton, the traumatic floggings, the troopers in the Park, Swinburne in St John's Wood.

Theobald Wolfe Tone who, back about the same time was snubbed by Mr Pitt and thought an Irish republic would be a good idea, saw those same faces when, getting out easy from a charge of treason, he was on his way to America. The ship he was sailing in had just cleared the Grand Banks when it was stopped by three British frigates: the *Thetis*, Captain Lord Cochrane; the *Hussar*, Captain Rose; the *Esperance*, Captain Wood...

... who boarded us, and after treating us with the greatest insolence, both officers and sailors, they pressed everyone of our hands save one, and near fifty of my unfortunate fellow-passengers, who were most of them flying to America to avoid the tyranny of a bad government at home and who thus, most unexpectedly, fell under the severest tyranny—one of them at least—which exists. As I was in a jacket and trousers one of the lieutenants ordered me into the boat as a fit man to serve the King, and it was only the screams of my wife and sister which induced them to desist. The insolence of these tyrants ... I have not since forgotten and I never will.

He wasn't to be allowed to forget them. The same faces were on the deck of the captured French frigate, the *Hoche*, and Sir George Hill, ancestor of the aforementioned Lord George and a college contemporary of Tone and a violent and narrow-minded man, was to point to him and say: "That man is Theobald Wolfe Tone".

That happened over there in Lough Swilly, around the long arms and deep bays of this dark indented Donegal coast, and Sir George Hill may well have owned the land on which this house stands. We are here in the corner between the fire and the wall. We are happy and warm with firelight and Courvoisier. Under the rancid eyes of Bonaparte I imagine I can hear the beat of the ocean on Mullachdearg strand. The children of this house were blessed by having that strand as a playground, right at the back door. Even if it is dangerous for swimming. The sea there always seems as it advances, gathers strength and stature, topples down and shatters on the red shelving sand, to have more colours in it than the sea has anywhere else. Or it had all those colours 42 golden years ago. Or perhaps the colours were only in the eye of the beholder.

This is a calm winter night 40 years later, and the sea out there can only be grey all the way to the Grand Banks and beyond.

ON A DOORSTEP IN DERRYBEG

It's so long now since I stopped overnight in the Donegal Gaeltacht that it seems odd to me that a nineteen-year-old in a green pelmet of a skirt, and more thigh showing than would seem natural in anybody except a giraffe, should wish me good morning and a happy Christmas in Irish.

My mind, it may be, has been conditioned on Jungian principles by ancestral memories of the daughters of Erin, *Inghinidhe na hEireann*, hands on their wild harps, tresses flowing as in Lady Morgan's Glorvina, a forerunner of Edna O'Brien, long, green, gold-embroidered gowns sweeping the earth, chaste toes showing like mice peeping out from holes at the bottom of a bag of oatmeal: the sort of ladies who once in a hallway in Camden Street, Dublin, lifted their skirts an inch or so to step over a young fellow called Joyce who had collapsed drunk on the floor after hammering on the door with his stick and roaring: "Come out, Fay. You can't keep us out of your whorehouse." Fay, one of two famous brothers later of the Abbey Theatre, had been rehearsing the actresses among the daughters.

Where have all those long skirts gone? What would the brusque priest, Larry Murray, man of Dunleer and Minnesota, founder of the Gaelic college a few miles away at Rann na Feirsde, have said about skirts that were little more than pelmets? He was a bit of a Puritan but he didn't object to dancing as long as it was Irish dancing. It's possible that he wouldn't have noticed if the Daughters of Erin went in their pelt, provided they behaved themselves and did it in Irish.

The dogs are barking from house to house but not until after twelve noon on Christmas Day. The dogs of Gweedore show some respect for the ancient decencies. But the dogs of the Rosses and Gweedore still constantly and enthusiastically chase motor-cars and that's a surprising thing on a road that during the summer carries so much traffic. Mayhap the dogs only bark at motors in the winter when the place is quiet and the road near empty. My friend stops his car and screws down his window and barks back at the dogs. That startles the dogs. By now they know enough about the world they live in to know that motors shouldn't bark.

Standing at the door I look with the eyes of 40 years ago on Gweedore, the crowded coastal belt between the bare mountains and the sea breaking white around a dozen islands. *Ganntanas talaimh agus tiugh na dtoighthe*, they used to say, scarcity of land and multiplicity of people. Joe Maguire from Fintona in Tyrone, told me in the 1930s how in earlier years he travelled this coast, selling his goods to those who could afford them, fishing the rivers when the notion took him. It was then still classified as a congested district: a brutal and exact, yet ludicrous description. Joe fought at the Dardanelles and survived, not tha that has anything to do with Donegal, but it helps to place him in time. He lived to see here fine houses where hovels had been. But even Joe, were he with me here this blessed morning, would be amazed, and pleased at his amazement, to see the face of prosperity that smiles back at me from this section of the homes of Donegal.

My mother's mother could look from the threshold of her farmhouse near Drumquin in Tyrone and on a clear day see 60 miles away the tip of the white cone of Mount Errigal, the Cock of the North. She looked west. From where I stand now I look east and there seven miles away is the entire mountain, as distinct as Fuji-Yama.

On clear days then when the old grandmother glimpsed the faraway mountain she'd say: "Ah, the poor Donegals, the poor Donegals". For she thought of the people from these places as they were in her time, some of them without a shoe to their foot, young men and women and children standing like cattle, to be hired out by the season, in the fairs and markets of Omagh and Strabane. We hadn't that much in Tyrone, but at least the fields were big and free of stones and there were trees and hedgerows and we didn't have to tether the cows.

In the 1930s on the Courthouse hill in Omagh I saw a strong Presbyterian farmer from near Newtownsaville feeling the bicep of a young fellow, as Georgian cotton-planters used to do with black boys and girls in the slave-market. The young fellow and his friends on the Courthouse hill talked the loveliest Irish which further encouraged the farmer, and his friends, to think they were dealing with animals.

Then my mother had actually known Patrick MacGill when she was a young girl and he was a servant-boy, a poor Donegal, in Young's of the Hollow near Drumquin, County Tyrone: a chastening experience that he was to remember when he wrote *Children of the Dead End*. MacGill, who died a few years ago in the States, was a sort of Donegal Gorki and the first writer ever to tell the truth about the lot of the Irish migratory labourer and of the Irish navvy on construction jobs in England. Young of the Hollow and his incredible skinflintry are still legendary in that part of west Tyrone. It was said that he'd go into a shop in Drumquin and say: "Two pounds of the good bacon and four pounds of sarvint-boys' bacon". *Id est*: Limerick ham for himself and American streaky long-bottom bacon for the labouring men.

Once in a spasm of revolt the sarvint-boys approached him and boldly did outspeak: "Mr Young, we're tired atin' dry bread. Could we have a bit of butter or jam or syrup or treacle?"

"Do you say your prayers?" says Young.

"We do."

"Do ye say the Lord's prayer?"

"We do."

"Well, the Lord himself said: Give us this day our daily bread. He never said a word about butter or jam or syrup or treacle."

He had his counterpart, of course, in other parts of Ireland, in Darby O'Leary, the Galbally farmer in County Tipperary:

I well recollect it was Michaelmas night,
To a hearty good supper he did me invite:
A cup of sour milk that would physic a snipe
And give you the trotting disorder.
The wet old potatoes would poison the cats,
The barn where my bed was, was swarming with rats . . .
. . . But such woeful starvation I've never yet seen
As I met with old Darby O'Leary.

In reality, and as immortalised in balladry, the lot of the servant-boy was not an overfed one. In the townland of Drumragh close to my native town of Omagh there was, just a little before my time, one Johnny Pet Wilson who made his corner in local history as perhaps the meanest man who ever lived. On the Courthouse hill once Johnny hired a "wee runt of a Scotchy" and so far forgot himself as to get drunk with his hired hand who, not to be niggardly about it, got as drunk as his master. For once, Johnny Pet was paying. They staggered home and to bed, and at about four in the morning Johnny routed the Scotsman out of the doss to look after the cattle. "Hae ye no gone to bed yet, mon?" Jock said. But when he saw what was walking behind Johnny he, according to the story, took off with a roar and was never seen again in that part of the country.

For Johnny, like the mountainy farmer in Drumlister in the comic dialect poem by the Rev. Marshall of Sixmilecross, wore the Indian meal bag like a shawl to keep away the cold, and led about with him on a halter—as if it were a pet poodle on an ornamented lead—a gentleman goat of distinct odour, prodigious hornage and malevolent appearance. In the days of my boyhood Johnny Pet's house was abandoned, the orchard around it running wild, and we used to peep fearfully through sagging fence and unkempt hedge to see the parading ghosts of Johnny Pet and the goat. Several of our elders had seen them. We used also steal the apples, if taking from a ghost and the ghost of a goat could be called stealing.

The first story I ever heard told in Irish over there a few miles away in Rann na Feirsde concerned just such another farmer as Darby O'Leary and Young of the Hollow and Johnny Pet Wilson.

In the establishment of this generous man and his hospitable wife the seven or eight servant-boys (in age from seven to seventy) ate in the barn, supping thick *brothan* (porridge, oatmeal or Indian) and buttermilk out of one huge basin. Each man dug a hole for himself with the spoon, poured the buttermilk into the hole and then supped around it. Once a pet goose belonging to the farmer's wife joined the mess and the oldest of the boys was delegated to cross to the house and ask the *bean a' tighe* (woman of the house) for a spoon for the goose. That was the first funny story I ever heard in Irish—and it wasn't all that funny.

Ah, the poor Donegals: the world of rocks here was hard in those days but it was home, nor was it half as hard and as heartless as the labouring life on the big farms of the Lagan, from Omagh all the way, say, to Manorcunningham and the fringes of Derry city. And beyond to Fifeshire and the gutters of Glasgow, the Rat Pit that Patrick MacGill wrote about in his most savage book. It was "all so unimaginably different and all so long ago". Or was it? Strange stories still come back from the potato fields of Scotland and from the men who navvy on the big construction jobs.

Once upon a time when the decent people at a spot in these parts called Kerrytown took a spasm of seeing visions, I talked in a small hotel on this coast to an ageing Scottish Presbyterian lady. We were holidaying in the same hotel. It had a great view of the islands and the open ocean.

This lady was a verra industrious body as was once said in her ain countrie about Auld Hornie, Satan, Nick or Clootie, and most of her holiday she spent in a chair outside the house with her spectacles on the tip of her nose, and her grey hair in a tight bun, and her knitting needles going at socks as if she were knitting for the entire peoples of Africa and India, and determined to make them all good Presbyterians—at any rate up beyond the balls of the legs or as far as the socks would cover. She never knitted anything but socks.

She was so hard at it all the time that she could never understand what myself and my two companions, all younger then, were doing at all that unChristian gadding-about. Finally on this Sabbath morning, when she wasn't even knitting but reading a sombre-looking buik—no, it wasn't the bible but almost certainly anither gude Ane—her patience broke an' she spaik oot. (This thing is growing on me, and I had better revert to as near to standard English as what education I ever had brought me.) She asked us where we were going. So I told her about Kerrytown, and how the people over there had imagined that they had seen this and that in the way of religious apparitions on the side of a great rock: the mother of God, Bernadette of Lourdes, a monk saying mass; that we were going over ourselves not to see apparitions, for none of us had ambitions that way, but to look at the place and at what was going on there. She closed her book and looked at me long and severely. "At home in Scotland," she said, "there are bodies who speir helpies in Loch Ness." Or words to that effect.

I'll never pass this road through Gweedore and into the Rosses without thinking of her. She may have had her misgivings about popish practices and credulities. Or she may have been accepting the reality of the other world and of visions and glimpses given to us here; and her honest logical mind saw no difference between people seeing a serpent in a Scottish lake and seeing among the rocks of Donegal the woman who crushed the head of the serpent. We never got down to the committee stage about the matter, which was just as well because, although one of the three of us was a clerical student his theology, and mine if any, would never have been up to it. Serpents, though, scarcely belong in theology—with that one notable exception.

We went on to Kerrytown and saw nothing except rain on grass and heather and stone walls, and a few people kneeling in the rain and looking at a big rock and quietly saying their prayers. Was there a big rock, I try to remember, at Ardboe in east Tyrone—there was one in Lourdes— when some people there stepped on the fringe of that other world which none of us can afford to scoff at? There can be a great variety in visions.

But this now before us is not the rock of Kerrytown but the big balancing stone of Crolly, and the only visions I ever saw around here were the young women who went to Colaisde Bhrighidhe in Rann na Feirsde when I was a young man, carrying a stick as was my custom and writing dreadful poetry, by the Lord, in the silent watches of the night, and keeping a fine phrase-notebook, and being idyllically and idiotically happy. All those laughing girls gathered like flowers around the big stone in all those faded snapshots. Dear, dead women with such hair too, what's become of all the gold. . . ?

Well, not dead, by no means, but scattered here and there and, like myself, getting no younger. Although I met one of them the other day and she told me she was a grandmother, but she didn't look a day older than she did when we sat out a sudden shower in the shelter of this balancing stone and held hands and spoke broken Irish, falling back now and again on memorised songs and *filidheacht* (poetry) to keep the talk going, and saying *Dia ar sabhail* (God save us) and *Tá sé ag cur go trom* (It is raining heavily) and such Wildean *bons mots* a lot more often than would seem necessary in any normal conversation; and listening to the Crolly river, which has to be one of the world's most perfect short rivers, leaping from pool to pool all the way down from the Lake of the Yew Tree to the gothic glen which we used to call the Ramparts which is halfway along the only genuine shortcut to the Rosses.

That sentence is damn nearly longer than the Crolly river but, like the wild mountain water itself, I was carried away:

Cloud-begot, mountain-bred,
Heather-nursed child,
Innocent, beautiful,
Winsome and wild,
Here she comes dancing
O'er boulder and rock
And in many a waterfall
Shakes her white frock.

That was Standish James O'Grady writing about what stream I know not. In the Eyeries of west Cork? In the Dublin-Wicklow mountains? But it will serve at this moment for the river that goes prancing and dancing down below there to the bridge at Crolly. Where just a while ago on this bright, cold, quiet, coloured morning my friend and myself were contemplating a windowful of Crolly dolls, created in the factory whose roof is visible from here. They winked back at us, they were the laughing girls that once gathered around the big stone: this one was Róisín from Donnybrook in Dublin, that one like Eibhlín from Bally-hackamore in Belfast, that one had a touch of Maruna from Tyrone, and that one in a dark dress was Éilis, a great dancer who is now a nun. Are things what they seem or is visions about?

The river, as clean as Eden, leaps from pool to pool and, because it leaps down to the gothic Ramparts on its way to the sea, it reminds me of Joris, and this has nothing to do with Robert Browning and bringing the good news, whatever it was, from Aix to Ghent. Or was it vice versa?

The Ramparts, tá fhios agat, was a place where young couples from the summer college in Rann na Feirsde went when they wanted to be alone —or together. Joris was a lively and amorous young man of eighteen and as fine a fellow as, in this life at least, I've met or am liable to meet. But he wasn't too hot at the Irish: for the reason that he had gone to a public school in England, and then his father, who was a lawyer in the Irish midlands, wanted him to go to University College, Dublin, for which he needed some preliminary stammerings of the ancient tongue of the Gael. So he came with me to the happy peninsula beyond this big stone here and, within two or three days, had given the business of learning Irish up as a bad job, and sunk backwards into silence more intense even than the silence that was before the jabbering hairy folk came out of the caves or down from the trees and made the first efforts at speech. For Father

Larry Murray who ran the college and ruled the peninsula would not have appreciated even a jabber if it sounded as if it had the flimsiest origins in *Bearla*. One word of English, detected, heard or overheard, and you took the first transport out from this Big Stone of Crolly.

In those days my phrase-notebook was, as the old randy mountainy Kerrywoman said about something else altogether, the wonder of three parishes: if it wasn't in my head or on my tongue it was in the book in two or three languages. So a scholar from Benburb, using the deaf and dumb signs and other pantomime aids, gets across to Joris that if he starts to keep a phrase-notebook he might get closer to the undying Milesian soul which we were so splendidly expressing in our pidgin Irish. A week later a man from Oldcastle notices that Joris has a notebook, a fine sable hardbacked edifice, and he's mean enough to have a peep and to tell us about it afterwards. We are mean enough to listen. Never saw anything like it, we hear, for scholarship, research, attention to detail: one page to each horse and everything there that you'd need to know, mare and sire, date of foaling, races run, wins, places, favourable mentions, always prominent and the rest, odds given, jockeys up, possible prospects, and all written in neat and cryptic *Bearla* with numerals in Arabic.

The breaking-point came one day when Joris with the face of a hunted man, handed me a sheet of paper on which he had written: "For God's sake get me a woman who is able and willing to speak the language of Chaucer and Shakespeare". That was the only time I ever broke Fr Larry Murray's iron rule about the speaking of Irish-only, once you had passed this big balancing stone. It was also the only time I ever pimped in two languages: something that everybody should try once, as part of a liberal education.

Thereafter Joris would return from the Ramparts under the cloak of kindly night that covered even the enormity of speaking English, and sit on the side of his bed (we shared a room) scrubbing the cowdung off his clothes with a nail-brush and saying again and again: "*Dia ar sabhail*". Those three words he did learn, and very good words they are.

The Big Stone of Crolly stands in the townland of Leim a' tSionnaigh, or Foxleap. Would Foxleap Stone be a fine name for it? Whence and how, I wonder, did the groins of the brae that the brook treads through get that name?

THE POET DIED IN INDIA

The young poet from Belfast and myself are walking along this narrow road. The year is 1940. He is twenty and I'm a year or so older. He is tall, a slow walker, bronze-haired, a gentle quiet soul and somewhat given to melancholy. He is doing Celtic studies in Queen's University, Belfast. He has a girlfriend in Queen's and as far as I remember she hasn't come to this Donegal Gaeltacht with him because she hasn't a word of Irish and doesn't care if she never has. This is grievous to him and he doesn't talk too much about it. But he broods.

He broods so much that, being a poet, one line of a certain poem almost moves him to tears. It is the last line in this most beautiful verse:

> *A sheacht n-anam deag do bhéal, do mhalaid, 's do ghruaidh,*
> *Do shúil ghorm-ghlé far threig mé aiteas is suairc;*
> *Le cumhaidh 'do dheidh ni léir domh an bealach a shuibhal*
> *'S a charaid mo chléibh, tá na sléibhte eadar mé agus thú.*

The beauty of her mouth, her curving cheek, her hair would draw not six, but seventeen, souls out of Shakespeare's puritanical weaver. For her blue bright eyes he would abandon all drollery and content:

> *With loneliness after you I can hardly see the road I walk,*
> *And love of my bosom the mountains are between me and you.*

You get the idea? She is faraway in Belfast, he is here with myself and many others in the stony Rosses. Errigal, silvery, clear-cut, with all its ancillary mountains, is there between them.

It's the sort of thing that worries a man of twenty, particularly if he is madly in love and given to poetry. Yet as Joe Maguire of Fintona once said to me, when he then was about the age that I am now, and we were flogging the stream one wet day along the vale of Dibben up above Glenties: "When you make my age you'd rather be dropping a fly over that pool or blowing the froth of a pint than putting an arm around the neatest waist in Ireland."

As I walk with the lovelorn poet, going up the slope towards Siopa Searcaigh (Sharkey's shop), I swing a stout ashplant, beheading the wayside thistles, and talk a lot in the vain hope of moving his mind away to something other than the ungaelicised female, his half-regained Eurydice, on the other side of the mountains. Then suddenly I notice that he isn't listening, that he isn't—by Aengus the god who also was lovelorn—walking with me at all; and I look back and there he is sitting on the roadside grass, his hand to the side of his head, a dazed look in his eyes. What has happened is that, in my hilarious beheading of the thistles, the ashplant has come full circle and caught him the most thunderous buffet, adding to his other woes a lump the size of a tennis-ball.

He is so gentle and good that he doesn't even reproach me. It is one of those things that you feel sorry about for the rest of your life, and I am to remember it four years later when the news of his death comes back to me from as faraway as India. Whither he had gone as a young officer in I forget what British regiment. Where he was to die not wildly in battle but killed by a truck in a road accident, killed casually, you might say, when the great armies, beset with the memories of centuries, were turning over in their nightmares.

O, friend of my bosom, the mountains are between me and you.

I search the house for a book that contains one of his poems, the *Faber Book of Irish Verse*, selected some years ago by Valentine Iremonger and Robert Greacen. But did any man ever find among his books the one for which he was really searching? It was a fine poem about a cat.[3]

All this I talk about to a friend of later years as we sit on a Christmas day on a rock above the sea in Rann na Feirsde, the only two men to be seen in the world, at ease in a mellow honey-coloured sunshine that seems just impossible at this time of the year and on that unsheltered coast. The mountains that came between the sad poet and his beloved are our secure shelter against the east wind, and never did I see those mountains, or the whole land and the colours of rock and heather and small field, look more beautiful. A sun in winter gives the place something that even high summer could not give.

"Someone," says my friend, "has given us a gift of Donegal."

All to ourselves, and this place for me with all its memories.

That endless wet August and the rain coming, not down from above, but sideways at you on a most ill-mannered wind bred on the Atlantic; and a crowd of us lodging in Teach Neide Franc, or the house of Neddy Frank O Grianna, and wondering to Mananáan MacLir, god of the sea, and whatever gods there be in these parts, would the rain ever cease. One day it does so, and the clouds break, and all the men of the house then, all naked to the waist and led out by a big Presbyterian schoolmaster from Milford on Mulroy bay, all kneeling in a solemn circle to worship the sun. . . .

Old Cormac McGarvey walking barefoot every morning to a flat flagstone at the corner of the house. On his head a sailor's cap, a relic of some half-forgotten deepsea voyage. In his fist a twisted stick, nothing so grand as the blackthorns you see in the shops nowadays that shine like the toes of patent shoes and that, I'm told, are cut and soaked in glossy paint in Italy, and after a while the paint comes off and takes the skin of the stick with it, because a good blackthorn no more needs paint than good wine a bush. . . .

Old Cormac, I say, looking down at the sea and across the lagoon of sheltered water to the White Strand, and sniffing the wind this way and that. Far out the ocean is whitening around the three rocks that the legend says are not rocks at all but enchanted children. Old Cormac then giving us a good foreview of the weather for that day and often for the day after, although Donegal weather, as a rule, is better taken a day at a time. Cormac told the weather by the smell of the wind. . . .

Mící Pháidí who could tell a story as well woven and golden as his pants and coat were patched and ragged, saying " '*Se tá*" to my friend, Labhras O Lochrann from Cookstown, and Labhras saying " '*Se tá*" back to Mící, and the two of them repeating that comprehensive affirmative through a long conversation, like Chippewa Indians in the diplomatic wigwam. . . .

Another rogue of a storyteller sitting on a rock, smoking his pipe as only a wise man could, and giving, day after day, to an eager and guileless note-taker from the USA an instalment of the serial story then running in the *Irish Independent* with subtle changes in style and terminology to give it the authenticity of folk. It was Philip Rooney's horse-racing novel *All Out To Win* and, years afterwards, when I told Philip the story, he was delighted to know that he had found his place in the *Fiannuidheacht*. . . .

And yet another storyteller, the glint of mischief in his eye, telling to a pride of clerical students who hadn't much Irish, a series of stories about a merry wandering fornicator, *an fear beag ribeach rua*, the little tattered red-headed man, who even in these permissive days would be no fit company for clerics. . . .

Maire John, ripe as a pippin at the age of 80, singing with the honey voice of a bird, "set upon a golden bough to sing", that the summer will come and the grass will grow, and the green leaves come again to the tips of the branches, and her love will come with the whitening of day. And running to embrace him, when he enters her house, the big-limbed schoolmaster from Milford. She is so small she can hardly reach up to his waist. When she was young she had a great name for being fond of the men. . . .

Brighidh Chormaic telling me how her brother and my friend, kindly Hudi with the drooping moustache, died: "*Thainig sé isteach ar an urlar, agus cliabhan monadh ar a dhrium. Chuir sé a lamh ar a cheann agus dubhairt sé: 'Tá pian millteanach i' mo cheann.'*—He came in on the floor and a basket of turf on his back. He put his hand on his head and said: 'There's a dreadful pain in my head.' "

Brighidh walking with myself and some friends who are travelling the short cut to the Rosses back the other way to Gweedore. She is small, apple-cheeked, silver-haired. She stands on that ridge up there, waving and waving, as long as she can see us, or we her. Is it a trick of this heavenly winter light or is somebody still standing up there waving farewell: the spirit of this place as, perhaps, only the young can ever know it?

Hand on the swelling lump on his head the young poet who died in India sits forever on the side of that narrow road. Another young fellow forever walks on, swinging a stout ashplant, beheading the roadside thistles.

The fine red strand at Mullachdearg has a capacious car-park now and a well-surfaced road leading into it. This cold off-season morning there are no cars to be seen except, of course, the one we've come in. For some odd reason you never reckon the car that gets you there among the disturbers of the ancient peace:

> We stand beside the crying sea
> That in an endless monotone
> Chants loud its bitter litany.
> No other sound, but where on high
> Some whirring, wailing sea-birds pass;
> A herding-boy's shrill distant cry,
> The seawind in the coarse bent grass. . . .

That's the way it is this winter morning now that the reverberation of the car engine has died away. That's the way it was 30 years ago but the way it will never be again on a sunny weekend in the summer. All the lonely silent places are giving up their secrets; and the Brazilians are making motor-roads through the Amazon jungle; and the small dark-skinned fruit-eating Tassadays have, after centuries of secure hiding, come out of the rain forests of the Philippines and given themselves up to the world we live in. Could nobody have warned them in time? But then too long living on fruit and tadpoles, their other chief article of diet, could weaken anyone's judgement.

Out there on Owey island, though, the people are more cautious than the Tassadays. The wit of the people of Owey is well known and if there's a wryness in that wit, that's likely because of the close contact with the low lowlands of Scotland.

Beyond the wide lovely spaces of Cruit island, which must be a sore temptation to any man who would want to beautify the world with a

holiday camp, runs the swift water of Owey Sound, narrow but dangerous. There's a story about a zealous young priest, fresh from the seminary
and new to the place and the people, who noticed after a while that a
considerable number of men on Owey never bothered to cross over to
the church on the mainland to go to confession. So he crossed to the island
and cornered the laddoes and asked them why not.

"Well, the way it is, Father," they say, "you see the Sound out
there."

"I do."

"It looks well with the sun on it, but it's not the safest water in the
world. The way we look at it is that it's too far to travel for a venial sin,
and too dangerous for a mortal sin."

The summer places have come to the Donegal coast, the new hotels with
fine grants from the Tourist Board (Bord Fáilte), the new white houses
for people escaping from wealthy suburbia and bringing suburbia with
them, the new motel in lime-white concrete, the trailer and the caravan
and, below on the water, the compulsory cabin cruiser.

All quiet now as we sit here in the empty off-season, but what will it
become in succeeding summers as more and more people, able to pay the
high prices, gratify their passion for sites and build the new suburbia on
sea? Some of the summer citizens are, though, by now as well-established
and as much part of the place as the Big Stone at Crolly. Brian Friel, the
playwright, for instance, got here a little after St Colmcille left, and there
may be among the *muintir na haite*, the people of the place, a tendency to
point him out as one of the sights—like Mount Errigal on a clear day—
even if some of them may feel timorous about taking part *i ngan fhios
dobhtha*, or unbeknownst to themselves, in one of his plays or stories.

But will all the summer people respect the genius of the place: that is,
the *genius loci*, not Brian himself, nor Peadar O'Donnell even, nor the
brothers O Grianna, Seamus, Seosamh and Sean Bán of the sweet voice,
nor that courageous wanderer, Patrick MacGill, but the thing that made
them all what they are: the spirit that lives in and the voice that speaks
from rock, and from thornbush twisted and thwarted by the wind, and in
evening by lonely little lakes with the gulls crying around them; the
ghosts of memories at the corners of roads and old homesteads, small
fields and gardens walled stoutly against the Atlantic wind? That's a
long question.

> *... memories of old vanished faces,*
> *Cabins gone now, old wellsides, old dear places, ...*

"Hould on there now," says my friend. "Yeats or no bloody Yeats, you can have a bit too much of ghosts at the corners and damn all else, of melancholy memories and the thatch all fallen in and the nettle and docken growing out of the cracks in the abandoned floor. Didn't a great and knowledgeable man in the town of Dungloe tell us that Dungloe was doomed and done for if it hadn't been for tourism? Isn't it a good thing that life, even if it's only for the summer season, should come back to the sites that the emigrants left?"

A sound argument, indeed, but then I think of St Kevin's holy Glendalough, the glen of the two lakes, in County Wicklow, and what that car-park by the upper lake has done to the gloomy shore which skylark never warbled o'er—according to Thomas Moore's melody about how St Kevin pushed his fair pursuer, Kathleen, into the water. Brightened it all up, for sure, that car-park did and killed the good smell of earth and flowers and trees with the stench of petrol. Even if a skylark did elect to warble there you couldn't hear him now with the noise of the revving engines. St Kevin's ghost would be dismayed.

But if people want to go to Glendalough in cars they must have somewhere to park them. Certainly: but couldn't the parking-lot have been placed well back down the road towards Laragh, and let all but the maimed and the halt, who could be carried, walk the rest of the way? The place was once, wasn't it, a place of pilgrimage, and not an appanage to the seafront at Bray, with transistors and picnic lunches on the holy ground of the seven churches?

This, by way of diversion, is the tale of the dentist and the king of the big island.

The dentist was cycling slowly past a house in west Donegal when he was halted by roars of agony, and a woman running out of the house and waving her white apron at him. It wasn't the woman who was roaring, but a man and he was inside the house.

"Dentist," she says, "would you for the sake of Patrick, Brigid and Colmcille come into the house and pull the tooth of the king of the big island? He's this hour landed and come up from the shore and his agony is a sight to see and the roars of him will take the milk from the cows."

"No tools of my trade have I with me," says the dentist.

Six roars came out, so loud you could see them.

"Do something," she says, "for the sake of the son of Mary who suffered on the cross."

Four roars, mad bellowing bulls in stampede, followed the six.

So in went the dentist and what with hot water and a pair of sterilised scissors, and a strong finger and thumb, and the grace of God, and the king's son to help hold the king down, a tooth two-and-a-half inches long was removed and the roaring, and the echoes of the roaring, died away.

"The luck of the companions of Fionn MacCumhaill on you," says the king to the dentist—for that was about as close to Christianity as his salutations could come. And to his son he says: "*Faigh an tairgead*—Get the money."

"No money," says the dentist, "let it be friendship between us and my deed for the day."

"Money it must be," says the king, "for it's unlucky to refuse what has been offered and the cooper is entitled to the value of the tub."

Then out steps the son and opens the fork of his father's trousers, and puts in a finger and thumb, and takes hold of a string, and pulls on the string and up comes a purse, and he opens the purse and gives a gold sovereign to the dentist, and he closes the purse and drops it again down the leg of the trousers, and he buttons the buttons and that's that.

"The way it is," says the king for he saw the dentist looking in amazement at the door of the strongroom where he kept the money, "the way of it is that we don't trust them in Ireland."

The big island is out there, a heavy-headed sea monster lazing on the surface, carrying on its back a remote people, separate and apart, not renowned for hospitality: perhaps descendants of sea-rovers who came from Noroway, from Noroway, from Noroway o'er the foam, and were marooned there by their more amiable fellows.

Once they were in schism with the Church of Rome: the second great western schism. They defied the bishop of the diocese, wouldn't let the old priest off the island, nor the new one on.

Once in British days they refused to pay rent or rates and the British, remembering Palmerston, sent a gunboat from Galway to collect the money. The islanders knelt and prayed. God alone knew, Flann O'Brien used to say, what Gods they prayed to but the story is that the gunboat sank, all hands on board, at the mouth of Galway Bay.

That's the big island out there, beyond Bloody Foreland, the end of the north-west of Ireland and, so, of Ulster.

THE CORPSE AND CONSTABLE KEENAN

The name of the house in which we have lived for a few days is Errigal View, and it sounds much better in Irish. It would sound better still in

Latin for Errigal, as I've said, is the Latin word for a praying-place: *Oraculum*. The Gaelic leaves the Latin slightly frayed around the edges.

You can, in fact, see Errigal from the doorstep or from any of the front windows, or from the roof or the chimney-stacks if you had occasion to find yourself there: not all of Errigal down to its roots in the long water of Dunlewy, but enough of it to let you know that you're looking at that distinctive mountain and not at Mangerton or Scawfell or the Brecon Beacons or Donard or Shasta or Kilimanjaro.

You could, of course, confuse it with Fuji-Yama, the shapes are not unlike, but even though the fuchsia grows well here in the season you'd want to have been up very late the night before to waken in Gweedore and think you were in Japan.

Errigal, the tip of it, stands up like a giant conical hat above a black ridge. The giant who is wearing the hat is hunched and hiding behind the ridge, ready to straighten up and display himself when the cold rocky coast is softened a little by the sun. There is, too, going to be sunshine. The radio says that the rest of Ireland and the most of Europe is devastated by bad weather and the east wind; and the hapless Italians, who aren't as used to it as we are, find themselves up to their necks in slush. But here on this north-western shore where we have taken refuge from the camarad-erie of a Dublin Christmas and the consequent debility, the air, even if it is cold, is still and bright and indescribably beautiful. Birds fly quietly here and there on the mysterious business of the morning.

Groups of walking people, an occasional motor-car go down to Derrybeg church, there below in the hollow. Smoke comes in puffs, then steadily from a score of chimneys, no pollution, the warm perfume of peatsmoke on the frosty air. The roosters are awakening, a certain embarrassment in their crowing, as if they know they've slept it out and that the men and women are on the move before them. Tentatively the dogs begin their talking from house to house.

Did Constable John Keenan of the Royal Irish Constabulary really see what he said he saw down there in the hollow at the end of January in 1889 at the time of the Gweedore evictions? He had been posted at the gate of the house of Fr James McFadden, the parish priest, who on behalf of his people had defied what then passed for law and order: the rights of landlord against tenant, the rights of the rich over the poor. A warrant was out for the priest's arrest and had been passed on by District Inspector Markham of Dungloe to Sergeants Daly, Carey, Dunning, Timulty, Walsh, Finn, Quinn, Dillon, Kielly, McQuade, Woods and Burns, and their several assistants, for local execution.

It's an odd feeling to find the name of your grandfather in that roll-call even if spelt with an extra consonant, an "l" of a difference. But it's good to know that that sergeant, and for all I know all the others as well, never did a damn thing about the warrant. District Inspector Martin from Ballyshannon had to—or had the ill wit to—come here to Derrybeg to apprehend the priest, and to meet a rough and bloody death down there in the hollow that's as quiet now as Eden before Adam.

It's not that cold this morning that I can't wrap my old frieze coat around me and sit on the low stone wall by the roadside and meditate on what Constable Keenan said he saw. Behind me the sun is coming up good and Errigal's a black pyramid against the new light, and the heather is burning brown and the sea too bright to look at.

Constable Keenan said that about midnight a terrible shower came on and he went inside the priest's gate for shelter. My God, a January night in Gweedore, and the man was earning his pay and whatever allowances went with it.

While he sheltered there he saw a police officer in full uniform lying prostrate at the hall-door. "When the shower cleared he examined the spot very carefully but there was no trace of the officer to be seen. It was on the very same spot that Inspector Martin was killed a few days later."

No reason on earth, and less under the earth, to doubt such things.

There's a friend of mine in South Bend, Indiana, a woman of fine intelligence and from my own hometown, who writes me letters, many of them involving a quite staggering total recall of people and places she hasn't seen or heard tell of for the best part of 30 years. From her letters I steal this story about a friend of her girlhood, a lassie we'll call Joan Smith, one of eight children:

Joan was unabashedly fond of the boys, was cool and calculating about them. She was attractive in a hard sort of way, with jade-green eyes. Lacking any imagination at all, she yet told me a story one time that shook me—and in these days of the cult of ESP I sometimes wonder about it. Joan died shortly after I came here: to my regret, for she was young and wanted so much from life.

Anyway, at one time she worked in an ice-cream parlour in Derry and apparently didn't bother to write home much. Her mother was worried and, on learning that I was to visit Derry, asked me to contact Joan. I found the place she worked, along the Strand in Derry [now in rubble] and duly gave her the message. With her usual cool she shrugged her shoulders and said: "Tell her I'll be home tomorrow for my grandmother's funeral". Startled, I said: "Your grandmother isn't dead. I saw her this morning, alive and well." Joan simply shrugged again. Next day she *was* home. Her grandmother *was* dead and Joan *was* at the funeral.

When I asked her how she knew, no telephone, no meeting, she said she had seen her grandmother beneath a tree along the Strand, dressed in her usual attire, black dress and black shawl. She didn't move or speak. She simply stared. She was a gaunt woman with deepset black eyes. Neither spoke. Joan went on to work. Joan was always very close to her grandmother. She was so matter-of-fact about everything, and that was the only time in all the years that I knew her that she evidenced any belief in the supernatural.

One would not normally look for evidence of extra-sensory perception in the dayroom records of a barracks of the Royal Irish Constabulary. But the story is, anyway, that down there in the hollow, with the Atlantic gale blowing the mad rain around him, Constable John Keenan had his private vision.

A certain mysterious thing did go with the story of Fr McFadden and the fight that he made to keep their homes for his people. As far away as Tyrone and when I was a boy you could still hear the story of the RIC man who was cursed for making shorthand notes on a provocative sermon the priest preached. Ever afterwards, it was said, the poor devil could be seen walking the roads, making all the time imaginary notes on the palm of his left hand, and the implication was that he was still note-taking in some horrible hereafter: "I proceeded to the parish church . . . I apprehended . . . I cautioned the defendant . . ." Forever and forever. A more than Dantean vision. Or Flann O'Brien's third policeman.

In Omagh we had an RUC man (Royal Ulster Constabulary)—of a lesser breed admittedly than the RIC, the last of whom with their fine polished boots and good speckless suits were the greatest walkers to funerals Ireland has ever seen—an RUC man who had a nervous thing, so that he nodded his head sharply every few steps he took. It was comforting for us wee fellows to hear that he hadn't been cursed by Fr McFadden or any of his ghostly allies, but merely shell-shocked in the Kaiser war. There does be an astonishing variety even in curses.

But had I here and now the gift, or curse, of extra-sensory perception, or the power to walk back into the past as the two maiden ladies, Moberly and Jourdain, said they did in the gardens of Versailles, or as Alain-Fournier made the big youth do in that weird novel, *Le Grand Meaulnes*,

I could on this quiet morning re-people the empty road and that hollow by the church of Derrybeg.

The weather in 1889 stays so wild that out of a congregation of about 2,000 only four or five hundred came to twelve o'clock mass. That is more than enough for what's to happen. They wait after mass and when Martin shouts at them to go home some one voice calls in Irish: "Let no man stir". No man does. The priest steps out in soutane and biretta, and breviary in his hand. The police close around him. The highly-excited inspector draws his sword, grabs the priest by the collar.

Martin might have lived if the rumour hadn't got around that he had been fuming about bringing the priest back dead or alive, if it hadn't been for that naked sword. As it happened he was stoned to death on the spot down there where the constable said he saw the fetch: a hard death in wild weather in a hard land. At what split second in such a tormented episode does a man know he is doomed?

The inscription in another church, high on a hill at Ballyshannon, says that he was foully murdered in the 45th year of his age: "A brave officer, Loyal to his Queen and Faithful to his Country, he died doing his duty, faithful unto death. *Sic itur ad astra.*" The inscription is surmounted by two RIC men leaning on their rifles.

Well, it was one way to go to the stars to which, we have been told, all men must, or is it may, return. But there are nobler ways to go than to have the head clobbered off you by the stones of Gweedore for tearing the thatch of the cabins of the poor. Duty, stern daughter of the voice of God, the things that get done in thy lousy name. And a dirty class of a queen it was that would ask a man to give his life in such a task.

Enough of my meditating. The god-fearing people, the grandchildren and great-grandchildren of the hard men who did Martin in, are coming quietly out of the church in the hollow. The car engines are vibrating, rending the peace. The sun is high. Errigal is a shining blue-and-white cone. The dogs and cocks are in high chorus.

Allingham, the poet, died in that same year and is buried in that same churchyard in Ballyshannon above the winding banks of Erne. From the grave of one poet you can look from Donegal, across the bay and around the buttresses of the mountains into Sligo, to the place where, under Ben Bulben, another poet lies buried.

You are also looking from the province of Ulster into the province of Connacht.

5

TO SLIGO TOWN

The salmon are not in the tides as they were of old.
My sorrow, for many a creak gave the creel in the cart,
That carried the take to Sligo town to be sold,
When I was a boy with never a crack in my heart.

W. B. Yeats:
"The Meditation of the Old Fisherman"

WEST FROM THE OLD BROADSTONE

All of a sudden it occurs to me that what I wanted to be all my life was a station-master. But in a small rural station and in the golden days of railways. For there aren't that many railway stations in these times and the demand for masters is down.

I am sitting in the Sligo train which has stopped to rest at Dromod, on the Shannon in County Leitrim. Like the salmon in the creaking creel in the cart referred to by the old fisherman, with the permission of Mr W. B. Yeats, I am on the way to Sligo town, but am intrigued by the possibility that if I turned wilful I could change here and take a bus to Ballinamore. Which some day I may do, to see what pollution from piggeries and fertilisers has done to Lough Garradice.

The book on the table before me is *Bullet Park* by John Cheever, by no means his best book but, being by John Cheever, it has a lot of good things in it. Believe it or not, this is what I am reading when the train stops and I look out at Dromod station which, fair enough, I have seen many times before, but never quite as I see it now. Cheever writes:

> Sometimes you step into a tackroom, a carpenter's shop or a country post-office and find yourself unexpectedly at peace with the world. It is usually late in the day. The place has a fine smell (I must include bakeries). The groom, carpenter, postmaster or baker has a face so clear, so free of trouble that you feel nothing bad ever happened or will happen here, a sense of fitness or sanctity never achieved, in my experience, by any church.

Sir Winston Churchill talked, with some reason, of the dismal spires of Tyrone and Fermanagh: but in Omagh on the Strule we couldn't agree with him. For under these spires of which the townspeople are proud, they, people and spires, have mostly managed to live together in civilized fashion.

In the Clogher Valley at Carleton's cottage, with Annie McKenna and a four-footed friend. See note to "To the Lake of the Salmon".

Seamus Heaney, the poet from the Lough
Shore who watched the eels and the
thatcher and looked into deep wells.

Right: When Dublin had "taught him
to be wise" with Inniskeen in the far,
far background—and as Patrick
Kavanagh's friend, John Ryan, saw him.

The Big Stone at Crolly—and dreams of fair women.

Below: Conical, white with shale, Errigal Oraculum, a praying-place, the Cock o' the North, guards Gweedore.

Coolbanagher: A Gandon jewel on a midland hilltop.

It may or may not be properly called the Spanish Arch,
but it is a genuine part of old Galway.

Below: Like Marius, delighting in elegant decay, George Moore would have been
shaken if he could have seen in vision the centre of Galway City as it is today.

From Cloghereeva the tennis-playing officers could have looked down on the glimmering lake.

Below: A moment of meditation by a Tipperary stream: in the Clare Glens near Nenagh, a place of great natural beauty splendidly gothicized by a landed family in the nineteenth century.

Bianconi, and many others, walked here by the Main Guard in Clonmel.
The sidewalk came after Cromwell.

The Suir and Kilsheelan Bridge.

On the road to Cork, Ireland's "great vision of the guarded mount".

So was it John Cheever trumpeting from suburban America, or was it my new vision of Dromod that made me think how fine it would be to be the master of a small rural railway station? There's a fine big red house out there and, stuck onto it, a smaller red house. Would they, now, be for the master and his man? There's the road to Ballinamore, and beyond. There's a small slow stream, and flat land, and the suggestion of the infinity and peace of the Shannon. Life here could have something monastic about it. Passing trains could divide the day as bells do in religious houses.

Men who run, or ran, small stations are, or were, almost always good gardeners, or they could get somebody to garden for them. The passing traveller eyed with delight the beds of bright flowers. Was it the station at Mostrim-Edgeworth (as I prefer to call it)[1] that was always winning prizes for its appearance long before the modern Tourist Board started the Tidy Towns Competition which really has given a facelift to the towns and villages of rural Ireland?

This, too, would be a great billet for a fisherman. Masters of small stations and men who work in forests should be a long step on the road to happiness and if any of them are not, and are just more-or-less miserable like the rest of us then I don't want to hear from them.

Edward Thomas wrote a poem about remembering a place called Adlestrop just because his train stopped there and lazily released steam on a scorching sunny afternoon. Adlestrop was in the middle of nowhere but the poet never forgot it.

Myself I remember Dax in the heart of the French pine forests, because of the evident joy of some navvies stripped to the waist in the fierce heat and sluicing the grime off each other with a hosepipe. And because a scholarly friend of mine, a mercurial professor with a vein of high fantasy, told me that a certain travel agency had once mislaid at Dax a train-load of Irish clerical students on the way to Lourdes. Were they ever found? Where are they now? Still wandering in Les Landes: wild hermits of the woods?

My train moves on towards Sligo. Another day then for Ballinamore and the lakes of Leitrim.

Below Carrick the Shannon sprawls through amber water-meadows, a sore place for floods. And this is the bright clean town of Carrick-on-Shannon where Tom Maher of the Bush hotel will tell you anything you want to know about boats on the big river which from Dowra all the way down to Limerick is as much a chain of wide lakes as a river: below Limerick it is a splendid sweeping estuary. In Carrick and elsewhere they may tell you how the Norfolk Broads are an overcrowded puddle.

D

And this is the town of Boyle, burdened with history, from medieval monks and a noble abbey (Mainistir na Buaille) to the fine stone house in which Mia Farrow's mother, Maureen O'Sullivan, daughter of the British officer in command of the Connaught Rangers, was reared. The town sits happily on the Boyle River which flows from the austerity of Lough Gara to the richly-islanded and wooded Lough Key and thence on to the Shannon, and over the ridge to the right is Lough Arrow. Three splendid lakes.

And this is Ballymote which also had its monks and ancient manuscripts and still has, beside the railway, the massive walls of the castle built 674 years ago by the Norman, Richard de Burgo. And the hogbacked mountain, with the caves, dark holes in a shining white escarpment halfway up, is Keshcorran (Ceis Corran), the Hog or Sow of Corran, a harper of the Tuatha de Dannan, that enchanted shadowy people who were imagined ancient gods. To the harper as a reward for the sweetness of his music they gave the fertile plain, Magh Corran, over which the train has just passed.

And in a camp on Ceis Corran Diarmuid O'Duibhne, matinée idol of the *Fiannuidheacht* or Fenian Saga, left Gráinne, the golden and wilful, and went foolishly to hunt on Ben Bulben mountain his taboo animal, the boar: and, sorely wounded, was basely allowed to die by Fionn MacCumhaill, jilted and infuriated leader of the Fenians, who had chased Gráinne and Diarmuid round and round Ireland. But a cynical professor I know says that Fionn wasn't after Gráinne at all but after comely young Diarmuid. All of which was a long time ago and most likely not at all except in the coloured imagination of our remote ancestors.[2]

These are the lovely little riverine towns of Collooney and Ballysodare and the mills owned by the Pollexfens. When John Butler Yeats, the portrait painter and a great talker, father of another painter and of a poet, married one of the Pollexfens who were a broody quiet people, he said magnificently that he had given a tongue to the seacliffs. In God's truth he had: and over there beyond Sligo town and under the long rampart of Ben Bulben, where the mythical Diarmuid died and where six young men were shot dead in the civil war of the '20s, the poet is buried in Drumcliff churchyard, as he willed to be:

"*Under bare Ben Bulben's head*
In Drumcliff churchyard Yeats is laid,
An ancestor was rector there
Long years ago, a church stands near,

By the road an ancient cross—
No marble, no conventional phrase;
On limestone quarried near the spot
By his command these words are cut . . .

"Cast a cold eye
On life on death.
Horseman, pass by!"

The first time I travelled to Sligo I set off from Dublin from the old Broadstone station, something that nobody has done for a long time nor will ever do again. The Broadstone, a fine stone structure, no longer a railway station, is now used for other purposes by Coras Iompair Éireann: the Irish semi-State transport company.

The reason why I started from Dublin and not from my native Tyrone was because I had been visiting relatives in Dublin who were going to visit relatives in south Sligo, and I was taken along. The result of my going that roundabout route was that I grew up thinking that Sligo was a lot further from Tyrone than in actual mileage it is.

So that it always seemed odd to me that Mick Leonard who went to secondary school with me, and who played left-back in Gaelic football for County Fermanagh, should have a western, strongly-sibilant, almost-Shligo accent when he came from a place as nearby as Garrison on the Fermanagh tip of Lough Melvin. That little village of Garrison has always seemed to me to be the still centre of peace, asleep as it is on the glimmering lake, and with all the beauty of Rossinver Braes running seawards towards Kinlough in County Leitrim. Yet it is part of the horrors of our time that the craze for blowing-up things, the Irish gelignite tradition as I once heard it referred to by a very black humorist, has even brought destruction to Garrison.

From Sligo, on that first trip, I went home to Tyrone by the old railway that opened up to the traveller the beauties of Lough MacNean:

Farewell to the hills of Fermanagh from Garrison round to Belcoo,
And the tall purple mountains of Leitrim and shady boreens I once knew.
For I've wandered from home and relations, far away from each well-beloved
*   scene,*
That will live in my memory forever, like the shores of my loved Lake
*   MacNean.*[3]

In one day coming up from Tubbercurry in south Sligo and going on to Enniskillen, the county town of Fermanagh, crossing the border between

Blacklion and Belcoo, you passed through two of the three railway stations that then adorned the tiny town of Collooney. One line came from Limerick, one from Dublin, one went on to Sligo and one went off on a wild stagger through Leitrim to the Erne and the northern counties. It was my friend, the late Philip Rooney (whose novels included *The Golden Coast, North Road,* and *Captain Boycott*) who told me how those three stations got the young fellows of Collooney such a name for wildness that there was even a ballad about it:

> *A dreadful dream I fain would tell,*
> *I dreamt I died and went to hell,*
> *And there upon the topmost landing*
> *Some prime Collooney boys were standing.*

That's the only stanza I can remember out of ten or twelve of the Dantean piece called "The Parish Priest's Dream". The point that Rooney made was that the real wild men from Galway and Mayo used to pass through the town on their way to the Scottish potato-fields, walking from one railway station to another, their tickets stamped: To Collooney and Ex Collooney. They might stop at a few pubs and raise a mild ruckus as men from Galway and Mayo have sometimes, under extreme provocation, been known to do, and the ruckus might even be renewed on the train so that, because of the stamps on the tickets the checkers knew the ticket holders as the wild Collooney boys. That's what Philip, God rest him, told me but we must remember that he came from Collooney. Even if he once did so weaken in his loyalties as to admit that Seán Ó Faoláin had said that the only notable thing about Collooney was that Yeats had found a rhyme for it. "But then what," said Philip, "would you expect from a Corkman like Ó Faoláin?"

On that first journey on the Lough MacNean train the rain came through a hole in the roof of the compartment. A girl going back to school in Enniskillen fell down the wet iron steps of the footbridge in Collooney. She was fielded by me. She may have been the first girl I ever loved. Even if I never knew her name or never saw her again. She made me feel like a hero. She certainly came more rapidly to my arms than any woman I've ever met since.

ANCIENT VOICES BELOW THE CAVES?

Keshcorran mountain still has for me the sinister magic that it had when first seen 45 or so years ago: a crouching animal of a mountain, a wounded animal with gaping holes in its side. Even before I knew what the name meant that was the way I felt about the mountain.

Even in sunshine it's seldom a cheerful mountain. Those holes could be the gateways to the *facilis descensus* to Avernus. It was named not only after that man of music Corann the harper who when the Tuatha de Dannan paid him for his music with a fertile plain must have been nearly as well-off as any long-haired showband singer. No, the mountain was also named after the brute beast that was killed there: the Hog or Sow of Corran.

And the first thing I ever heard about the mountain was that bits of the bones of bears and wolves had been found in those gaping caves and were to be seen in Dublin in the National Museum. That was enough to afflict a young fellow with awe and when, daring the unknown, I clambered up the steep slope and entered the caves it was to go squelch like Browning's Caliban in the pit's mulch mire and in moist and odorous dung left behind by the brute beasts sheltering from the mountain's wind and rain. The caves I'd read about in school stories had sanded floors, sheltered nooks, buried treasure, pretty nearly everything except central heating. But those dark holes into which I walked until I sank to the knees were dank, dreary, dripping, depressing, dirty and all dung.

Potholers are crazy people. After the lunacy of clambering up rock-faces just because they are there comes the worse lunacy of crawling into the bowels of the earth because the caves are there. Robert Penn Warren, though, did squeeze a good novel out of that nuttiness, and a novel with a lot of sanity in it: *The Cave*. But I've never yet heard of a speluncar or potholer who was crazy enough to try to make his way into the cold slimy entrails of the Sow of Corran. Let's hope I'm not putting a mad idea into somebody's head.

The Sligo train as it climbs up from Boyle presents you with a fine view of the rush of the Boyle river and the faraway light of Lough Gara where once upon a time the Sligomen lived in crannogs. Some years ago the lake-level fell and the crannogs, ancient lake-dwellings, were revealed. Then there's the infinity of the west and the wide plains of Mayo as you see them from Kilfree junction. Or from where the junction used to be. There are grass-grown platforms, a few empty ruinous sheds: the west-bound line to Ballaghadereen no longer exists:

> *Ballina, Ballinrobe, Balla and Bohola,*
> *Newport and Foxford a few miles below,*
> *Then on to Inistreigue and down to Manulla,*
> *You'll always find true friends in County Mayo.*

Then beyond the abandoned junction and over to the east is the swine-shaped mysterious mountain with its caves and the tracks of the animals.

One sunny day about twelve years ago I came with three friends, one of them an American, to the long meadow at the foot of the mountain. The mouths of the caves were dark above us. The steep slope of gentle grass below them looked inviting in the sunshine: if you didn't know the caves, that is.

So up the mountain with the three of them while I sat at my ease in a corner of the long meadow to read a book. Those caves of Kesh I had had again and again. Never once had they looked like that happy cave in which the robbers that Gil Blas met on the road from Santillane to Salamanca lived in comfort and hoarded their loot. Up there Ali Baba would be up to the backside in clobber.

The figures of the three climbers became smaller and smaller on the steep flank of the sleeping animal. The mouth of the largest cave swallowed them leaving me to luxuriate in the fantasy that the last of the bears of Ballymote might be somewhere inside and that my friends would suddenly reappear, electrically scattering like Keystone cops along the green and gentle place. At that moment there was nobody to be seen in the world except myself and one black bullock.

Then I heard the voices, people shouting and laughing as though they were quite close, yet the sounds were also faint and faraway, if you know what I mean. There were also sounds of music. I stood up and walked to the gap in the hedge and looked down the byroad to the main road between Boyle and Ballymote. Nobody to be seen. The plain of Corran glittered in the heat. The black bullock went on grazing. The voices, the music were no longer to be heard. So I sat on a fragment of a drystone wall and went on reading my book.

There could be several explanations. The simplest would be a good lunch with wine, ample but not excessive, in the Southern hotel in Sligo town, and the tendency of middle-aged men to doze and dream after a good meal. Just at that time, too, I had finished reading, and writing and broadcasting about, Maire MacNeill's great book *The Festival of Lughnasa*[4] and my imagination, such as it was and is, had been much affected by her account of those places, on hilltops or by lakeshores where for centuries our ancestors had met to rejoice over the first fruits of harvest and to honour the god Lugh.

What I had written a few days previously was:

After the reading of this book so many places in Ireland will be changed utterly for me, made richer, peopled with the shades of gods and heroes who have not perished, have not even, as the character said rather weakly in *The Bending of the Bough*, retired to the lonely hills but who live on as part of our ancestral imagination.

It was, indeed, the imagination of the people transforming history and local fable, creating symbol, that inhabited the hills with gods and fighting men and even with Christian saints.

From the caves of Keshcorran—a striking photograph of them illustrates the dust-jacket of this book—you can look down on the plain that the Tuatha de Dannan gave to Corann, the harper, in repayment for the sweetness of his music; and the mountain of the caves itself, crouching like an animal, recalls forever the enchanted sow, Caelcheis, that was killed there by the hunters of Connacht and their hounds.

By the banks of the Barrow St Moling the miller asks the mythical pagan mason, the Goban Saor, to make a church for him—St Moling being also a myth. Christian and pagan co-operate and the church is made out of the wood of one of the sacred trees of Ireland, the Yew of Ross. For payment the builder asks of the saint as much rye grain as the church will hold. So the saint asks him to turn the church upside down, which, being done, the saint is constrained to work a rye-making miracle to keep his part of the bargain. Pagan and Christian contend in the working of wonders.

At Meelin's Rock near Duhallow in County Cork, a mystic maiden called Maoilin—her name has been comically anglicised as Miss Moylan—escapes from an unwelcome marriage by soaring across the valley to the rock which opens before her. . . .

And so on. With a head rattling with such images, and with a belly full of good food and wine, a man in a lonely meadow on a sunny day might easily hear music and voices with neither instruments nor people to account for them. Also, when I sat down in the long meadow I was aware that I was exactly on the place where the people of the plain of Corran used to gather to honour the god by ritual and jollification.

There is also the possibility that I did really hear the voices and the music, a suggestion that the three speluncars treated lightly when, unclawed by any Ballymote bear, they came down to the enchanted meadow.

Yet what happened to the American that day might well go to prove that there was enchantment in the air.

He was, and is, one of those Manhattan Islanders who wouldn't walk from here to the bathroom if he could find a cab to carry him. It was a wonder to the three of us that he had exerted himself to the extent of clambering up to the caves. Perhaps since his people were Irish he may have heard, in ancestral memory, some echo of the bay of the hounds as Diarmuid heard it in the night when he lay with golden Gráinne up there on the mountain: "And day in its full light came to him afterwards and he arose and said he would go where the hounds had bayed." So off with him to death by the boar's taboo tusk and the treachery of Fionn, great captain of warriors.

The American was not so disastrously affected. We went on from Keshcorran by a narrow dust-road so intimate that it seemed even to lead us through the kitchens of the farmhouses. We came to the Bricklieve mountains and into a genuine Valley of the Dead. Nowhere in Ireland that I know of does there seem to be such a concentration of cairns as at Carrowkeel.

The mountains had taken possession of the man who all his life had been calling cabs. He bounded from cairn to cairn like William Wordsworth or the wild mountain roe. But at the ultimate cairn the enchantment or the wine had worn off and the man was sadly feeling his feet. The scholar of the party was explaining how our remote ancestors carried the corpse up the mountain, cremated it there and entombed the ashes. The American asked: "Couldn't they have cremated him first and carried him up afterwards?"

That sunny comical day is as far now into the past as the night when Diarmuid heard the call of the hounds.

My train goes on through Ballymote and Collooney and Ballisodare to that striking view of Slish mountain, to Yeatsians it is the rocky highland of Slewth wood and mountain. Lough Gill is there unseen in the hollow:

> *Where dips the rocky highland*
> *Of Slewth Wood in the lake,*
> *There lies a leafy island,*
> *Where flapping herons wake*
> *The drowsy water rats. . . .*

There's a blunt finality about Sligo station, and it isn't just enough to say that it's a terminus and that I was reared close to a junction where, before dirty politics did away with the railway and allowed the old station-buildings to decay, you could change for Fintona, Irvinestown,

Enniskillen and Bundoran, and even Ballinamallard where, then, only one Catholic lived but she was an old lady and she died. And change, too, for Derry, Belfast and Dublin and all intermediate stations.

Bundoran on the sea was also a terminus yet I never felt there, as I always do in Sligo, that I've completed an important journey.

HIGH ABOVE THE GLIMMERING LAKE

At Sligo railway station in 1920 the lady of the house in which I now sit met a charming Black-and-Tan, an ordinary unassuming member of the rank and file.

He would have been a most good-humoured little fellow if he hadn't been weighted down to the bleeding Irish earth with bandoliers and bombs and pistols and carbines, all carried to preserve the king's peace. Also he didn't seem to like the Sligo children. He looked suspiciously at two or three of them who were loitering about the station. He said, "They're all spies". The lady who came from this house, high above the glimmering and most beautiful lake, didn't disagree with him.

The Irregulars (they had also called on the poet, Mr Yeats, in his tower down near Lady Gregory's place at Coole and had a bit of a poem written about them) called at the house and took away a tent belonging to one of the lady's daughters who was at that time in London but had not had the good fortune to take her tent with her. Tents were not much in use in London that season. The Free Staters called and were even worse-mannered than the Irregulars. They demanded food and beds. The lady of the house locked into their rooms the two daughters of the house who were then at home.

The Staters demanded guns. The master of the house, who was a descendant of one of Marlborough's generals who was granted land in Ireland as a reward for his generalship, gave to their leader a German pistol that an Australian had brought to him from the western front. There was one bullet in it and it went off by accident and caused some confusion, but nobody was hurt.

The lady of the house who, in a varied life in good society, had met everybody from George Meredith to Maggie the Rag, wrote in her book: "Shortly after we left Ireland for good". The master of the house decided that although Ireland had done its bit for the family, from the battle of Blenheim onwards, it was now: "No good". But earlier on in those bad times of the breaking of empire the garrison officers used to come to this house above Lough Gill to play tennis:

As long as the English regiments were quartered in the various towns we felt pretty secure. They were very popular and often came out to Cloghereeva to play tennis, dine and dance, but they must leave before dark. Deep down in all our hearts was an anxiety that they should get back to their barracks without an ambush, and we changed one of our tennis-courts, surrounded by trees, so that it should not provide shelter for a sniper.

Lois, the girl in Elizabeth Bowen's novel, *The Last September*, goes prowling alone in the wet shrubbery near her home in County Cork and surprises life "at a significant angle" when she sees an armed man short-cutting secretly across the demesne. She decides that Ireland is the cause of his haste. But she realises that she cannot "conceive of her country emotionally: it was a way of living, an abstract of several landscapes, or an oblique frayed island moored at the north but with an air of being detached and washed out west from the British coast".

Lois (or Miss Bowen) was a lot more subtle than the lady who 50 years ago lived in, and left, the house I'm sitting in now. Yet, subtle or not, Maud Wynne did stumble over a Bowenish situation in the gossipy book she wrote: beginning with her father who was a lord and a great lawyer, and she herself the aunt of a man now notable in Irish life—and in international sport. The title of her book, published 36 years ago, is: *An Irishman and His Family: Lord Morris and Killanin*.

The room I sit at lunch in, with a nun and a learned lady from Sligo town, has one of the best of the views or visions of Lough Gill. Any view of Lough Gill has something about it of the beatific vision. This spacious room was not here in the days of the Irregulars and the Free Staters, nor in those earlier days when Cloghereeva was a dower-house of the Gore-Booth family. It is part of the new building that, along with the original house, now goes to make up St Angela's College of Domestic Economy. Since it is a corner room and on the first floor it has this lofty and comprehensive view of Lough Gill.

A hard north-east wind rubs the lake the wrong way but the dark revolving sky is showing signs of cracking with light. There are no ghosts in this new room nor, it would seem, in any part of the old house nor in the grounds around it. The Staters, searching for guns, and beds to sleep in and food to eat, the Irregulars commandeering the girl's tent, the British officers playing at tennis where no sniper could get in on the play, have all wended on into eternity on the track of Thomas Carlyle's Merovingian kings. They will be followed in due course by bombers and liquidators and hurlers on the ditch, and what will any of us be remembered for?

The fire burns bright. Above Slish mountain the sun finally cracks the sky, a shaft of light falls on Gallagher's island. It is, I reflect, a very good thing to be invited to lunch or dine in a college of domestic economy. This would also be a fine place for an aspiring young man to find a wife, both because of the outward appearance of the young women and for the sake of the young man's digestion.

Cloghereeva has happy memories for me. In this room which is well-shelved with books and is the common-room and library for the students, and of a quite daunting elegance, we refresh those memories by looking at photographs taken on a prize-giving day twelve or so years ago. The faces of Padraic Colum and Sean White and myself look at me out of several photographs. The long skirts the nuns then wore, move the young women, students of the present, to laughter. Sean and myself had acted more or less as guard of honour for the poet Padraic all the way from Dublin. He sat like a prince in the left front-seat: alert as always, good-humoured, reciting a poem now and again, or demanding a song, or exact information on topographical details. Crossing the Curlew mountains he asked: "And where are the Curlew mountains?"

"We're crossing them."

"Not much in the way of mountains," he said cheerfully. He was seeing taller mountains that, in much travelling, he had crossed. So we argued that they had been big enough and rough enough to see a battle and the bloody end of Sir Conyers Clifford, Elizabethan captain. His head, was it, to the Castle in Dublin, and his body to his wife to be buried on an island in Lough Key? Red Hugh O'Donnell had a brutal sense of period. That was before warriors bombed Dresden from the air or Derry city from a parked car. We are not more savage, not any more of the killer ape than the Elizabethans or the Irish who fought them. The ape simply has worse (better?) weapons than his hands or the sword.[5]

Padraic had written about the road round Ireland and, as cosy as a man in an armchair by his own hearth and the pile of turf against the wall, he had travelled the road round the world. Another poet, a man from my own county of Tyrone, once marvelled to me about how Padraic had lived for half a century above Central Park where everything, and a lot of it bad, happens and keeps happening, and yet had never lost his vision of narrow winding lonely roads and quiet country places, and drovers and shuilers, and men from the fields coming softly in. He had even been mugged and robbed on the streets of New York. He had a great calm.

His vision was part memory and part hope. He had the temperament that might even find hope in these our unhappy times when a few seconds can turn a street busy with shoppers into a bloody shambles, and when (our technology being so advanced) the paratrooper or the Provisional can relax in the evening and see on teevee the fruits of his day's work in broken glass and burning buildings, screaming women, dead bodies or (as a touch of cream on the trifle) a crying, shocked, half-blinded child with its forearm protecting its wounded eyes.

O'Leary the Fenian, whom Padraic knew well and talked a lot about, said that there were things a man might not do, not even to save his country. In his innocence he was probably thinking of something mildly dishonourable, like telling false-hoods. He might have gone further and said that there are actions that cannot save a country, or anything else, that hatred and bloodshed breed, in Ireland in the coming times, only hatred and bloodshed. The year after I was born and a mile from the house I was born in the Dromore murders happened, as I've said elsewhere: three men, all friends of my father, were liquidated. Fifty years ago. The memory still lives while we fashion a multitude of memories for the future. The Peep o' Day Boys and the Defenders are still out there in the dark as they were almost 200 years ago.

These are black thoughts, but they come inevitably in these times between me and the happy room and the sunlight now creeping like quicksilver along the lake from the Collooney end towards Dromahair and the spectacular falls on the Bonet river, and the odd shape of the mountain called O'Rourke's Table: "the *ceannabhan* of the mountain tops of Ireland".[6]

The House of the Stars and Stripes

This journey begins at the House of the Reveries. I call it that because the poet Yeats mentions it in the movement of his autobiographies that he called *Reveries over Childhood and Youth*. Some of his relatives once lived in the house. It is over 200 years old. It is in perfect condition and very beautiful.

Long before I was aware of Yeats, beyond the few poems that turned up in a primary-school reader, or beyond hearing grownups say that there was a Sligo man who was a great poet, I envied the people who lived in that house. It had what I then thought and still think a house should possess: its own private stream, a sizeable one, a mountain stream with trout in it, curving in the most friendly fashion around the front garden. To go to sleep or to awaken to the sound of such a stream would bring me as near to happiness as I could imagine.

Reconciled sadly now to the knowledge that I'll never own such a house, it is still good to enter and to meet the fortunate people who do own it, and to admire the house and what the *fear a' ti* is doing to preserve it. It occurs to me also that it is the second house I was in this year in which there are five daughters. If I should enter a third such house before the year ends I'll be entitled to a wish. Heaven when I die? Or just a house with its own private stream?

Under this roof that is 200 years old and in a house that the great poet visited as a boy, we talk about another part of Sligo altogether—that shadowy sleepy land to the south around Templehouse Lake, the place where the great folk-musicians came from: Michael Coleman, Jamesy Gannon, Michael Gorman. The man of the house himself comes from those parts.

So I say that Michael Gorman, the fiddler, who partnered Margaret Barry, a singing woman of the travelling people, and partnered her even in the Albert Hall, that Michael once told me that he learned to play the fiddle from Jamesy Gannon when they were working at the building of a house for people called Devaney. Jamesy wrote the notes of the music on ceiling boards that were afterwards built into the house. Music built the towers of Troy, and it is pleasant to think that music written down and played should go into the building of a house in the neighbourhood of Templehouse Lake; "a beautiful lake about two miles long and one broad and as charming a sheet of water for the size of it as one could meet with in any part of the country". So I find it described in Tadhg Kilgannon's *Sligo and Its Surroundings* and so I have seen it for myself.

"Those Devaneys now," I say, "were related to relations of my own who were also called Devaney."

My host says: "There are a lot of Devaneys in the neighbourhood of Mucklety mountain."

Which is enough to start us on our journey southwards from the House of the Reveries. First by Collooney, with many learned references from the company in the car to the horse fair of Farniharpey, more ancient even than the fair of Ballinasloe in Galway, but gone, as indeed Ballinasloe has also almost gone, into the shadows. Or worse still, been mechanised, modernised, motorised.

No [a correction comes from a learned Sligo lady], the horse fair was held twice a year at Carrignagat, the scene of Teeling's victory for the French and the rebels in 1798. The monthly cattle fair that was held at

Farniharpey was important because of the strategic situation of the place, midway between Sligo and Ballina in County Mayo. Many prosperous farmers, mostly Protestant, lived in the hinterland. Oddly enough, until comparatively recent times only black cattle were sold, and these were subsequently shipped from Sligo Quay.

You could write poems about the black cattle of Farniharpey, the wild horses of Carrignagat.

On by Coolaney, honoured by Yeats in "The Land of Heart's Desire", and by the Ladies' Brae, and within four miles of Easkey and, for the fun of it over to the village of Bonniconlon where, according to the story . . . But this is the story and one of its implications could be that Bonniconlon is still part of the Garden of Eden. For a publican from that place, they say, went on a holiday to Paris in the high and haughty days of the *maisons tolérées*. He saw everything that money could buy: the two fat ladies with the dildoes, the Alsatian dog and the mulatto lady, the blue lady and the giant, the cinema show, etc. Then he came back home to Bonniconlon, said nothing at all about the sights he had seen until one night the clients in the pub challenged him to talk about his travels. He gave it deep thought and pulled twelve pints in the process. Then when the place was respectfully expectantly silent he said: "The way of it boys is this, that here in Bonniconlon sex is only in its infancy."

On into the dark Ox mountains and by Lough Talt which must be one of the most austere of Irish lakes.

And down to Tubbercurry and to the back of Chaffpool hill which gives its name to that spring-morning and Schottische tune "The Chaffpool Post" as Templehouse Lake gave its name to the reel tune that the great Coleman played.

Forty-three years ago a boy on holidays over there in a cottage on the far side of Chaffpool, heard that tune first on a record made in the States where Coleman died. There were in that cottage other records also made in the States: of John McGettigan of Carrigart in north Donegal singing "Cutting the Corn in Creeslough", one of the last and best of the songs of the Irish emigrant:

> Oh Danny she'll wait as she whispered goodbye
> There was just the least trace of a tear in her eye
> And a catch in her voice as she said: You might stay
> But please God you'll come back to old Creeslough some day

So well McGettigan might sing that song, for Carrigart is only a few

miles from Creeslough and in Carrigart the singer had gone to school with
the boy's father and after schooldays emigrated to the States.

There were records of somebody singing a fetching song called
"Whippoorwill" which never seems to have been revived, and of somebody else singing "Lullaby of the Leaves", and of somebody else singing
"My Heart is where the Mohawk flows tonight". Many years later that
boy grown to a man (myself of course) coming by train along the
Mohawk from Buffalo to New York City, remembered that cottage and
those records, and the gardens behind the cottage, the black currants and
the red; and the day he got twopence from a tinker for helping him, as
the man picturesquely put it, to find his ass—a black donkey that had
gone astray.

He remembered also the musical shlow Shligo speech of his handsome
dark-haired cousin talking about the big house up there: Doherty's of
Chaffpool. He had learned to ride a bicycle on Chaffpool hill.

His cousin was, in the politics of the time, a Blueshirt. But his chief
companion in that place was a boy a few years older than him who lived
in a fine farmhouse a few fields away and who, oddly enough, went to
school in Dumbarton, Scotland, but came home for the summer holidays.
That boy's father was a returned American: a description that, because of
air-travel and the decrease in the Irish quota, doesn't mean anything
anymore. He was a kindly man but a stern old-style Irish-American
republican to whom the fascist tendencies of the Blueshirts were detestable.
On the brace over the hearth in the huge country kitchen he had pinned
the Stars and Stripes.

One night the cousin's house was raided and the Blue-shirt parapher-
nalia taken out and burnt by masked, armed men. Tempers were somewhat frayed after that. But the visiting boy from the Six Counties kept
coming and going between the two houses, undisturbed and possibly
unknowing. In those days when you were ten you didn't know much
about politics. The young ones in Belfast today are much more
knowledgeable.

We cross Chaffpool hill. The big house that the cousin had talked so much
about is an eyeless ruin. The cousin's cottage is closed and shuttered, the
cousin and his wife dead and gone. Was John Healy right when he wrote
about emigration and his dying native town and the depopulation of the
west? Charlestown, in Mayo, the town he wrote about, isn't so far
away.

So with trepidation we approach the House of the Stars and Stripes.
The door is opened by a young man who says, more or less: "We know

who you are. We were expecting you for a long time." He is one of three brothers, sons of the man of the house, nephews of the boy who went to school in Dumbarton.

There are places that feel as much like home as the place you come from.

TUBBERCURRY HAD THE BEST TEA

As far away as the town I was reared in Sligo town had the reputation for being a good place to go shopping in. It came second in that way and in that part of the world only to Derry city itself. I'm talking now about the 1930s. And God save Derry!

Nobody in Omagh, now, would have thought of going to Enniskillen to look for bargains. Enniskillen people were regarded as being clannish and inhospitable to strangers. This, as I grew up, I found to be quite untrue and some of the happiest weeks of my boyhood were spent there fishing for perch under the shadow of Portora hill where Oscar Wilde and Samuel Beckett and others went to school, rowing down the widening waters of the Erne to Devenish which is one of the loveliest of our medieval holy places, getting to know a young lady who worked on the staff of *The Impartial Reporter*, a Unionist newspaper that once upon a time gave Barney McGlone full freedom to write a nationalist column. Old Trimble who owned the paper had given his word to McGlone and that was that. Honour among Ulstermen, Orange or Green.

Nor would any Omagh person have dreamt of going to Strabane (which thanks to the Provos is now a burnt-out wreck) for the shopping. Young fellows went to Strabane looking for loose women. With the exact same hope young fellows came from Strabane to Omagh. All this, also, as I grew up I found to be quite pathetic wishful thinking.

But connoisseurs, or connoisseuses, in the shopping business did go all the way to Sligo and that was 66 miles if you went through Bundoran. They declared that they came back satisfied but then there are people who would travel to Bokhara and back for the sheer joy of a bargain:

> His glint of joy in cunning as the farmer asks
> Twenty per cent too much, or a girl's forgetting to be suave,
> A tiro choosing stuffs, preferring mauve.

Tubbercurry also had the best tea. Why this should have been I do not know. From the tops of the mountains of Muckelty and Knocknashee no tea plantations were visible and it is to be assumed that Tubbercurry got the tea that everybody else in Ireland got. Yet my mother used to bring home, to Tyrone, tea from Tubbercurry and sure as God it always tasted better.

Jack B. Yeats once, half in fun, told a friend of mine that he learned to paint by leaning over (he may even have said spitting over) the Garravogue bridge: the second bridge, that is, in the centre of Sligo town and the last before the water turns salt: the bridge that has the cataract and the music of falling water to mock the grunts and belches of the traffic. When the river is at the top of its form it's quite easy to see what the painter meant. The smooth black water turns the corner, holds its breath for a while and hesitates when it realises what's in store for it, then takes the plunge: breaking up into all shapes and patterns and colours, revealing in a moment all the beauty it had stored up during its long reverie two miles upstream in Lough Gill.

Beyond the other bridge you can still hire boats and pull at your ease up the brief Garravogue into all the wonder of Lough Gill. Which was what a schoolfriend of mine and myself did one year when we were holidaying in Bundoran. The hiring rate, as I remember, was a shilling for a boat for the afternoon and the evening. Being from an inland town we knew little or nothing about boats beyond poling a half-submerged punt around the shores of Lough Muck on hot summer days in pursuit of the shoals of perch. For some odd reason the twelfth of July was always the best day for perch fishing. Was it that the weather was always perfect when the Orangemen marched out to celebrate the battle of the Boyne? Or that the fifes and drums had by remote control some odd effect on the fish?

Landlubbers both, we paid our shilling by the Sligo river and sat in and rowed like heroes, a little fearful that if the man saw the shape we were making he would take the boat back from us. Up to that time neither of us had seen Lough Gill. We knew it was there and that was all. We may even have been thinking of it in terms of our own local pond, Lough Muck, Loch na Muice or the Lake of the Pig, which isn't quite the same sort of thing as Lough Gill.

With our eyes towards Sligo town and with our backs before us, as is the way with men and even with liberated women who row boats, we were in the heart of Lough Gill before we knew we were there. Never have I found words for what we felt. We sat for a long time, not rowing, just looking, just thinking, the lake was very still. We beached on a green island, Gallagher's island, where tall trees grew all about. We were part of every story that boys had ever read or dreamed about islands. We helped an old woman who lived alone on that island to tether a carnaptious goat. We drank tea in her house. The very chickens picking on the green seemed to have a prouder air about them than any chickens on the common mainland. The hills and woods around the lake rose and fell in green and grey and blue and the deepest purple. In a defensive way we felt very sorry for Lough Muck.

Many years later I read in the papers how the woman on that island had died tragically and alone, burned alive in her own house. Hearing things like that is part of what we call growing up.

6

RETURN TO COOLBANAGHER

WHERE THE GREAT HORSES RUN
The town of Newbridge in the County Kildare, on the main road from
Dublin to Cork, has on this mild pearl-coloured morning in late March
all the appearances of one of the better-looking small towns in the States:
automobiles in two steady streams, a glistening coloured supermarket, a
lacework pattern of overhead wires. But the effect, if a little alien is not
unpleasant; and I seem to remember Newbridge in the death and the
doldrums, caught between the passing of the great armies and the coming
of the new industries that were to give the place another and, perhaps, a
better life.

Once, along with the nearby Curragh of Kildare, that windy open
plain where the great horses run, Newbridge was one of the principal
training-camps for Britain's imperial army. During the second world war
it was still well-crowded with men in green uniforms, the new Irish
army. After that there was a lull until the new industries appeared: part
of the Irish economic development of the last twenty years. We hear a
lot about it and it is, indeed, a reality. This morning Newbridge is a
bright lively town and very easy to look at and, like Naas, and Kilcullen,
and Kildare town, and all the other towns around the Curragh, it thinks
more of running horses than it does of anything else.

Newbridge is on the River Liffey, the Anna Livia Plurabelle of Mr
James Joyce, a goddess river and, just here, as beautiful as any teenage
goddess before she swings back eastward to be polluted and turned into a
stinking hag by the city of Dublin.

We go on across the Curragh of Kildare, the words of an old song in our
ears: the young woman's lover has left her to enlist in the British army.

> *A livery I'll wear*
> *And I'll comb out my hair,*
> *And in velvet so green I'll appear,*
> *And straight I will repair*
> *To the Curragh of Kildare,*
> *For it's there I'll find tidings of my dear.*

Far to the left is the still surviving military camp. With its annexe of interned patriots, God help us. To the left also is Donnelly's Hollow where, in the old days, Dan Donnelly, the Irish bareknuckle boxer, struck down Cooper, the English bareknuckle boxer. Donnelly being hard-pressed, a landed lady leaped into the ring and cried out that she had her whole estate on him. Whereupon, for love of the old land and out of chivalry, Donnelly felled the Saxon. The marks of his feet as he walked away from the fight are still to be seen on the green ground, and you are invited to see if your pace can match his. It will—if you're an adept at the hop, step and jump or if you're an abominable snowman. Years after, in poverty, Sir Daniel Donnelly walked the streets of Dublin, bearing a title given to him as a sort of a joke, but carried by him in innocent pride. He was a big man and it was said that his arms were so long that he could, without bending, scratch the backs of his knees. His right arm, a little the worse for wear, is preserved in a glass case in a pub called the Hideout in Kilcullen. A ballad was written about the battle, and Jack Butler Yeats, although it all happened long before his time, painted a picture of it. But Colm O'Lochlainn, the Gaelic scholar and ballad-collector, told me he had made a special study of that painting and that he could find neither Donnelly nor Cooper.

All this is to me more marvellous than the *Book of Kells* also to be seen in a glass case in Trinity College, Dublin.

To the immediate right, as we cross the Curragh, is the race-course where one of the richest races in Europe, the Irish Derby, is run. Far to the right is the hump of the Hill of Allen, sacred to the memory of Fionn MacCumhaill and his warrior companions: Conan the Bald with the mocking tongue; Goll MacMorna who wrestled with God on the Fenian meadows; Oisin, the poet, the son of Fionn who went for 300 years to the land of youth with Niamh of the Golden Hair and who—weary of vain gaiety, vain battle, vain repose and homesick for mortality—came back in the end and met St Patrick and his shaven men, and realised sadly that times had changed.

Sacred, but not sacred enough. Gravel pits and quarries have made brutal wounds in the side of the Hill of Allen: the machine is a worse monster than any ever met with in a Fenian nightmare.

Kildare town has its round tower and its associations with St Brigid whom, some people think, may have behind her the shadow of a more ancient flame goddess. It has Japanese gardens, the result of one man's noble eccentricity, which people who love the lovesomeness of gardens, God wot, come to see. It has the national stud which people who love horses come to see and which justifies the maxim of the Irish horse-belt that women are the best thing God ever made . . . after horses. Beyond Kildare there's a long straight road through water-meadows to Monasterevan where John Count McCormack, the singer, a fine gentleman that I first met in the company of Maud Gonne MacBride and Jack Yeats, once lived in Moore Abbey on the banks of the Barrow. For on the road from Newbridge we have crossed a watershed. The Barrow goes not east like the Liffey, but south to meet the Nore and the Suir and to make one of the great valleys up which the Normans came 700 years ago.

Beyond Monasterevan, and into the county of Laois or Laoighis or Leix or, as it once was, Queen's County after Mary Tudor of the sad tumour and the fires of Smithfield, and I am in familiar territory.

The old bridge that once humped over the canal has long been flattened out. But so clearly do I remember sheltering from the rain under that bridge while my two companions and myself ate our lunch of brown bread, garnished with sour apples picked from roadside trees. After that we walked seven miles home to examen of conscience and long-table (feast-day) dinner with talk and all. My two companions are now learned and reverend Jesuits, if you know what I mean. A lumbar spine saved the Jesuits from me, and me from the Jesuits.

But in that flat fertile land apples were to be found in more places than on trees. Down to the left there, below the crossroads of Brittas where a few houses bravely but vainly try to add up to a village, there's a beautiful little Protestant church, an exact replica of Cormac's medieval chapel on the Rock of Cashel. At least that's my memory of it, but it's a long time since I've seen it.

My tale is—now that at last the truth can be told—that once in the golden harvest when the midland people were bringing home the sheaves, three holy Jesuit novices visited that little church and found, to their delight, that the church porch was stocked with sheaves of grain and pyramids of the most delicious apples. So they weakened a little, as David did over the loaves of sacrifice, and scoffed some of the decent Protestant apples. It was a long time ago and the fault has been confessed and penance done, and two of the apple-eaters have been piling up merit all these years. About the third there is nothing to say.

Laois, it occurs to me, must have been, may still be, a great county not so much for wild apples as for cultivated apple-trees left abandoned and unkempt in the oddest places. There was nothing quite like that in the careful north where I came from. There was a whole desolate orchard by an empty house that three of us discovered one day in the course of a long walk. Brown bread never tasted better than on that day.

And ahead on the ridge there, as we leave Brittas behind and drive on towards Port Laoise (once called Maryborough after that same sad queen) there were apple-trees around the old coaching inn. That particular building, in those days seemingly on the road to ruin, with walls cracked and beginning to sag stirred the imagination with thoughts of tired horses heading for Cork or Dublin or Limerick, pulling and straining wearily up the long muddy slope, coming by lamplight to all the shouting and bustle of the hostelry. Mr Pickwick and Dingley Dell and all that. All silent and desolate when I walked these roads 40 years ago: how pleasant to be able to say, like Mangan's old German, that they were golden years. But not silent or desolate today. For the new trade in travellers has pulled a threatened building out of the past and the Old Inn is alive again.

Standing at Old Inn you could see, if it weren't for the new forestry, the great rectangular house where the Earl of Portarlington once lived and where the Jesuits lived until quite recently, and where the novices learned, in the deep silence of the woods, to pray. It would seem that that placing of houses in solitude was something the Jesuits did when they came back to open life again after the suppression. Their very nature, taken from the mind that formed them, sets them moving among men. But the desert places were chosen for what we call the formative years. So a Jesuit told me recently, and he couldn't be wrong, could he?

Today the style is altered and an esteemed newspaper colleague and friend, who lives in that part of North Dublin city, tells me that three Jesuit novices were seen wearing sailors' ganseys and drinking pints of Guinness in the Dollymount Inn adjacent to which is the new novitiate. This I take to be a humorous or—as Flann O'Brien would have said—a quasi-humorous exaggeration. But what a welcome change the pints would have been from brown bread and sour apples.

Over the new forestry the high-sailing tips of the Wellingtonias still stand up defiantly, and can be seen for quite a distance. They mark the line of the main avenue that led up to the earl's house and is now a grass-grown wilderness, awesomely silent. But the rarest people once passed that way. The avenue, they say, was laid with red carpet for the visit of the royal and concupiscent Edward the Seventh of England. A good mile of red carpet to make Irish ground fit for the feet, or the coach-wheels, of the bearded playboy.

Being reared in a garrison town where the permissive society had an early birth, and having that sort of mind, I often wondered, even when I

was a Jesuit novice, what room in Emo Park King Edward had slept in—
and with whom. But I never brought the matter up as a topic for conversation at recreation which was sometimes in English, sometimes in Irish,
sometimes in Latin. Irish would have been the best of the three in which to
discuss the capers of his majesty, and my Irish, picked up in west Donegal,
was mostly love ballads and bad language. But the holy rule forbade.

In the nearby town of Mountmellick in the workhouse hospital (I hope
and pray that it has now a nobler name) heroic French Sisters of Charity
worked among incurable cases. It was part of our novitiate training to visit
those cases, and some of them would have made strong men take to their
heels: Shaky Whelan who shook all the time; the dropsical case with
sores on his thighs as wide and deep as teacups; the groaning man with a
nightcap on his head to hide a growth as big as his head again. There, in
that house of death, I met an old man and up-patient who had been a
boy-bugler in the army on the occasion of the visit of the royal lecher.
Trumpeter, what are you sounding now? Strumpeter?

He was small, neatly-dressed, grave, slow-spoken and wore a well-
clipped, pointed beard. He looked at the ground as he spoke and said
that all men believed in the same god. He was old and saintly and I was
young and callow and at the time we both believed it. But it seems to me
now that his god and the god of the blackguard for whom he blew the
bugle must have been two different people. Or, at any rate, the two men
who passed but made no contact somewhere down there where the
avenue is lost forever in deep grass and forest, looked at the deity from
different angles.

At the crossroads beyond Old Inn you can turn left to follow a narrow
winding byway to the chapel on Maryborough heath, despite, as I have
said, the town of Maryborough being called now, in Irish, Port Laoise.
But Port Laoise heath wouldn't sound the same.

Sharp and rugged beyond the heath is the Rock of Dunamase, an
ancient Celtic fortress plundered by the Vikings in 844. It came to the
Normans as part of Strongbow's dowry on his marriage to Aoife,
daughter of Dermot MacMurrough, King of Leinster. The wild O'Mores
took it from the Normans but in 1641 Sir Charles Coote, a great robber,
took it for himself—or the English. Eoghan Roe O'Neill, the great Irish
soldier, Don Eugenio back from Spain, was there during the wars of the
Confederation, and in the end the fortress was shattered by the
Cromwellians, Hewson and Reynolds. The ruin remains.

Closer at hand, and just visible above high hedges, and looking like the
last splinter of a rotten tooth, is what is left of Moret Castle where,

according to Sir Jonah Barrington, an ancestress of his stood on her battlements and watched the wild O'Mores hang her husband because she wouldn't surrender her castle to them. Her reasonable if unaffectionate argument was that while she could always get another husband it wasn't as easy to get another castle. The husband seems to have been a poor loodheramawn of a fellow and she may simply have been glad of the chance to get rid of him. The story is told of other chatelaines and other castles in other places, but Barrington claimed it for his family and he was such a crafty old liar that it's hard to gainsay him.

The turn to the right brings us to the tiny village of Emo, and above Emo is Coolbanagher. It is well-mentioned on the signposts. Coolbanagher church is famous, for in it, in perfect delicate miniature, Gandon the great English-born architect of the Irish eighteenth century, who adorned Dublin with the Customs House and the Four Courts, set his seal here upon a midland hilltop.

Walking these roads, as 40 years ago I did, with companions, as an embryo Jesuit (if an embryo or tadpole can be said to walk) it seemed perfectly natural to look up at the slim spire of Coolbanagher, and to begin to talk about the decent church that topped the neighbouring hill. Coolbanagher was perfectly cast for the part. Indeed, Coolbanagher had in its line of rectors at least one perfect replica of that rector of Auburn, loveliest village of the plain, "a man he was to all the country dear". A plaque on the wall of the interior of the church commemorates him:

Rev. George Stopford, M.A., for thirty-three years rector of this parish. During a long residence among his people he was justly beloved and respected by them as their faithful Christian pastor and their sincere friend; and when his health forbade continued residence with his parishioners, his affection for them remained unchanged, and was marked no less by anxiety for their temporal good than for their better and more enduring interests.

Goldsmith could have cast that into musical couplets.

On the road ahead of us, between Emo crossroads and the village itself, there's an Irish soldier back from Cyprus, as we find out, walking home from the Curragh of Kildare to somewhere in the neighbourhood of Portarlington. By all means, he'll take a lift. By all means, he'll detour with us to take a look at Coolbanagher. When he was younger he had often walked all the way to Coolbanagher just to look at it, and to listen to the peace of the place, and to look at the view from the hilltop: that way and all the way to the Wicklow mountains, that way across the melting blue plain towards Rosenalis and the Slieve Blooms.

"In Cyprus," he says, "I saw a lot of churches."

The remark brings a new element or dimension or something, a new colour rose-red as Petra (according to the vile Newdigate poem), or red as the rocks of Utah (as I saw them with my own two eyes), into the greens and pearls, quiet fields, low motionless skies, of this Irish day.

We cross the stone stile into the green churchyard, even the graves are green, and daffodils grow and blow around "the mounds that hide the loved and honoured dead". The names of the place are here, stylish resounding names and, by no means, ancient Irish: Chetwood, Allardyce, Odlum. A plague tells us how, because of Lord Carlow, the son of the Earl of Portarlington, James Gandon came here to build this church; indeed it was, as the world or, at any rate, the Georgian Society knows, Lord Carlow and John Beresford who brought Gandon to Ireland.

The church that stood here before Gandon made this gem had a mysterious and fiery end, and the instructive leaflet that you can pick up at Coolbanagher does, I feel, give up the story too easily. If the Church of Rome could produce Chesterton's Father Brown then surely to St Patrick the Church of Ireland should be able to come up with a sleuth who could find out what really happened on this hilltop on the second day of February in 1779. This is what the leaflet says:

On February 2nd, 1779, the church at Coolbanagher according to local tradition, was locked on the outside during Sunday service, and the straw-thatched roof was set on fire. The records of the lawsuit which followed have been lost and maybe it is as well. The rector at the time, Anthony Fleury (1736–81), was known as the crossest man in Europe.

At that time, or at any time, that was a considerable record to hold. Anthony Fleury's bad temper may have been the cause of the fire. Cross men are inclined to make other people cross. It's possible to imagine him in the pulpit when the flames began and to speculate on how exactly those flames affected the tenor of his pious discourse. But who was his pyro-maniacal adversary? Between them they cleared the ground for the genius of Gandon. Lord Leitrim, the one who was assassinated on the shores of Mulroy bay, in 1878, once seized a church for non-payment of the rates. That was a good way to keep the bishops in their place. But to burn the roof because you don't like the preacher comes as near to genius as makes no difference.

Rector in a Wheelbarrow

Aline, Countess of Portarlington, the last great lady of her family to live in the house which the Jesuits have now vacated, has the rare distinction of being commemorated in two churches and by two denominations. Her name is here on the wall on the hilltop. Down below in the Catholic church in the village is her tomb with a catafalque that bears in splendid marble her recumbent sleeping image. For Aline became a Roman Catholic and, it was said locally, worked and prayed that her house, and the house in which Edward, the royal lecher, had once stayed, would one day be inherited by a religious order.

Well, for many years she has had her prayers granted and her work rewarded, but now that the house steps back, as we pious boys used to say, *in mundum*, or into the world, is there, I wonder, in the halls of high heaven one discontented countess?

Just now, as I think in this way, a gigantic shadow strides across the graveyard grass, a ghost with a stride so tremendous that he might shake out of their sleep the Allardyces and the Odlums, not to mention the Chetwoods; and might perturb even the marble repose of Countess Aline who went over to the other side in more ways than one. He could never have approved of Countess Aline.

William Dudley Fletcher was rector here for twenty years, from 1907 to 1927. He had a fine beard and was a well-known controversialist: "A writer of pamphlets and letters to the newspapers, he was described by Newport White, Regius professor of divinity at Trinity College, Dublin, as not so much a pillar of the church as a column of *The Irish Times*." It was said around here that he carried his controversial zeal to the extent of stopping the Roman Catholic children coming home from school and putting them rigorously through their catechism, his nose keen for the odour of Romanist error. "He had a great belief in the curative power of bog-water: standing in it, in bare feet helped rheumatism. When he suffered from phlebitis, he arrived at the church door from his nearby rectory, pushed by his man in a wheel-barrow."

To the church and the parish, a zealous group of a mere 28 families who have spent a lot of money in repairing roof and steeple, this bearded bog-watered eccentric passed on some treasures. For one: a drawing of the church interior that he bought when the Portarlingtons sold out at Emo Park. For two: an ancient stone font that was found in the pleasure grounds (i.e. the ornamental gardens) of Emo Park. The font may date to the twelfth century. The informative leaflet says it was placed in the church "for safety" in 1927 by the same Dudley Fletcher. The local comic story is that the bearded rector, having heard that the jays were on the way, leaped into action, dripping perhaps from his footbath of bog-water, to purloin the font before the Ignatians could get their hands on it.

Was the font trundled up this hill, I wonder, in the same barrow that carried the phlebitic preacher to the pulpit?

If the story of the hasty removal of the font isn't true, it should be, for Dudley Fletcher would seem to have been one of the last of a fiery and intransigent breed: the breed, say, of the Rev. Caesar Otway of the early nineteenth century, a scholarly author and antiquarian of the Church of Ireland (episcopalian) who completely lost his cool when confronted by the Church of Rome. Leaping around heaven where, it is to be hoped, phlebitis is no more, and possibly addressing a civil word to the countess now that she is disconsolate, Dudley Fletcher may rejoice in the work done by the Guild of Friends of Coolbanagher, by the Georgian Society and by Mr Hugo Duffy, the architect. Coolbanagher still stands—renewed and refreshed. The Jesuits have retreated to Dollymount strand where Stephen Dedalus saw the wading girl: "Her slate-blue skirts were kilted boldly about her waist and dove-tailed behind her. Her bosom was as a bird's, soft and slight, slight and soft as the breast of some dark-plumaged dove. But her long fair hair was girlish; and girlish, and touched with the wonder of mortal beauty, her face."

The ancient font is where Dudley Fletcher willed it to be.

In the pleasure-grounds between the big house and the weedy lake does there still stand the statue of Socrates to which a zealous novice once addressed his rosary under the impression that he was praying to St Joseph? Ah well, Socrates was also a very patient man, with extra marks for patience because he had Xanthippé to listen to. The Virgin made less noise, we hope.

Does the statue of Diana still sneer from the fringe of the tangled woods beyond the lake? Sneer? Diana? Because part of her nose had fallen off, an accident that gave a decidedly sinister cast to the countenance of the queen and huntress, chaste and fair.

Seated by the stone stile at Coolbanagher with my friends and the Cyprus soldier, I say absently: "I could write a book about this place."

"You did," says Sean my friend, "alas, you did."[1]

So I say to the Cyprus soldier: "Would you be too young to remember Father Arthur Murphy who was parish priest below in Emo?"

"I heard of him," he says. "He had hair I was told as white as silver."

He had, indeed, as I remember him. He had also a deep devotion to Saint Ignatius and a consequent attachment to the sons of Ignatius who lived in the great house in the woods. Their coming, for him, into the lonely life that a rural parish priest can lead must have been a godsend.

All silver hair and rubicund smiles, and with the peculiar strutting step of a ballet dancer or a soccer footballer, he would walk with the fathers up the refectory floor to the rare feast-day dinner. Rare; for although we all know the joke about the old Dublin woman who, passing the Jesuit house in Gardiner Street and sniffing the steam of cookery ascending from the area, said that "the Jesuits were a grand atin' ordher, glory be to God", it would still be wrong to give the impression that the life lived in the woods of Laois was anything but rigorously austere. Yet careful organisation, and a lay-brother who happened to be a natural cook, did work wonders; and the story was that after one decent meal, Father Arthur said with great good-humour: "Ye take the vow of poverty, we keep it."

It was his wish to die and be buried in the Jesuit gown and I have heard that his wish was granted.

"And Master McCloskey," I ask, "would he be retired now?"

For one of the stints or chores or swinks (they were called experiments) reserved for the novices for their spiritual betterment was to walk, gowns tiresomely flapping around their feet, black wings blowing in the wind, to the schools at Emo and Moret to teach catechism to the chisellers. The teachers must have rejoiced that that drag at least was removed from the daily aggregate drag.

So one got to know and appreciate Master McCloskey who could talk endlessly about Father Burke's refutation of Froude, which must have been among his favourite books.

Walking back up the avenue, which had been but a side-avenue in the earl's days, the mind rejoiced in the idea of the comic-homeric pursuit around the United States of a half-Norman English historian by a half-Norman Irish priest: the priest trying, as best he could, to lecture where the historian had lectured and to cast, as he considered, the lie in the fellow's teeth. In this midland quietude Master McCloskey must have brooded a lot and rejoiced a lot over that battle of brains: Burke and Froude were as alive to him as Dempsey and Tunney.

In there to the right, on a slope where the new trees were then no bigger than Michaelmas daisies, the earl's strawberry beds were going wild, but that little taint of wilderness gave them a flavour that no tame cultivated strawberry could ever have had. In the walled garden, old Tracy the gardener, a relic of the past, grew splendid peaches and talked forever, in a voice sorrowful with pride, about his begonias. Now the trees are giants and the strawberries and the novices and Old Tracy are gone.

Let me, sitting here on the hilltop, with two old friends and the Cyprus soldier, hope that the peaches, the begonias and the walled garden remain. Even in this unsubstantial pageant of a world something must endure.

To my companions on the churchyard wall I say: "There was this novice who was a bit of a joker. Like myself, he's a layman now. He washed his hands a lot. He was, you might say, a compulsive handwasher, not such a rare phenomenon as you might think. We used to call him Lady MacBeth. What else? But he hated shaving. And one day, teaching catechism in Emo school, he found that his pupils were unable to control their giggles. He located the eye of the hurricane and asked him what it was all about. No answer. Giggles and more giggles.

" 'Go up,' says he, 'and tell Mr McCloskey you were impudent.'

"Then a little later, through the open doorway that leads into the next room, he hears the tearful voice: 'Please, sir, I wasn't imperent. I only whispered to Dinny Meehan that the skewdent needed a shave.'

"So the joker of a novice afterwards says: 'Watch your facials. Use Gillette and a good lotion. The conisoors in Emo school are hard to please.'

"It was that same novice," I say, "who thought up the tactic: How to find Fun at a Quarter of Charity."

"Now what," says the soldier, "would a quarter of charity be? We don't have them in the army."

"Well it was like this. One novice would kneel down on the floor of the conference room, the Father Master, *Pater Magister*, of Novices, *Novitiorum*, presiding. Then one by one the other novices would stand up and point out the faults of the kneeling penitent. Oh, nothing serious. Peccadilloes. There was no opportunity for anything else. Something like: He rushes up the stairs three at a time. Or: He slops his soup.

"For humility, you see. And to make community life smoother."

"I see," says the soldier. "The sergeants would love it on the Curragh of Kildare."

"This joker of a novice had ideas for saying something like: Father, I think Brother Smith shouldn't slip out at night to drink in Allardyce's pub in Emo.

"Then *Pater Magister* would be supposed to say: 'But does he, brother?'

"And the joker would say: 'No father, but I don't think he should.'

"There were other suggested statements. Like: 'Father, I don't think Brother Jones should keep turnips under his bed.'

"And so on. Of course none of these remarks ever actually got made."

"Ah well," says the soldier.

We all stand up.

"You actually went on your knees like that," says the soldier.

In the laughter that followed we drove west.

"We wore the gown," I say, "when we went to teach in the schools. But on walks we wore any old clothes. For a long time the local people thought that the novitiate was a school for the sons of families that had come down in the world."

All gone now, all ghosts in these woods: the earl and his Catholic countess, the lecherous king; the old man in Mountmellick workhouse who had been a boy bugler when the king went over a mile of red carpet, down the avenue between the soaring wellingtonias; the old silver-haired priest, the teacher brooding on Froude and Father Burke, the Jesuit fathers, the ragged novices walking the roads, eating brown bread and green apples; the bearded minister conveyed to church in a wheel-barrow.

Our way is west from Coolbanagher and away from this woodland of ghosts. But then every corner of every field has a ghost that talks to somebody.

On to the town of Portarlington with its Huguenot houses, quiet walled gardens tucked away from the street; and that sombre-looking old house where the boy who was to be the Iron Duke, the victor of Waterloo, went to school. He wasn't much of a scholar, but then he managed to get into the army where scholarship might have been a disadvantage.

In Portarlington, outside Alo Donnegan's pub, we drop the Cyprus soldier and, being the eldest member of the party, I can talk learnedly about the day in 1932 when I saw Alo Donnegan and Bertie Donnelly performing at the Tailteann Games in Croke Park, the big Gaelic Athletic Association stadium. It's sad to think that there may be young people in Ireland in 1978 who from that last sentence may be misled into thinking that Alo Donnegan and Bertie Donnelly were hurlers or Gaelic footballers and not among the greatest of track cyclists. There may even be young people who think that Dixie Dean was a precursor of the Beatles.

All things in Ireland remind me of something else. We go on by Mountmellick and Rosenalis and Dunne's castle to which the white horse, riderless, its master dead, came back from the battle of Aughrim.

We skirt the Slieve Blooms and cross the Barrow where it's little more than a stony creek, which you'd find hard to credit if you've ever walked the old towing-path by the sleek ample water from Graignamanagh to St Moling's where Mad Sweeney at last found peace. Standish O'Grady compared the river Nore, whose chief man-made ornament is the Norman city of Kilkenny, to a shy novice meeting, above New Ross, with a seasoned abbess: the Barrow.

On to Birr where a journalist I know once picked up a telephone in a bar to find himself talking to Queen Elizabeth (the second) who has relatives in the vicinity. Something had gone wrong at the exchange. And where long-ago the Galway hard-riding country gentlemen (parcel of drunken louts) burned that same hotel in the course of a party, and earned for themselves the name of the Blazers.

On across the Shannon at Portumna where Domhnall Cam O Suilleabhain and his hunted people at the end of the wars of the great O'Neill, crossed in midwinter without the aid of a bridge, and beset by foes who should have been friends.

But what happens on the far side of the Shannon is always another story.

7

ALONG THE CLADDAGH

There were lovely ladies along the Claddagh
All taking the air by each garden tree,
All taking air in the quiet evening,
And none so lovely as my lady.

Then I stepped beside her most entertaining,
Making fine talk on the rounded sea,
"But ah," she said, "you I cannot marry,
For a bold Spanish man said bravely to me:

'Oh be my lady, and in Limerick laces
Your delicate ways shall airily pass,
With quiet feet in your blue pampooties
And guinea hens on the daisied grass'."

F. R. Higgins: "The Spanish Man"

MORNING AT GALWAY HARBOUR

Elisa Johanna from Groningen is one girl I don't expect to meet at nine o'clock in the morning in Galway city. Yet here she is, disgorging a mealy substance that a man, passing by like myself, tells me is fertiliser. Puffs of wind come now and again from Galway Bay and take some of the stuff with them in the direction, roughly, of Lower Abbeygate Street. The man and myself pick the grains out of our eyes, then stand a bit more to the west and continue to watch the unloading operation. Who wants to be blinded from Groningen—or fertilised?

Elisa Johanna is not alone. Close beside her the *Hurnay* from Lubeck is loading timber; and the *Naomh Eanna* that joins Ireland to the Aran Islands, and the *Galway Bay*, are still enjoying the morning slumber that's made all the more sweet by the knowledge that somebody else is awake and working; and the monstrous *Egee* from Caen is sucking in black ore from the mines of Tynagh. The ore is stored on the quayside in a crazy sort of structure that at a distance looks like an oriental pavilion. There are, I know, various views about the value to Ireland of the present mode of exporting a portion of her bowels to far foreign fields yet it does make for activity in Galway harbour in the early morning.

It's a good fifteen years since I last walked in Galway city or around the harbour, or any closer to them than Paddy Burke's Oyster House at Clarinbridge when Paddy, God rest him, was there to give the full warmth of a Galway welcome. Why it should be fifteen years, or why one should be as close as Clarinbridge without coming on to Galway, I can't exactly say. But my journeys in these parts in those years always seemed to be from Clare to Dublin or Dublin to Clare by the high exciting road along the ridge of Slieve Auchty where you strain your eyes all the time for the first glimmer of Loch Graney or Loch Cutra; or by a detour to view Black Head and the white stony Burren of North Clare and to meditate on the ancient ruins of Corcomroe Abbey and on Yeats's vision of Dermot and Dervorgilla.

It helps a great deal to appreciate the strange moonscape of the Burren —the name means Big Rock—if you read those descriptive lines at the beginning of Yeats's "The Dreaming of the Bones":

> *Somewhere among great rocks, on the scarce grass,*
> *Birds cry, they cry their loneliness.*
> *Even the sunlight can be lonely here,*
> *Even hot noon is lonely.*

Then if you found yourself in the Burren and wanted to get back to Dublin, it was hardly a detour and always a delight to call to see Paddy Burke, particularly if you had known him long before the English Royal family and John Huston started to visit his place; and if you had feasted well with Paddy, on black velvet, on bread and smoked salmon or Galway oysters, then it seemed the part of a wise man to slink back to the comparative safety of Dublin and leave Galway city until the next time round.

For, drunk or sober, a man may stay in Galway city at least a day more than he meant to.

The last time and the time before that I was at Galway harbour at this hour of the morning I was on my way from the Castle hotel in Lower Abbeygate Street to the Aran Islands. The Castle hotel is to the Aran Islands as Hong Kong is, or was, to the British empire, a foothold and trading post on the mainland. In days of more uninhibited roistering the older people on the islands used to say about the behaviour of the younger people: "We don't know where the devil is by day, but by night he's in the Castle hotel in Lower Abbeygate Street."

On no previous morning, though, in Galway harbour did I see so much

E

business afoot. This may be a sign of the Irish economic revival, about which we have read, and a good thing, too, we suppose, and long overdue. But to get away from the noise and dust of it I do, more or less, what George Moore, the novelist, did, about 70 years ago and walk on and out as far as I can go with the living rugged Corrib and the crazy gulls to my right, and the bay, grey with white splurges, and the sullen hills of Clare ahead of me.

There was a *feis*, or Gaelic cultural festival, to be held in Galway city and a Gaelic League secretary in Dublin had told Mr Moore that his musical cousin, Mr Edward Martyn of Tulira Castle which is over there by the town of Gort and now the residence of Lord Hemphill, would be there to judge the traditional singing. Lady Gregory and Mr Yeats would be there also. Mr Moore who, on his own whimsical admission, couldn't bear to be left out of anything, took off for Galway. Seventy or so years ago.

Cousin Edward is there, as endearingly comic as Cousin George always made him seem to be. Mr Yeats is made to talk as, indeed, he may then have talked. The walk that the three of them had around Galway makes some of the best reading to be found in the three volumes of Moore's *Hail and Farewell*.

A lovely day it was, the town lying under a white canopy of cloud, not a wind in all the air but a line of houses sheer and dim along the river mingling with grey shadows; and on the other bank there were waste spaces difficult to account for, ruins showing dimly through the soft diffused light, like old castles, but Yeats said they were the ruins of ancient mills, for Galway had once been a prosperous town. Maybe, my spirit answered, but less beautiful than she is today. . . .

And later on, when they came to the harbour:

. . . we continued our walk down the wharf, thinking of the great labour spent upon it. The bringing of all these stones, and the building of them so firmly and for such a long way into the sea, could only have been done in famine times. A long wharf, so long that we had not walked half its length when Yeats and Edward began to talk of returning to the *feis*, and leaving them undecided, staring into the mist, hoping to catch sight every moment of the black hull of a hooker, I strayed on ahead, looking around, wondering, tempted to explore the mystery of the wharf's end. Yet what mystery could there be? Only a lot of tumbled stones.

Oh, what gentlemanly melancholy, what a dying fall, and Marius the Epicurean meditating on the meaning of the sun-warmed stones of the decayed, ancestral villa. All bullshit, Mr Moore!

But what would Moore in his pose as Marius have had to say about the black guts of the Tynagh mines sailing off, as he did himself, to gallant France? Or of that stout wench from Groningen scattering her fertilising dust in the dacent eyes of Irishmen?

From the point of this wharf Moore saw some laughing Galway girls wading in the salt pools. One of them was so brazen and so daring that she hoisted her kirtle right up to her waist. George seemed to think that her performance was for his benefit. It may well have been—although he was a little bit given to self-gratulatory whimsies of that sort. Didn't he think, or pretend to, that every young nun he met anywhere was mutely appealing to him to be rescued?

But what, I wonder as I head back for the Spanish Arch, would Mr Moore think of Salthill nowadays on a Sunday in the summer or of the men at the swimming pool there who complained in letters to the papers that their privacy was being shattered by young women in bikinis?

Women, we all know, can be a nuisance at times, particularly in pubs, if there are any pubs left. But women sober and young and by salt sea pools and in bikinis might have moved Mr Moore of Moore Hall to talk not only about mermaids but even about Aphrodite, not in Aulis but in the cold Galway sea. He would have given the matter serious thought—and brought Cousin Edward along to embarrass his modesty by the sights—nor would the letter he wrote to the papers have been one of complaint.

INTRODUCTION TO A LOBSTER

Galway is the city or town in Ireland most possessed by water: living water, wild water, clean water, sea-water, river-water, lake-water, but not water in the whiskey except you add it yourself.

The restless bay at my back, I walk under the Spanish Arch and over the roaring Corrib, and along by the canal which is the most restless canal I've ever seen. It never seems able to make up its mind, to rest content with its lot in life and stay where it is. It always seems as if it had half a notion to go back with a rush, engulfing all before it, to the tumult of the original stream.

Then when I pass the crowded friendly university college and the vast cathedral—empty at this hour of the day, except for the Lord himself and two whispering nuns, and myself with my audibly creaking knees—I am assaulted by all the wild airs and memories of Connacht. It doesn't seem to matter there which way the winds are blowing. They all come at you from the long chain of lakes, Corrib and Mask and Carra and Conn, when you stand on the big bridge at the fringe of Galway city and look northwards in the general direction of Cong.

It's the most exciting bridge in Ireland, making a man want to be young again, and a boatman or a hunter or a spearer of salmon, or a character in a novel by that good man, the late Walter Macken who couldn't be totally happy anywhere except in the west.

The crowded friendly college: for like all our colleges, and like most colleges elsewhere it's crowded and not so long ago the students were making their protest for what the Germans euphemistically used to call elbow-room. It is a friendly college, which may be because it partakes of the character of the city. The group of students that I lectured to there one evening leave a pleasant impression on the memory, particularly a young man in whose father's house I once was, not far from the town of Boyle in County Roscommon and close to the grave of Carolan, the blind harper and composer whose eighteenth-century music is splendidly played today by Paddy Moloney, the piper, and the Chieftains: and close to the grave of the mythological god and cyclopean monster, Balor of the Evil Eye.

This young man says to me at the end of the night that most of his fellow students read nobody except John McGahern and Edna O'Brien. This gives me matter for thought long after the young people have gone and I am sitting alone, sipping and reading, in the only hotel in the world in which I was ever introduced to a live lobster.

This day long ago I was in the bar and a man came in with a bag and put the complicated splendidly-designed creature on the counter. He was still the dull colour of the Galway rocks that hadn't protected him well enough. The red radiance would come later when, for the delight of men, and of women too, he would be boiled alive. The man who brought him in solemnly introduced him to everybody in the bar. There was much laughter and extending of hands in mock salutation. Let it be said, in some slight extenuation, that we were all half tipsy. But nobody was tipsy enough to reach the hand too far forward. The mechanism of the creature fascinated me. His eyes were out, as Mrs Mulligan used to say, like organ stops. He saw us, for sure. What he thought of us we will never know.

John McGahern went to University College Galway so that it's reasonable that students at Galway would want to read him. But there's a lot more to it than that. The centre of the truth may be that until Edna O'Brien and John McGahern came along no Irish writer that I can think of ever really spoke to the young. In terms of patriotism, yes, and the rising of the moon, and "did that play of mine send out certain men the English shot". But not about more domestic matters, like masturbation, around which adults and the ages have built a mythology and a theodicy, or about the passing or failing of examinations, or the domination of a strong father, or a mother dying slowly of a dread disease; or about young girls wondering what it was all about and being determined to find out. Most of us seem to have been born with minds as matured, to put it nicely, as that of the changeling in the cradle who speaks with the voice of an old man, or that of "the eagle cock that blinks and blinks on Ballygawley Hill" and is, according to the Sligo poet, the oldest thing under the moon.

When I describe McGahern as the Frank Sinatra of the Irish novel I mean no denigration—if the word is permissible. Sinatra fans will wonder why I bother to hedge the remark. When Sinatra first set his audiences screaming he did so because he appealed to young people who had problems that they thought a scream might solve.

All this, of course, may be just a special quality of our time, and here I give up theorising and look from the most exciting bridge in Ireland at the white wonder of a shower gathering high in the air above the Corrib. There's a lot of quite audible screaming in the world we live in.

A GAELIC GODOT

Once upon a time I lived in a suburb by the sea in which there was an ordinary size of a public-house, not the type of pandemoniacal filling-station the size of Donnybrook bus-garage and every bit as homely and comfortable, that you get now in the new Dublin suburbs. Into that house one day there wandered a nobleman from the other side of the eastern sea: a stout tall man with a pale face, pale eyes that didn't look at you, straw-coloured hair and a drooping moustache. He was also a dipsomaniac and no harm to him for that, for some of us are just as far gone, except that we're noisy as well. This man was inoffensively quiet. He stayed with us for a long time, three months or more, yet he was never really with us. He lived somewhere in the neighbourhood. He was on duty punctually every morning when the pub opened. He sat alone at one end of the counter and sipped large brandies. He sipped two bottles of brandy *per diem* and gave offence to nobody. With the coming on of closing time he washed down the brandy with two bottles of Emu burgundy, which comes from wherever emus come from and good luck to the men who make it. Then he went home to bed. He never staggered.

As he sipped his way through the long and arduous day he looked and stared moistily and steadily at the shelves of bottles behind the bar, and spoke to nobody, and, we all, the locals, left him in the peace that he clearly desiderated. It seems a better word to use in relation to him than merely: desired. Sometimes he stared or looked at the auctioneers' advertisements in the newspapers.

Once I saw him in the centre of the city, in a bank, and I thought: of course, the money has to come from somewhere. The brandy and burgundy in that surburban pub alone—none of us had ever seen him drinking anywhere else—was, even in those days, costing him £47 a week. Not even a nobleman, perhaps not even a top executive, could afford it nowadays.

Once, doubting the patents of his nobility, I looked him up in Debrett. I had easy access to Debrett because I worked for my bread in the leader-writers' room of a certain Dublin daily newspaper where a Debrett was maintained because that newspaper was then such a respecter of tradition that right into the 1950s it topped the social-and-personal column every morning with some such throbbing message as: "Lord Footmagoory is 92 today". The leader-writers, who were supposed to do so, kept forgetting to keep Debrett up-to-date with the ravages of death so that quite frequently deceased and long-buried baronets found themselves socially and personally celebrating their birthdays.

Anyway there in Debrett was my drouthy nobleman, a lot larger than life, generations of him and acres and acres of wide and windy English land. A vision I had of coastal erosion, an ocean of brandy and burgundy beating on the shores of the ancestral estates, acre after acre slipping away and sinking into the silent deep. There rolls the deep where grew a tree.

Gradually the news leaked out that the nobleman was there waiting for his agent to catch up with him to purchase a property, house and all, somewhere in rural Ireland. That would explain the interest—if interest it was and not just something to stare at instead of the bottles—in the auctioneers' advertisements. Suppose, I said to myself, the agent never comes. Suppose the nobleman is left sitting here forever, sipping brandy and washing it down with burgundy, staring at photographs of desirable properties in their own grounds—forever and ever.

Being at the time a young man with literary aspirations I could see the novel taking shape: I never thought of it as a play, knowing nothing about the theatre. At that time nobody in the neighbourhood of Dublin much mentioned Samuel Beckett except Con Leventhal (who was his close friend) and Kate O'Brien, Philip Rooney, Tommy Woods (Thomas Hogan), John Jordan, John Montague, Sean White, Owen Quinn, Anthony Cronin and myself who had all luxuriated in *Murphy*. The two who waited for Godot were not even there, as yet, to wait for Godot.

The agent, as it happened, turned up and read the riot act and blamed everybody within sight and hearing for allowing his lord and master to expend that £47 a week. But as we all agreed it wasn't on us he spent it.

Now what, in the name of God, has this got to do with Galway? Simply this: that I'm sitting here on my first visit to the Gaelic theatre, the Taidhbhearc, watching a superb Godot, wonderfully performed, directed by Alan Simpson who was down in the train with me from Dublin. Alan is a good man to travel with for he knows the country as only old army men or ordnance-survey chain-men could know it, not so much by towns and mainroads as by hills, fields, marshes, fences and small streams.

He also knows his Beckett and was, you might say, one of the first in the business in these islands, and Galway, it seems to me, is the sort of a place in which Godot might turn up; for the races, for God's sake, and speaking Irish. Everyone, according to the old ballad, turns up for the ecumenical races of Galway:

> As I roved out through Galway town to seek for recreation
> On the seventeenth of August, my mind was elevated.
> There were multitudes assembled with their tickets at the station,
> My eyes began to dazzle and they going to see the races.
>
> It's there you'd see the pipers and the fiddlers competing
> And the nimble-footed dancers and they tripping on the daisies.
> There was others crying cigars and lights, and bills of all the races
> With the colours of the jockeys and the prize and horses' ages.
>
> It's there you'd see the jockeys and they mounted on most stately,
> The pink and blue, the red and green, the emblem of our nation,
> When the bell was rung for starting, all the horses seemed impatient,
> I thought they never stood on ground, their speed was so amazing.
>
> There was half a million people there of all denominations,
> The Catholic, the Protestant, the Jew, the Presbyterian.
> There was yet no animosity, no matter what persuasion,
> But fáilte and hospitality inducing fresh acquaintance.

John Butler Yeats, the da, said that in New York everything happens; in Dublin nothing happens except the occasional insolvency. But then New

York is not a city, New York is the world compressed, and everything means everything good and bad and in-between, and too much of it all at the same time. Galway is a small city, a distinct memory of the middle ages, and things happen singly and are more often than not liable to be pleasant. Old Galway friends of mine, some still alive, some gone to God or Godot, used to keep saying during the week of the races: "This place isn't what it used to be. You should have been here in the old days." That always set me wondering what they did in the old days that they weren't doing all around me at that living, present moment.

There was the story of the two hearty heroes who found all the pubs so crowded that they couldn't get a drink in comfort. So they bought a barrel at a backdoor, a full one or a half-barrel or a tierce or a half-tierce or whatever, and carted it off towards the bedroom they were sharing in the Southern hotel. This was before the Southern was modernised and all tarted-up, and it had then a deep stairwell down which you could look from the topmost floor to the space now, and then, outside the dining-room. On that space, as our heroes entered, a cocktail reception was going on. Their room was up at the roof. So they climbed and then looked down on the reception and listened like two ancient mariners to the merry din, and grew dizzy with temptation, and broached one end of the barrel and unloaded the lot like a tempest on the well-dressed throng below.

That was a bit before my time, but I do remember the pint-drinkers' club in a certain backroom. For initiation you had to drink seventeen pints one after the other and then buy a round for everyone in sight. The rules were framed and on the wall. Membership was naturally exclusive.

Opening off the backroom was a sort of hallway with a blind stairway, roofed over to make a larger room above. The great joke was to send a half-tipsy stranger in there looking for the gents and then listen attentively for the thump as he ascended the truncated stairway on the road to nowhere and his head made contact with the ceiling and he came reeling out again. I was a victim once. The echoes of the laughter are with me still. That backroom and the pub before it are now gone or transformed into a prosaic shop. Perhaps I *was* here in the old days.

But after the play is over tonight and whether Godot turns up or not, a party of us will go down the street to the Castle hotel and talk learnedly for a while. That knowledge leaves me well content for I have happy memories of the Castle hotel in Lower Abbeygate Street which is the true gateway to, and from, the Aran Islands.

A VERY CONFIDENT EAGLE

For it was from the Castle hotel in Lower Abbeygate Street that I set out one morning many years ago to have my first meeting with the late Monsignor Pádraig de Brún—Paddy Browne. The first real meeting, that is, for over the years I had encountered him at the sort of Dublin social function at which you never really meet anybody and at which the only happy people are the boys of the old brigade who go along with the simple, honest intention of freeloading.

On the morning of that meeting I was not at all at my ease. To begin with, it was an excessively dark November morning. The fog was as thick as wet cobwebs over almost deserted streets, and over a Corrib that for once seemed sullen. A large part of the previous night had passed in learned discourse in the Castle hotel, interspersed with songs in Irish and the *Béarla Gránna*, and in the company of fine Connacht friends, three of them from over the sea in Inishmore.

Because I had talked too much by night, I was in no great form for talking that morning, and I knew that to talk to Paddy Browne you had to be in a manner of speaking on your toes. Hadn't he, in John Huston's house, talked Jean-Paul Sartre out of it, so that the Frenchman had to give up and go to bed early? The legend even went on to say that Huston had frightened the philosopher back to France by telling him that every second priest in Ireland was a similar sort of polymath and could talk like that.

Looking out of the hotel doorway at the network of mist, trailing like Spanish moss in southern forests, from corners of old Galway stone, I understood why Dr Johnson when he was indisposed was wise enough to have Edmund Burke kept away from him. There is a time for not talking, particularly with a man who knew the pure mathematics and had translated Dante into Irish; who stood over six feet and had about him the style of a very confident eagle. To make it still worse I was supposed to write an article about the man.

One of my three friends from Inishmore island walked with me through the fog as far as the bridge over the canal where the campus begins. He was a considerable help to my morale. His last year as a student in Galway had been the first year that saw Paddy Browne as President of the College. The Inishmore man had nothing but good to say about the president's wisdom and kindness, as far as the students were concerned. The wilder the student the more liable the president was to talk reasonably to him if he in his turn had any sort of an argument or half-argument to offer. The mind of the eagle didn't expect to find perfect reason anywhere.

Consoled thus, I went on all alone, fog all around me.

A warm well-lighted room was further consolation on that drear November morning. Then when the eagle-man spoke he said: "Sit down. What'll you have? I've wanted to meet you for a long time." No better way in the world to make a man feel at his ease. We went on happily after that. Then an hour before lunch Michael Scott, the architect, joined the company. It was a day to remember.

There was one quite extraordinary thing about Paddy Browne. He seemed to know just that little bit more about everything than anybody else did. This was all made evident without any overbearing pedantry, with no straining effort to prove that he was a knowledgeable man, no dogmatism, no talking down to people. From that day I can remember several aspects of that side of the man, but this one may serve for the moment.

We had been talking about a murder case, not a recent one but a sad thing from the tail-end of the last century. It was a long way from the Himalayan air of the higher mathematics or the reshaping of Dante into Irish verse. The case had for a long time interested me, and still does, and I had hoped that some day it might take the shape of a novel. Everything that I ever could find to read about it I had read, and had visited the place where the dreadful thing had happened, and talked to old people who had memories of it—or the memories of their parents. But two details of the case had defied all research and any explanation. Paddy Browne was able to explain them to me. Then after a while he said: "I wonder should you write that novel. They were sad poor people and it was a long time ago."

He set me wondering too, and I'm wondering still. Behind the great granite face there was a brooding kindness, not only for the living, but for the privacy of the dead.

Back to the Castle hotel I went in high good humour to rejoin the three men from Inishmore. After further learned chat they walked me to the railway-station, collecting on the way three hardy travelling men or tinkers and bringing them with us into the station bar. The barman was uneasy. But he listened to the eloquent speech I made on behalf of the travelling people, agreed with the argument that we were all travellers from the cradle to the grave. An hour or so later I stepped (staggered?) gracefully onto the Dublin train, and away east the road with me.

When next I met my good friend from the ultimate islands he looked at me sadly and said: "You were the cunning man to leave when you did for Dublin. You got our travellers into the station-bar. We had the honour and glory of getting them out."

But there is no creeping fog this blessed day. Galway is bright and the Corrib loud and happy.

Once I knew a lady who lived so close to the edge of the Corrib that in the livingroom of her house you could hear the slap and the struggle of the salmon on the ground when they were scooped out of the wild water. That detail makes me think of an early poem of Austin Clarke, the fine love poem with lines about the salmon, shattering the air into silver when the chill grass ends their leaping: and that in turn sets me thinking of some of those dazzling fragments from the sagas.

"And lovely was the character of that island, full of wild apples and melodious birds. . . .

"He came to the crest of that hapless sea, full of strange beasts. . . .

"A branch of silver with three golden apples was on his shoulder. . . .

"And she made of the stones blue men and others with heads of goats. . . ."

Every fragment has enough magic in it for a day's meditation, certainly enough to keep my mind going as I walk back along Upper Abbeygate Street to the stone corner newly-cleaned and shining, and the ornamentations of Lynch's castle where once upon time the Mayor of Galway hanged his own son. For the sake of justice.

Thackeray who did so well for a lot of Ireland in his *Irish Sketch Book* didn't make much out of Galway. But then he struck bad weather here and spent his time looking out the window at the rain on Eyre Square, and reading an old book about the celebrated highwayman, Captain Freney. He saw nothing of that urban quality in decay which, since he was to write *Vanity Fair*, would have interested him and which George Moore, in *Hail and Farewell*, was to describe so excellently.

Moore and W. B. Yeats on that day in the early years of this century walked behind Moore's musical and religious cousin, Edward Martyn:

through some crumbling streets to the town house of the Martyns, for in the eighteenth century the western gentry did not go to Dublin for the season. Dublin was two long days' journey away: going to Dublin meant spending a night on the road, and so every important country family had its town house in Galway. My grandfathers must have danced in Galway, there being no important towns in Mayo, and in fine houses, if one may judge by what remains of Edward's . . .

When Yeats and Moore and Martyn looked at it 70 years ago the Martyn town house was a ruinous tenement, marble chimney pieces high on naked walls that were under the threat of demolition. But Moore who seems to have loved Galway in decay and mighn't have liked the lively look of it in the 1970s, had a "scattered vision of ladies in high-peaked bodices and gentlemen with swords . . . dancing in mid-air".

Cousin Edward, as Moore nastily pointed out, didn't see the vision. Thackeray missed it because the weather was wet and he knew nobody who could show him around.

THE RED MAN, THE PANTHER AND THE BEAVER

This pub in Eyre Square as I first remember it was a place where you might easily lose an eye if you were a tall man and happened to brush against the peaked tweed-cap of one of the other customers: caps that bristled with or were festooned with salmon lures and artificial flies. The one thing that made you feel happy was that the fish were reasonably safe while those fellows kept their caps on their heads. The female customers were not so adorned. Germaine Greer had not been heard of.

As far as I remember there was even sawdust on the floor in those days, and a feeling in the air that everybody had just crossed Ireland on the same train that had carried George Moore as far as Mullingar before he parted company with it and went to Westport and the Marquis of Sligo's place to meet the mythical Alec Trusselby and (thanks to the Celtic scholar, Kuno Meyer) to write *A Story-Teller's Holiday*. But now the sawmills, like the woods of Kilcash, are down, and the floors are freshly hoovered, and the fishermen have no panache—that is, if there are any of them in the place at all.

Most of the customers seem to be young, that is under 40, people out of offices for lunch, college people. They are drinking beer and soft drinks and eating well in a long bar that was not there at all in the old days. Would these young people even talk of the old days as my friends in Galway were once inclined to do?

Where the barbed and bristling anglers once trampled sawdust there is now a classy restaurant with uniformed waiters, and a stylish mock-Elizabethan gallery around it, and good food, and pictures on the wall. This friend who went to college with me in another city and has a professional interest in the old days—he's an historian—sits with me and we eat large portions of the good food. When fed we will go back as far into the old days as Anach Cuain on Loch Corrib where in 1825 the people were drowned for whom Blind Raftery wrote the lament:

Má fhágaim-se sláinte is fada bhéas trácht
Ar an méad do baitheadh ag Anach Cuain. . . .

This time round, I tell him, the thing I liked most about Galway city was the hand-printed welcome I saw in the windows of the city's best shop—to my way of thinking. There it was for all to see, welcoming me to Galway, mentioning me by name, and when I say that the shop is one of the best bookshops I've ever been in, everyone who knows Galway will know that I mean Kenny's. Going east the road you won't as far as I know meet anything like it unless you have had the good fortune to browse in Bernard Stone's Turret Bookshop in Kensington Church Walk where, all of a sudden, you could be as far as the middle ages from modern London. I say could be, for, alas, the glory of that shop has now departed. Going west the road you might come to Jim Battle's place in Peachtree Street, Atlanta, Georgia. There could be a dozen or more others, for I haven't been everywhere nor in every bookshop. All I mean to say is that Kenny's books and antiques, and Kenny's gallery in Salthill, have added a new dimension to the life of a city that was always multi-dimensional.

To speak of books new and secondhand doesn't mean much. There's nothing secondhand about a great book. Augustine Birrell who looked after his library said: "When a new book is published, buy an old one". And walking on the Dublin quays the other day I brooded over the decay in my time of the Dublin secondhand bookshops, the teetotal extinction of the sidewalk barrows. The point is made particularly obvious at one corner where there was once a shop where treasures could be found for a few pence: that's a cliché, but it was true. There's damn all in the neighbourhood now but a selection of gaudy paper-backs, and the reading of them would be unlikely to create Francis Bacon's full man; and even at that the prices are crazy.

On a day that's appropriately overcast we head out for Anach Cuain.

There was another pub once around that corner, and off Eyre Square, and thinking of it brings back to me comically the sort of thing that can happen to a person in Galway. For once, upon a good summer, I acted as guide on the road round Ireland to an American professor and his wife, having first fairly warned them of the alcoholic hazards of rural travel. Not quaking morasses any more, nor rough rugheaded kerns. But like meeting a lot of friendly people and not getting at the right time to the hotel into which you had booked, and missing your night's sleep and the proper vitamins, and so on. They were quiet brave people and they tightened their lips and said they'd face it. So we travelled Leinster and we travelled Munster and hell to the thing happened to us—we could have been cycling in the Malvern hills where the last thing that happened to anybody was when some poor ploughman saw things on a May morning in the middle ages.

We came even to Limerick city and passed through sober and un-scathed. We passed by Lady Gregory's Gort and saw all that we should see, lakes and woods and swans: and at Ballylee the symbolic tower in which the poet, Yeats, had lived. We came to Galway and Salthill, and on our first night there the proprietor of the hotel told them about his experiences in the United States: which was interesting but not exactly riotous. When I warned the professor fellow that getting to Galway was one thing but getting out of it could be another, he smiled in a tolerant fashion.

Then at ten o'clock the next morning I called on a scholarly old friend of mine, told him about the pair of decent people I had with me and how it was that we were on our way to Sligo to the grave of Yeats. We wouldn't have time, you see, to go the long way round the coast but if he could bring me to some nearby eminence from which, looking west, the Americans could get an idea of the Connemara scene, then I'd be grateful.

He said: "Love to, old boy. But the fact is, I'm on a diet. First mess of pottage punctually at noon. But I tell you what I will do. We'll go to (mentioning the pub that's not there any more) and have one drink. . . ." He held one forefinger in the air to show me exactly what he meant. "And while we're having that one drink I'll tell you exactly where to go so that you can give your friends a meaningful glimpse of Connemara."

That was ten in the morning, remember. At seven in the evening a relative of my friend came to remove him for his first mess of pottage. By that time the professor was quite happy in the middle of a shouting throng. His wife standing on a barstool was singing: "Rye whisky, Rye whisky".

We spent three good days in Galway. We saw neither Connemara nor the grave of Yeats but I learned the words of a Clifden ballad: "The Bogs of Shanaheever".

> Oh, my young life is past, and it makes me feel weary
> That in exile I'm cast on the plains of the prairie
> To hunt the red man, the panther and the beaver,
> And to gaze back with pride on the bogs of Shanaheever.

But here and now and in the present the historian and myself go on towards Claregalway and Anach Cuain, and in the end of all I miss the train the next morning, just by a few minutes, and go back across Eyre Square to the hotel where I was once introduced to a lobster. There I meet the best company and come back merrily on the next train, and sing and talk the whole way home, and when I get to Dublin discover that my baggage is still in Galway. It's quite safe, of course, but as I say: A man always stays a day too many in Galway!

8

HONEYMEADOW REVISITED

FROM THE BRIDGE OF KILSHEELAN

If I wanted to approach the town of Clonmel ideally I'd have myself delivered by helicopter, much less hazardous than by parachute, at about four hours before noon on a sunny morning on the bridge at Kilsheelan.

Nobody to talk to or listen to but the rooks and the other more mellifluous birds of morning. Nothing to look at but the sunshine on the wide silver Suir and the long levels of parkland by the water, and the dark forestry on the side of the mountain to the south: the darkness hinting at the cold deeps of Coomshingaun and Crotty's lake which have been and are and will be forever somewhere back there in the Comeragh mountains on the road to Dungarvan.

Nothing to look at except the world as God made it who walked in just such a garden in the morning: and why wouldn't he if he had any artist's pride at all in the work of his hands.

Well not, perhaps, exactly as he made it because a good deal of man's work has gone into this Munster valley since Henry the Second of England, with less right over it than I have now alone here on Kilsheelan bridge, gave it to Bill Burke, who built his castellated moats at Kilsheelan and upstream at Clonmel. He died in 1204 and had a fine funeral to the abbey of Athassel, which he also founded: and the Burkes are still here in large numbers. One of them even taught me when I was going to school faraway in O'Neill's Tyrone.

A shaft of theatrical light moves across the dark new trees on the old mountain.

If Oliver Cromwell had had helicopters, there never would have been an iron hand preserved by the Langley family up there at Coalbrook near Ballingarry, where the mines are—or were. For the helicopters could have dropped the Cromwellians down on top of the defenders of Clonmel and made unnecessary all that brutal fighting around the north gate in which a Cromwellian lieutenant, a Langley, lost his left hand. He had an iron hand made to replace it and his descendants, I once heard, had the hand in their possession until about 50 years ago. Where it is now? What do you do with an ancestor's iron hand when you don't want it any more?

Maxime du Camp preserved on a scarlet cushion the (somewhat withered) right hand of the assassin, Lacenaire, who turned to literature in the period of relaxation and reflection before they guillotined him in Paris. He was apprehended in the provinces and, a true Parisian, his chief worry was that he would be disposed of in those backward parts. Now there was a man who put first things first.

This wide river is as innocent of boats as if boats had never been invented. Whatever became of all the merchant craft that used to sail the Suir between Clonmel and Waterford and of all the Suirside sailors who used to man and command them? Has a whole way of life and lore slipped back into the shadows, to be recalled now only in the comic verse of Charles J. Boland, a higher civil servant who died in 1918 in a house called La Scala on the Vico Road, in Dalkey, which road goes round and round to end where terms begin? Nor would Charles J. Boland and many another be much remembered if it hadn't been for that great local historian, James Maher of Mullinahone, over there to my left (I'm looking downstream) in a valley near Slievenamon.

To the morning then and to the sleepers of Kilsheelan let me quote what the poet Boland wrote about the ill-fated voyage of the *Avondale* under the command of Captain Britt who had with him, to bear him company, his little son and his terrier dog likewise: and all the way up from Carrick, and even as they passed under this very bridge, nature seemed to smile upon their enterprise:

> *From Carrick town they made a start the morning bright and clear;*
> *Securely on the tide they sailed by Poulakerry's weir;*
> *Kilsheelan they did navigate and distant Derrinlaur,*
> *And if the final bridge was passed all danger would be o'er.*
> *O, brave Sir Thomas Osbourne, you little did suspect*
> *Against your bridge the* Avondale *was fated to be wrecked.*
> *The cruel pier in her poor side conveyed a dismal hole*
> *Scamandhering her precious freight of thirteen tons of coal.*

That was in the month of November, some 76 years ago. The waterfront correspondent of *The Clonmel Chronicle* covered the disaster:

On Saturday afternoon as two lighters containing cargoes of coal were being towed up the river Suir by a team of horses, from Carrick to Messrs Phelan's Stores, Clonmel, when, passing under the Sir Thomas Osborne bridge, the hind boat stemmed against the archway. As a result of the impact the boat immediately began to leak rapidly. The boatman, observing this, at once severed the rope connecting her with the other boat when she drifted some 400 yards down the river and sank. She happily rests in such a position that traffic can go on the river uninterrupted, and it will not be difficult to have her removed. She contains about thirteen or fourteen tons of coal.

Sunken treasure in the silver Suir: and I remember that the first gramophone record my elder brother, who was nationally-minded, ever bought was a record of Pipe Major Nelius Cronin playing, "The Lovely Sweet Banks of the Suir". There was a poem of the same name which long ago I came across in a brown-tattered, coverless book called *Songs of '48*. Trying to fit the words to the grace-noted music damned nearly drove me crazy:

> *Donleavy stood lone in the forest*
> *To list to the bells' merry peal,*
> *The sound made his young heart the sorest*
> *That e'er throbbed 'neath corselet of steel.*
> *They rang the gay bridal of Alice,*
> *A lady he loved, long and pure,*
> *Lost to him in the tyrant's grey palace*
> *On the lovely sweet banks of the Suir.*

Was his love long and pure? Or was it the lady? And who wrote the sad doggerel? Which to be fair to the poet I quote from memory, not having seen it in print since sometime in the late '20s or early '30s when that verse, read and memorised by a wee fellow in an Ulster town, seemed to contain all the romance that Ireland could offer: the lovely sweet banks of the Suir.

Down below me in the clear water the trout are going mad at their breakfast. A small brown terrier who has just walked all the way down from the village joins me on the bridge in my morning watch.

Richard Lalor Sheil[1] lived up the river there, at the first wall of the mountainside, in the big house of Gurteen Le Poer. He was a lieutenant of King Dan O'Connell, the Liberator, and one of our most mellifluous orators but he isn't much read or heard of nowadays. When Count de la Poer was living there in 1912 the writer of a guidebook complimented him on having greatly improved and beautified Gurteen and the neighbourhood:

... Wherever the hand of man could supplement the handiwork of nature.

Deer dot the green lawns and cattle stand kneedeep in the broad and gentle river. Brush, rather than pen, should portray the ravines of the Gurteen woods which clothe the hills from river-bank to summit, each possessing a characteristic beauty of its own.

I couldn't put it better myself.

THE DANCE BESIDE THE ANNER

It may seem odd to the three ladies who come to talk to me on Kilsheelan Bridge that I should be alone there in the early morning, a stick in my fist, and no luggage: and me neither a hiker bent double under a rucksack nor a travelling man with a budget. So I explain: that I was away west the road at the funeral of a great musician in the hard land of Muskerry, that a friend who was with me at the funeral dropped me on his way back to Dublin.

Seán O'Riada's heart-rending music, playing him to his early grave, has been in our ears all the way back, through Millstreet and Mallow, Fermoy and Lismore, Clogheen, Newcastle, Knocklofty, ever since the crowds had walked and driven on two roads down from Coolea where, close to Macroom, O'Riada spent his last years, then over the Sullane River and up under damp mourning trees on the road that O'Sullivan Bere followed in a bad winter to pray at the shrine of St Gobhnait who must have been musical because she loved the sound of honeybees. Seamus Murphy's symbolistic statue of Gobhnait now tops the hill above the shrine.

One of the three ladies of Kilsheelan has come, wheeling a bicycle, down the Tipperary slope from the village. She is heading for Waterford and the wooded mountains. While we talk we are joined by that wandering terrier, and then by Nelly Hogan who lives in that snug house on the left bank below the bridge, and then by her mother who is 71 and as fresh and good-humoured as living in such a beautiful place could enable one to be.

God began this beauty, and Bill Burke (William Fitz-Aldhelm de Burgo), who has been at rest in holy Athassel for 700 years, kept up the good work, and Count de la Poer added a bit, and the people who live here now have, even in this age of development or destruction, done nothing to take away from the appearance of the place. Leaning on

Kilsheelan Bridge and looking upstream you think that it seems so easy for Clonmel to be the handsomest town in Ireland.

What I'm now going to do is to walk to Clonmel and meditate for a while where the road crosses the River Anner which comes from the valley near Slievenamon to meet the Suir. This valley is all songs:

> She lived beside the Anner,
> At the foot of Slievenamon,
> A gentle peasant girl
> With mild eyes like the dawn,
> Her lips were dewy rosebuds,
> Her teeth of pearls rare,
> And a snowdrift 'neath a beechen bough,
> Her neck and nut-brown hair.

And the same man wrote about another girl from the same place:

> Alone, all alone, by the wave-washed strand,
> All alone in the crowded hall;
> The hall it is gay, and the waves they are grand,
> But my heart is not there at all;
> It flies far away, by night and by day,
> To the times and the joys that are gone,
> And I never can forget the sweet maid that I met
> In the valley near Slievenamon.
>
> It was not the grace of her queenly air,
> Nor her cheek of the roses' glow;
> Nor her soft black eyes nor her flowing hair,
> Nor was it her lily-white brow:
> 'Twas the soul of truth, and of melting ruth,
> And the smile like a summer dawn,
> That stole my heart away, one bright summer day,
> In the valley near Slievenamon.

Then I'll enter Clonmel at the place where Cromwell tried to enter it. A land worth fighting for, he told his sombre troops, and Black Hugh O'Neill and his men made them fight for it harder than they ever had to fight for anything else: and the Cromwellians found a bitter and bloody gate into the meadow of honey.

So with the pleasant Munster blessings of the three ladies in my ear—and that's more than Cromwell ever had—I set off walking. From the post-office in the village I send a dozen of the splendid postcards of John Hinde to people that I know would like to see the Suir. An old man standing by the postbox seems to doubt my physical ability to walk as far as the next turn of the road, let alone Clonmel itself. So just to show him I steam off at a good five miles an hour:

> This charge must rout the Papists out
> Cried Cromwell at Clonmel. . . .

What poem, now, did that come from? Night before last I thought I would find it in Joyce's *Ballads of Irish Chivalry* (the IRA, the UDA, and the UVF display a lot of that) in which book you have everything and everybody from the blacksmith of Limerick to the wind that shakes the barley. But it wasn't there. In the 1920s I saw it for the first and last time in the *Our Boys* and those are the only two lines that I remember.

The road to Clonmel is as wide before me and as empty of traffic as the river that flows away from Clonmel. The outline of the Galtees comes out of the morning haze ahead of me, and Slievenamon is clearly to be seen but still asleep over to my right: and the shadows of blind Sheehan from the Glen of Aherlow, and of the sad girl from the Vale of the Anner dying in a foreign city and hoping to meet her kin in heaven above, are with me as I walk. One song so sad and gentle as to be weakened by sentiment, the other as much made of iron as the militarism it preached against:

> Struck blind within the trenches
> Where I never feared the foe,
> And now I'll never see again
> My own sweet Aherlow.

My own great-grandfather was from those parts and I've stood often enough at the place where the high road from Tipperary town tops the ridge, and displays the most splendid inland view of mountain and fertile plain in Ireland, not to feel what Kickham felt when he wrote those lines. To look even once on all that, and then to know that never in the darkness of this life could you see it again, would be a fate only to be borne by or visited on the saints of God; and the blind, we may suppose, have a special claim to sanctity.

The contrast in moods of the two songs suits their subjects but also reflects the contrasts in the song-writer himself: Charles J. Kickham.[2] That man of anger and of iron could face up to and survive the English prison cells of the nineteenth century. That same man could have such a gentle romance with Rose Kavanagh, the Ulster poetess, that it was scarcely a romance at all but the brief greeting of two spirits never meant to be stained by the ways of this world. That deeply religious man could talk to bishops, telling them to mind their own business, as few men in Irish politics (there have been and are exceptions) have ever done, or do.

Oh, James Maher of Mullinahone, every man who feels anything about the spirit of Kickham, and of this land around Slievenamon which is the true heart of Ireland, owes a lot to your enthusiasm; and, as I walk, I remember a day twelve years ago when we stood with friends in the graveyard in Mullinahone and you read out Rose Kavanagh's lines from Kickham's gravestone:

> *Rare loyal heart and stately head of grey*
> *Wise with the wisdom wrestled out of pain. . . .*

While James read I was in two places at once: in Tipperary where my father's father's people came from long ago; in Tyrone where I was born and reared. Rose Kavanagh's grave is at the Forth Chapel in the Clogher Valley in south Tyrone almost within sight of William Carleton's cottage. An odd link between two Irishmen who may have resembled each other only in two things: they were writers and they loved their people. Yet Carleton as a boy when he went to the Forth to mass in the open air, long before the chapel was built, must have walked over the very sod that was to cover Kickham's second love. As Rose Kavanagh knew, his first love was that ideal Ireland that one feels only on such a sunny morning and in such a place as this:

> *His lifelong love—the land whose sacred name*
> *Throbbed to the last through his life's ebbing tide*
> *And lit the face of death with love's white flame.*

That day twelve years ago we went on from Mullinahone to Kilvemnon crossroads where I learned a lot about dancing the culm. But the Anner is ahead and another bridge to lean on and those of you who think that the culm is danced in a ballroom must wait to know better while I stop here and rest for a while.

The River Anner hereabouts has only echoes of Kickham of Mullinahone, recluse and rebel, of Kickham singing of the valley near Slievenamon, or of that older song about Slievenamon, the music of which Seán O' Riada arranged so splendidly, the words of which were so well translated by Séamus Clandillon, the piper:

The French, they say, are in the bay now,
The tall mast tapering on each gallant ship.
They'll make a stay now in our green Erin
For that's the tale I hear on every lip.
If true the tale is, then blest this day I am,
My heart like blackbird the thorn upon,
With the trump resounding and the swift steed bounding
On the sunny slopes of Slievenamon.

The words reassemble in my memory (haphazardly I fear) and suit well to the rhythm of my feet as I walk on towards Clonmel.

In the sunshine beside the Anner as it flows down to the Suir, which, always beautiful, is here at its best, a man could think of Maenads or Bacchantes dancing, thighs splashed with the blood of the grape. But etiquette being calmer, alas, I think instead about somebody once telling me about an amazon of a woman who used to dance the culm up by Ballingarry and New Brum where the coalmines are—or were. What madman ever thought that a new Birmingham, God preserve us, would arise in these Tipperary hills? Or was it some sardonic scoundrel, having a sneer at us, who thought of the name?

That dance of the culm I never actually saw but I heard it well described by a man at the crossroads of Kilvemnon. He grew quite lyrical about that broth of a girl, kirtle tucked up to her navel, stout brogues on her feet, leppin with hilarity and to hell with modesty. But no grapes burst and spurted under her bright and battering sandals. Because (and this is for the instruction of such untravelled people as do not know these parts of Munster) culm is, or was, a fuel compounded of yellow clay and Ballingarry slack and it makes, and this I can testify to, one hell of a fine fire. A fire like a brazier, Michael Pollard, the smith at Kilvemnon, said to me twenty years ago, and he gave me the best balance of ingredients: one bucket of yellow clay to two hundredweight of Ballingarry slack.

Stout ladies used to dance on the mixture either to give it the necessary texture and resilience, or as some faint memory of an ancient, fire-worshipping ritual. Then it was shaped into cylindrical briquettes, or croquettes, by a machine called a culm-gun or culm-shooter. The one that I saw looked like the sort of old-fashioned pump once used to inflate motor-tyres, and it could come also in a double-barrelled variety and, oddly enough, the mechanical genius who perfected the gun was, like the novelist, called Kickham.

They tell me you don't hear of culm any more, and the culm-gun is practically a museum piece, and the mines of Ballingary are in a state of watery torpor with some slight hope of revival, and the stout ladies like, once again, Carlyle's Merovingian kings, have all trampled their way on into eternity. Fire comes through cables or in cans and the fire-god needs no dances to appease him.

The first motor-car I have seen on this morning walk to Clonmel over-takes me, drives on a little, pulls up and waits for me to overtake it. Out of it step two men I know: a MacSwiney and an O'Friel. Northern ancestors of theirs could have been with that mysterious man, Black Hugh O'Neill, when he defied Cromwell and defended Clonmel.

But these two are old friends and on their way to the refurbished castle at Cahir (captured once and held for a while by my lord Essex) and they are amazed to see me hoofing it in that strange place at that hour of the morning. The beauty of Ireland is that you always meet somebody. The walk across the Mojave desert now would not—even apart from the aridity, the heat and the rattlesnakes—ever be liable to come up with a reunion like this: my plan to walk peaceably into Clonmel the way Oliver Cromwell didn't is now ending in a merry motor-ride. May the honeybees go before us and settle on the bottles, I mean the blossoms, as it is said they once did here for some mythical wanderer, thus giving us one interpretation of the name: The Meadow of Honey. There is another, more ancient meaning.

Clonmel, the bright and the modern, is also a town of unforgettable ghosts. And what a variety of ghosts: Cromwell and Black Hugh O'Neill, George Borrow and Carlo Bianconi, Laurence Sterne and Father Sheehy and even the anonymous convict of the old Irish song, " 'Sé Dubhach é mo Chas", awaiting death in his cell, remembering his native village, the keeping of the patron, the young active hurlers, the dance of fair maidens. Ever since Luke Kelly of the Dubliners sang with such sensitivity the translation by the nineteenth-century recluse, J. J. Callanan, I see the nameless eighteenth-century convict as a young man bearded and haloed by the wild red hair, as is Luke himself:

> *How hard is my fortune*
> *And vain my repining,*
> *The strong rope of fate*
> *For this young neck is twining.*

My strength is departed,
My cheek sunk and sallow,
While I languish in chains
In the jail of Cluanmeala.

No boy in the village
Was ever yet wilder,
I'd play with a child
And my sport would be milder.
I'd dance without tiring
From morning till even,
And the goal-ball I'd strike
To the lightning of heaven.

At my bedfoot, decaying,
My hurlbat is lying,
Through the boys of the village
My goal-ball is flying;
My horse 'mong the neighbours
Neglected may fallow—
While I pine in my chains
In the jail of Cluanmeala.

Next Sunday the patron
At home will be keeping,
And the young active hurlers
The field will be sweeping,
With the dance of fair maidens
The evening they'll hallow.
While this heart, once so gay,
Shall be cold in Cluanmeala.

There is no cloud in the sky as MacSwiney of the Battleaxes, O'Friel of the Foyle and myself sweep grandly for refreshment up to Hearn's hotel from which Bianconi's horse-drawn cars set out along the roads of Munster. It's odd in a way that there is no cloud, because it's well known that a Clonmel sky has never been without at least one cloud since Nicholas Sheehy, the priest from Clogheen, was hanged there in the March of 1766 because, as Billy Heffernan said in Kickham's novel, *Knocknagow or The Homes of Tipperary*, "he wanted to save the people from bein' hunted and the whole country turned into pasture for sheep and cattle".

Yet, cloud or no cloud, the ghost of Black Hugh O'Neill who slipped away from Cromwell and Clonmel to Limerick, and from Limerick into the shadows of history, must here and now be watching us. How could he not be? A MacSwiney and an O'Friel and a Tyrone man with a Tipperary name all stepping forward like heroes to drink the *vin du pays* in an hotel associated with the name of an Italian from the Lombard highlands of the Brianza who as a boy at a horse fair in Cremona (where the Irish brigade had once distinguished itself) had seen Napoleon Bonaparte.

Black Hugh would have appreciated the continental connection.

His ghost is a resplendent figure of a man of middle height and rather corpulent, about 50 years of age, dressed in a blue tunic and dark blue breeches, with black high top-boots, an Irish black glengarry with a gay feather, a mail breastplate and backplates. Very much with it.

He's as plain to my eyes as the pathetic "arboreal figure" on the 1798 monument, the work of James K. Bracken from Templemore who was a Fenian and a founder of the Gaelic Athletic Association, and the father of that Brendan Bracken who was so close to Winston Churchill. Time and again in Clonmel, as elsewhere in Ireland and in the world, history gets rolled up in a ball. But why must all 1798 monuments, at least all that I've looked at and pondered on, seem to be of sad fellows pleading for our pity. A friend of mine refers quasi-humorously to this statue as Bracken's Other Bright Boy, or the Shanavest.

But the rebels of 1798 rose in dark and evil days to right their native land, and defied cruel Lord Carhampton and vengeful General Lake and rabid animals like Hunter Gowan and Hawtrey White; and they must in truth have been very fierce and tough and desperate men. Yet I have still to see a '98 statue that has the verve of the verse in the old ballad:

We'll plant the tree of liberty at Lord Carhampton's gate,
We'll plant the tree of liberty and on him we will wait.
We'll keep him agitated till the Frenchmen do come in,
When we'll make a common begging-bag of Lord Carhampton's skin.

THE WHITE HOUSE AND THE MAGIC MIRROR
Every town that has a fine river should be compelled by some law or other to have a place by the river where people can walk. That seems so obvious as to be scarcely worth saying. Yet it's quite sad to think how many Irish towns, my own being one of them, would be guilty before that law if it was on the book. But not Clonmel which seems to me to have made the

best possible use of its river. Nor Westport in the County Mayo. Nor Macroom in the County Cork.

And I recall a lovely June morning on the bridge at Macroom, and a friend of mine and myself swithering (before breakfast) as to whether we should walk one way the three miles to Ballinagree, sacred to the memory of the Bold Thady Quill,[3] or the other way along the bank of the Sullane river where we could see the beginning of what might turn out to be a good walk or might, after 40 or 50 yards, end in nothing. We chose the river-walk, nor did we regret it, nor did breakfast ever taste better than it did that morning in the Castle hotel in Macroom: and Galway, of course, is (as I say elsewhere) the most water-possessed city in Ireland, triply-possessed by lake and river and sea.

But here and now in Clonmel there are ten swans before me on the clear water of the Suir. Eight of them are not yet quite white, but by their grace and vanity on the water they seem to know too much about the world to be still called cygnets. They may be just slow-whiteners who are going through a difficult period. Jack B. Yeats said in one of his novels that there is a shape that is simply called swan—or words to that effect—and this off-white eight have the shape for sure.

The two all-white creatures go before them, slowly upstream to where two branches of the glistening river meet again around a bushy island. Their reflections sail beneath them and set me thinking of Carlo Bianconi's magic mirror and also of how he once looked across the Suir and saw the vision of the white house.

He was a young fellow at the time, his biographers tell us, and a pedlar. On his back he had a box of prints weighing about seven stone and under that weight he would sometimes walk as much as 30 miles a day. Little wonder that he was ahead of his time in being ready to appreciate the benefits of wheeled traffic. His sore feet at the day's end would have taught him that much, even if he had never seen the first great coaches coming down from the Alps into Italy or the six-seater post-sleighs drawn by ten or twelve white horses.

He wanted to own much land and many white horses, as white as the two swans now leading their flotilla up the Suir. In Cremona he had seen, riding on a white horse, that little man who for a while was to rule Europe by the sword. Oddly enough, it was the fall of that little man, from his throne if not from his horse, that was to make it more easily possible for Carlo Bianconi to set up in the transport business: for, after Waterloo and the ended wars, horses to pull coaches were cheap and plentiful.

But that was still in the future as he walked by the Suir with a pack on his back: or rather, a heavy box of pictures on his shoulders.

As a strolling foreigner he had been set on in the town of Thurles by a parcel of roughs and rescued by a young fellow called Theobold Mathew who was later to become a friend—and also, as the founder of the temperance movement, a great preventer of fights by what you might call remote control. Bianconi had been befriended by a bootmaker called William Cahill and had, through him, made his first settling in the river valley where he was to find his home and, in the process, to put the Irish people on wheels as they had never before been.

He must have had some feeling, some premonition, about the place—in his bones and in his excitable Italian heart. Were there white swans like those on the water the day he looked across the Suir and saw the white house? "Money melts," he said, "but land holds as long as grass grows and water runs." This Tipperary grass would have been equal to anything he had seen anywhere. Much land he always wanted and many white horses, symbols of grandeur that make the automobiles of today, owned on the easy-payment system, appear handmedown and shabby.

There, through the valley in which he was to come into his kingdom, water runs as happily as it does anywhere in the world.

Halfway between Cashel and Holy Cross he sits forever on a moat, overlooking the Suir, and sees across the valley a white mansion. He calls there one day with his pack on his back and a manservant impolitely shows him the way out. But he knows that he will be back one day as owner, and he is: 42 years later.

That story of a wandering Italian boy in one of Ireland's loveliest valleys is to me one of the world's wonder stories. It makes Dick Whittington look like the prosaic English businessman that he possibly may have been.

Here by the Suir in the morning—and on this riverwalk it always seems to me to be a summer morning—is the proper place to read or re-read that wonder story, and be delighted by it: as I do, and am, now, with a word of thanks to M. O'Connell Bianconi and S. J. Watson, the above-mentioned biographers.

There is this about Clonmel: that to visit or revisit it you must do a lot of reading or rereading, from Borrow's *Lavengro* to the book brought out locally in 1960 for the tercentenary of Cromwell's siege, and even to that simple novel, *Travelling Men*, in which W. G. Dowsley imagined himself backwards in time into the boyhood of Borrow. Clonmel has a crowded history, and a lot of strange people have passed this way and been compelled to praise by the beauty of the place. Even John Wesley, who had eyes more for the other world than for this one, said that Clonmel was: "the pleasantest town beyond all comparison that I have seen in Ireland".

The river is before me, as bright as Bianconi's magic mirror. If I study it carefully I can see the easy morning town behind me. There was a great dog asleep outside a ladies' hairdressing establishment, and a queue of trucks at a weighbridge as I came down to the river, and the cries of children playing around a school, and a pub with its doors open to the sunlight of the street. And two young women met a third at the corner of the Main Guard: Youth and Beauty meeting beside old brown stone that had once housed men of iron. One of the two says to the third: "You're all out."

She is too, dressed to kill and pretty as a picture. They all are. Or is that just the way that middle-age, to put it nicely, feels on a fine morning? Then one of the two says to the other: "Do you know this girl?" And then to the third and in explanation: "I forget your name again." Chimes and tinklings of young happy laughter. The awkward moment passes so easily. Is it the sun and the fine morning or just the sight of young merry people that sets me to thinking: In Munster manners are better.

I walk past them and feel a little like the ghost of Carlo Bianconi. A few steps away, in a corner house facing the Main Guard, he first set up shop in this town. Some of the locals called him Brian Cooney: a reasonable stagger at an alien name. He bought up golden guineas. He sold, among other things, mirrors. In his window he exhibited a prize specimen, so big, so bright, so splendid, that old woman fainted and horses bolted when they saw themselves staring themselves in the face. The three beauties at the corner of the Main Guard would be unperturbed. Nowadays we know a lot more about mirrors. All that was before Waterloo.

Mirrors, a white mansion, wide lands, and always the horses as symbols of splendour. And Napoleon in the saddle at Cremona.

Do any of Brian Cooney's mirrors survive along the valley of the Suir? If I could look now into that big mirror what would I see? The clear bright river will answer for me.

I see a small boy in an Italian garden that belongs to his uncle, the parish priest. The boy in his play upsets the beehives and the bees take off. When he grew to be an old man he used to say that the stings he got on that day saved him from rheumatism in the damp climate of Ireland, and he held that honey would cure all ailments in men or horses.

It was only fitting that he should make his home here in the meadow of honey.

UP AND DOWN THE MOUNTAIN

One of the happiest things that could happen to a writer—after big sales combined with a respectable sort of reputation—would be to have his words cut in or fastened onto stone, and on view for all to read in his own hometown. Moses brought a book of that sort down from the mountain but they say he didn't write it himself.

Standing here by the lovely sweet banks of the Suir I read on the stone of the big bridge the words of the local poet, Charles J. Boland:

> *Do the feeble still venture to toddle*
> *To the quay, and sit down on the balk,*
> *And sun their old selves in the even,*
> *With the crows cawing loud in the trees?*
> *That's the spot, I think, outside of heaven,*
> *Where a heart wearied out would find ease.*

Not the greatest poet in the world, and I'm sure he never claimed to be, but he dearly loved his native place—and that may be some part of poetry.

The lame leg in the rhyming in the six lines is there because somebody did a little bit of editing. The lines are from a six-verse poem, eight lines a verse, purporting to be a letter written by an exile to a former sweetheart in Clonmel, asking about this place and that, about this and that person. The first two lines of the verse are:

> *Does your young brother mitch from the Model?*
> *Do the tinkers still fight in Poulslough?*

But who would bother to write up on a wall that boys mitched school or that travelling people had an occasional domestic upset? Yet it all sets me wondering if Moses, the travelling man, did any editing on what he brought down from the mountain.

My road is over the bridge and up the mountain that rises like a wall on the Waterford side. Up there, I feel, a man might grow young again and walk as lightly as the fellow in Allingham's delightful song:

> *One morning walking out, I o'ertook a modest cailín,*
> *When the wind was blowing soft and the early dews were falling.*
> *"Is our way, perchance, the same? May we journey on together?"*
> *"Oh, I take the mountain side," she replied, "among the heather."*

Across the river and into the trees, and high estate walls and the mountain very steep and dark above me.

The first signpost gives me the choice of Youghal or Cork city or Limerick or Dungarvan, and that's a lot of Munster or, indeed, of the known world. At the Hillview (how aptly named—some genius there) lawn-tennis club, a few people are pitching and putting: and as Laurel might once have said to Hardy, it must be confusing to find yourself pitching when you should be putting. Every bit as bad as being fro when you should be to.

At an insignificant little bridge a sign, with yellow letters on a black background, tells me and everybody else where the town boundary was marked in 1895. At the corner beyond the boundary a man digging in a plot and casting a thoughtful eye on two rooting pigs, points me to the shortest way up the mountain. Which is up suddenly from the Dungarvan Road, along a steep gravelly byway that, even though the trees are almost bare, becomes after a while a green, sun-splashed tunnel. Bronze bracken here and there and the crimson of mountain ash.

This could be twenty Irish miles from any town. No houses to be seen. Nobody to talk to but the birds. Nobody to talk to me except the brook which is talking very loudly, shouting at the top of its voice, down there in the ravine to the right, but completely hidden by the trees. This is no road for old or ageing men: not meaning only that it would be a way to walk if you were young and in love as the young, God help them, frequently are. But the sudden steep slope is hell on the knee-joints and the balls of the legs, and the rolling pebbles, each with a vicious life of its own, are sore on the soles of the feet.

The road levels with me (literally) after a bit. The trees fall away below and behind me. There's a house over there, old-style farmhouse and, on the slope below it, two men are building a new house, bungalow-style. A son of the old house getting married? The sounds of hammer and saw are shockingly loud after the silences, or natural sounds, of the woods.

At a small concrete bridge the stream creeps out from under a blanket of watercress and takes its first waterfall. Little does it know what's in store for it in the glen below. On a fragment of wall at a bend of the road some demon of the mountain has written with a paint-brush: "Glen Gap Skittle Alley." For, surely to God, nobody ever climbed up here to play skittles, a game that belongs in crowded places.

Five minutes more and I am at the highest house on the mountain and thinking naturally of the playright John B. Keane and of a joke in a play of his, *The Highest House on the Mountain*, a joke that I regret to say, sets me laughing every time I think of it. The soft-headed fellow in the play, one of two brothers who live a simple life in the highest house, can never forget a big man that he saw once in the town of Tralee, eating chops by the dozen or the two or three dozen, a man so big that he had seventeen buttons on the fly of his trousers. It may not be a joke for a wedding reception but to my crude mind it seems perpetually funny.

The dog from this here—and present—highest house comes out to talk to me, and then the man who owns the dog, and when I tell him that there's nothing in the world or in Waterford that I'd like better than a glass of water, he brings me indoors and the woman of the house gives me three glassfulls of cold spring-water out of the tap. It tastes like the rarest wine and I feel guilty standing there and wondering would it taste still better straight out of the well.

The noonday angelus rings from the radio, and it sounds real up here, a genuine angel's greeting, not vaguely absurd as it does when you see boozers in pubs doffing the hat and wiping off the froth, and gesturing and muttering for a minute. Not that there's any reason why boozers should not occasionally see an angel or pray into a pint.

Following the directions of the man of the highest house, I go up on a path that in wet weather would be a torrent, lost and smothered under mountain ash and furze. There are fresh horse-droppings in a place where you'd think no horse could walk, and in all the morning on the mountain I see no horse. Perhaps, last night the pooka passed this way.

Then I'm out on the open mountain with the whole beauty of the best part of the Suir valley at my disposal, the coloured roofs of Clonmel, the Galtees half-misted, and Slievenamon gracefully asleep over there: where Fionn killed Culdubh, the lord of Sid ar Femen, and became wise by catching his thumb in the jamb of a door—as good a way as any. That story of the salmon of wisdom and the scalded thumb I never could take seriously, no more than I could take seriously that silly tale about all the women racing for the favours of Finn around that mountain and so giving it the name: Sliabh na mBan, the Mountain of the Women.

For it seems to me at this moment that the mountain is so-called because some man once saw it just as I see it this morning: blue and silver across the valley, the exact shape of a graceful woman, symbol of all women, resting on the heart of the richest plain in Ireland. That's it, if you want a fertility symbol.

There's a mountain in Virginia, USA, called Dead Man Mountain. Some early settler gave it the name because when you look at it, sombre and shaggy with primeval timber, it really does look like a corpse laid out. By contrast, that blue and silver Irish mountain is this morning alive, sleeping gently perhaps and a bit late in the day since the noonday Christian bell has rung—but alive, alive, alive.

At Glen Gap, on my way down, the invitation to skittles is still open, but I can see nobody skittling. I take the road to the left, the one with the houses, as a change from the precipitous one to the right and through the lonely coloured woods. Not one person I meet doesn't bid me the time of day, even asking after my health as if it genuinely mattered to them. A woman, ascending in a donkey-cart, reads the *Sporting News*, published in the town below, the voice of a land that takes seriously horses and dogs and hurling. (The donkey, at his ease, does the navigation.) From where we meet I can look across the valley to Grangemockler where Boomerang, Eddie Macken's famed jumping-horse, was first owned by a man called Murphy.

To my left as I go on down there's a blue house with Doric pillars built back against the slope, and to my right a house whose front garden is ornamented with old iron pots of all shapes and sizes, everything but a famine pot which would take up too much space. It took 24 buckets of water to fill a famine pot and there is, or was, in the garden beside the rectory at Glencolmcille, in Donegal, a famine pot that was three and a half feet in diameter. There's a fine piece of useless information for you.

I am now in old Clonmel. Coming down into it this way I get the feeling that I've surprised it as Cromwell never managed to do, even discovered some secrets it was hiding: old walls, the multitudinous many-branched river, a silver weir, a half-submerged cot, a little park dedicated to Edel Quinn[4] and that hypothetical family that prays and stays together, a schoolboy tossing the core of an apple at a large lazy indignant trout.

L. M. McCraith in her priceless book, *The Suir: From its Source to the Sea*, said that the largest salmon ever taken out of the Suir weighed 58 lb and was taken on a feather out of a lady's hat because no other lure was at the time available. That must have been an impressionable, lovelorn salmon.

F

9

ALL THE WAY TO BANTRY BAY

ON THE GREY ROCK OF CASHEL

The best way to begin the long journey to the mountains of the south-west is not by picking the filling out of a tooth after lunch on the first day out. This happens to me quite simply in the middle of all the grandeur of the archbishop's palace (hotel) in Cashel with the renowned Rock of Cashel in, you might say, the back garden. The filling I have religiously preserved as one should preserve any relic connected with the ancient and holy city of Cashel.

The great basement dining-hall is crowded with quiet Americans. Their shining coach awaits them outside on a tree-lined avenue where over the centuries other coaches, with prancing horses striking fire out of Munster rock, have been. Their guide, counsellor and friend is telling them the ancient chestnut about the visitor who said that Cashel would be a fine town if somebody would only get that old ruin out of the way. In the case of Cashel the story may seem so obviously a comic exaggeration, but it is told in all truth about the town of New Ross in County Wexford. When fifteen or so years ago that impressive Rhineland-style town was tidied up and little gardens placed here and there like coloured steps of stairs climbing up from the big river made by the meeting of the Nore and the Barrow, a distinguished political visitor, on what we laughingly call ministerial level, said to one of the people who did the job: "A lovely town now if you only had that old ruin out of the way." He meant the remains of Three Bullet Gate about which the bloody fighting ebbed and flowed in the year of the Rebellion, 1798:

> *We bravely fought and conquered*
> *At Ross and Wexford town,*
> *Three Bullet Gate for years to come*
> *Will speak of our renown . . .*

There are four of us on this expedition into the iron mountains of the south-west: a Californian, the Manhattan Islander of previous journeys, a red-bearded Limerick man and myself. The quiet Americans troop before the four of us out of the hotel. They are younger than the groups who usually go in coaches, a sort of dedicated look about them and very clean for young people in 1977.

Out on the avenue a lady in late or latest middle-age, a cruiser of the Anglo-Irish class, horsey face and demanding neigh, is loudly looking for a boy to fetch her baggage. When she finds him she brings him to the boot of her car and burdens him to the ground. Is she trying to keep alive the upper-class gentility of the place? The coachload of Americans look on with a quiet curiosity, and take their seats and calmly wait for Ireland to come to them. The Rock, with its buildings, is over all and has been there for a long time. The Californian says: "Ireland has come down in the world when the likes of us are allowed at all into what was once the palace of an archbishop of the church by law established. Even if our unfortunate papist forefathers did begrudgingly pay tithes towards it."

He's a cynical man and his origins are far-back and Fenian in the meadows of Fermanagh.

A poet could well see visions on this Rock of Cashel. Cold chapel, the most part of 1,000 years old, arched empty windows, ancient tombs, crabbed symbolic carvings, tall tower, tiny heads that look out of dark corners with eyes that seem curious and alive.

Then out into the sunlight and the prospect of flat riverine land limited over there by the high Galtees, the most graceful or stylish of Ireland's mountain-ranges. The grey town sleeps at the foot of the Rock. It always seems to sleep as if unaware or trying to be unaware of the Rock, is perhaps a little hostile to an eminence that has survived from almost another world to dominate still the life of the town, in an age of machines and motors and new factories—one of them nakedly and painfully obvious on the plain below. The Rock may be some sort of an uneasy conscience.

You look down on the green lawn at the back of the palace that is now an hotel where generations of Protestant bishops walked and looked up at the Rock and to whom, also, the Rock must have been a sort of a conscience, an echo from the past and even in its own immutability a reminder that the world around it changes as the seasons do, but not with the seasons' recurrence. Archbishop Agar in 1749 must have been particularly tormented when he stripped the roof and left the ancient walls and tombs and carvings to the mercy of wind and weather, and as a nineteenth-century writer put it: "The stillness was only broken by the discordant voices of birds and beasts which shun the light of day."

And our greatest poet tells us that he did see visions on the Rock:

On the grey Rock of Cashel I suddenly saw
A Sphinx with woman breast and lion paw,
A Buddha, hand at rest,
Hand lifted up that blest.

The images cut in stone in Cashel, the beast with trefoil tail, the centaur shooting a lion with bow and arrow, were certainly capable of inspiring in Yeats the difficult and obscure poem that contains those four lines. For the Rock itself is, in all truth, a vision, seen either in the detail of arches and tower and old carven stone, or seen suddenly and startlingly from a distance. No one will ever forget his first prospect of the Rock of Cashel. For most of us, including myself, it comes on the road from Dublin to the south, or to Cork—if you prefer it that way.

The road ascends a gentle slope and takes an easy curve and there it is, not just a rock but a fantastic stranded ship, the original limestone that came up out of the fertile clay now horned and crowned with the accretions of the centuries—some of them of surprising architectural beauty, some of them creatures of fantasy like the crazily-elongated Celtic cross that a vain man set sailing like a mast above his family tomb.[1]

There was a time though when the outline of man's work on the Rock was simpler, when Cormac's chapel, the twelfth-century gem of the place—in fact a small exquisite Romanesque cathedral build at the wish of Cormac MacCarthy, King of Desmond—would have been clearly visible from a distance, and the traveller approaching could have thought in the terms used by a poet of the last century:

But to make thee, of loving hearts the love
Was coined to living stone;
Truth, peace and piety together strove
To form thee for their own.

A light, when darkness on the nations dwelt
In Erin found a home—
The mind of Greece, the warm heart of the Celt,
The bravery of Rome.

There was a time too, 1,500 years ago, when the *Eoghanachta* falling back from Wales where the Irish colonies had outlived their welcome, or their power, saw the naked rock and the rich land around it, and set up on it their kingship of Munster, and had enough Latin from across the water on their tongues to enable them to call it their *castellum* or, as it softened into the Irish, their *caiseal*. There it must have been, their vision, pushing up out of the green earth and trees, as striking if not as gigantic as the whale-back of granite called Stone Mountain that humps up over the red clay of the State of Georgia: and there for centuries, through varying fortunes, the kings of Munster ruled.

From the eighth to the tenth centuries they gave the place its greatest glory through a remarkable union of church and state in those four kings of Cashel who were also churchmen, most notably in the scholar, Cormac Mac Cuilenáin:

> *O, for one hour a thousand years ago,*
> *Within thy precincts dim*
> *To hear the chant in deep and measured flow*
> *Of psalmody and hymn.*
>
> *To see of priests the long and white array*
> *Around thy silver shrine—*
> *The people kneeling prostrate far away*
> *In thick and chequered line.*
>
> *To see the prince of Cashel o'er the rest,*
> *Their prelate and their King,*
> *The sacred bread and chalice by him blest,*
> *Earth's holiest offering.*

The famous Dr Murray of St Patrick's College, Maynooth, a nineteenth-century scholar, wrote all that in a highly ecstatic mood but he was also aware that in 1,500 years there are varied fortunes in history, and as much destruction as building. The wonder is that so much of something so conspicuous as Cashel—now being carefully restored as has been the abbey of Holycross further upstream on the river Suir—has survived those centuries: the taking of the rulership by the Dalcassian, Brian Boroimhe; the burning of the church by Gearóid Mór Fitzgerald because, as he told King Henry VIII of England, he thought the arch-bishop of the time was inside; the second burning in Cromwellian times by that O'Brien who fully and dreadfully earned his name of Murrough of the Burnings—the most notable pyromaniac in Irish history; the final unroofing by the Protestant Archbishop Agar. He was no puling pre-servationist. Did he walk on that lawn down there below and look up at the desolate skeleton of the centuries and feel easy in his conscience?

On these things you can meditate as you walk round and round the Rock, on it or below it—something you must do to get the true feeling of the place—through quiet side streets and roads heading off across the Suir valley, and even through one lovely laneway of little cottages: catching glimpses of the Rock from this or that unusual angle.

For my money, though, you must, to get the best prospect, turn your back on Cashel and go off towards the Glen of Aherlow. Go at least as far as Bansha which guards one end of the Glen as Galbally does the other. But who having gone so far on a clear day will not want to explore the beauty of the Glen? Then turn and come back, with the high stylish Galtees behind you, and forget for a moment that you have ever heard of the Rock. You can even imagine that you're a hermit of the tenth century coming for a while out of the fastness of Aherlow to look at the busy sinful world: you would, of course, have to do the journey on foot.

There must have been hermits in Aherlow, in a place that was remote even into the eighteenth century, and hermits did now and again break out. There's the legend of the hermit who had been a great hunting man, and who lived for years in his solitude until one day he heard a faraway hunting horn and, overcome by memory, rushed out of his cave and found a horse and went in pursuit, and was thrown and broke his neck. Nothing so accursed can happen to you on a journey that is in the nature of a pilgrimage from Aherlow to a place that is both historic and holy.

You cross the Suir at the village of Golden where the handsome river is islanded and many-channelled and where old crumbling Norman towers show that the place was once well-guarded. You are close to the most impressive remains of the Augustine abbey of Athassel, founded by the Norman, William de Burgo, and dedicated to St Edmund, the martyred king of East Anglia. How place is linked to place.

By the bridge at Golden there is that odd but interesting monument to Thomas MacDonagh, one of the executed leaders, and poets, of the 1916 Rising: and a reminder on the plaque that you should also remember the Normans who passed this way. Which, indeed, you may do: for their buildings and foundations which marked, and still mark, this rich valley, for their ruthless gait of going and their sins—or what Professor Curtis called their restlessness and versatility.

Then on towards Cashel, and a mile or so out look to the left and get what I think is the best angle on the Rock. If you can rid your minds and eyes of eighteenth-century estate walls and twentieth-century overhead wires you may still be able to see it with the eyes of that eremitical pilgrim who looked up to it from the plain and knew it as the meeting-place of holy men and kings.

We go on to the town of Cahir and I recall a happy meeting here twenty or so years ago, in the year of the first Cork film festival.

On the way back to Dublin from that wildest of all carnivals myself and a South African Jewish journalist who, for various good reasons, was not going back to South Africa, encountered here a poet and a friend of his who were down for the fishing. They leaned on the bridge under the shadow of the great castle and studied the water, and we joined them and stayed two jovial days in Cahir, and on the way back to Dublin lay in the sun on the grass on the top of Dunamase and heard the jackdaws screaming around the ruins of a castle that had changed hands so often in ancient wars; and steamed the last of the free champagne of Cork out of our clotted veins.

Where the poet then stood the four of us now stand and study the Suir as, indeed, once did Elizabeth's Essex and Murrough, the Burner O'Brien and many a Butler. This bridge of course, wasn't here all that time but the lovely sweet banks of the Suir were and the Swan of Avon knew about them and had his reference to the song about the girl who came from the Suirside.

As for Spenser he knew all the Irish rivers, or most of them, except that he thought they all flowed or should flow into the Thames.

The Norman Butlers of Cahir, we are told, like other branches of that great house, inclined towards the Gaelic way of life and a fragment of an Irish poem-book compiled (1566–76) for Theobald, third lord of Cahir, still survives. I have never seen it and it is unlikely that I ever will, but as we drive on, the staggering ramparts of the Knockmealdowns to the left, the humped back of the Galtees to the right, I mumble to myself a verse from the poet encountered nearly twenty years ago on the bridge of Cahir.

The poem first appeared in the *Irish Times* and is to be found also in *Poems from Ireland*, edited by Donagh MacDonagh, published by the *Irish Times* and with an introduction by the then editor, that most remarkable man, R. M. Smyllie. The poet, who afterwards died tragically, was Patrick MacDonogh, no relation to Donagh and the name is differently spelt:

> *Be still as you are beautiful,*
> *Be silent as the rose:*
> *Through miles of starlit countryside*
> *Unspoken worship flows*
> *To find you in your loveless room*
> *From lonely men whom daylight gave*
> *The blessing of your passing face*
> *Impenetrably grave.*

A white owl in the lichened wood
Is circling silently,
More secret and more silent yet
Must be your love to me.
Thus, while about my dreaming head
Your soul in ceaseless vigil goes,
Be still as you are beautiful
Be silent as the rose.

Sunlight not starlight is at the moment all over this splendid Munster countryside. We have a long road before us to the ruins of Dunboy, the fort of O'Sullivan Beare.

But my lord Essex who once battled his way into Cahir Castle might, at calmer moments and when the lutanist was playing, have appreciated those lines and even the Swan himself might have listened: and not even the sunshine can keep me from being overwhelmed by melancholy for dead poets and men and things long gone.

THE DARK CAVES OF COOLAGARRANROE

Kilcoran Lodge, a fine hotel, is up there to the right and the Mitchelstown Caves are down there to the left and it would be pleasant to have time to dine and wine in one and to cross the valley to visit the other: the cave where the Sugaun Earl hid in the days of Elizabeth's Irish wars, and was betrayed by the White Knight, and O'Leary's cave and O'Callaghan's cave and the Altar Cave and the House of Lords and the House of Commons and all the other wonders that I first read about a long time ago in the *Our Boys*.

No harm at all to Mitchelstown but the caves would sound much more splendid under the name of the townland in which they are actually to be found: the Caves of Coolagarranroe. A splendid name of which the caves are generally deprived simply because Coolagarranroe once belonged to the landlords, the Kingstons of Mitchelstown, a family long in conflict in everything from horse-whipping to total bloodshed with the indomitable O'Mahonys, the family that produced that rock of a man, the first of the Fenians,[2] left lonely and disillusioned in New York in the end of his days:

In a foreign land, in a lonesome city,
With few to pity or know or care,
I sleep each night while my heart is burning,
And wake each morning to new despair . . .

Not a single hope have I seen fulfilled
For the blood we spilled when we cast the die;
And the future I painted in brightness and pride
Has the present belied, and shall still belie . . .

Let no man venture to tell my story
Who believes in glory or trusts to fame;
Yet I have within me such demons in keeping
As are better sleeping without a name.

For many a day of blood and horror,
And night of terror and work of dread;
I have rescued naught but my honour only
And this aged, lonely and whitening head.

Those are four of the seven verses that Douglas Hyde wrote down as the lament in exile of John O'Mahony, scholar and revolutionary: and a rather better type of revolutionary, to put it mildly, than Ireland has produced in the last eight bloody years. The order of the verses I have slightly altered. They do not add up to the customary style of pugnacious, patriotic verse that the events of our time have polluted forever. But the heroes of our time (not comparing them, God knows, to John O'Mahony) could well meditate on those verses if they have the brains to meditate on anything.

Thanks to what one of those heroes has described as technological development (i.e. bombs in cars, bombs in books, bombs at mass, bombs in the morning mail) the present blood and horror could not have been imagined by O'Mahony in his worst and loneliest nightmare. Honour is now not so much spoken of, nor common humanity.

The present can at times seem darker than the pit down there under that rich sunny valley into which James Fitzthomas, the pathetic Sugawn Earl, lowered himself by rope to find refuge. He failed to find it. Three hundred and seventy years ago his pursuers came here after him, dragged him out and sent him to a darker place in the Tower of London where he died raving. In the account books of that hospitable building where so many lived and died as the guests of her or his English majesty this is written: "The demands of Sir John Peynton, Lieutenant of Her Majesty's Tower of London, for one quarter of a year from St. Michael's Day, 1602, till the Feast of Our Lord next. For James Macthomas (the Earl) for sayd time, at £3 per week, physicye, sourgeon, and watchor with him in his lunacy."

Housed, bedded and cleaned-out, as Paddy Kavanagh used to say, and held-down as well.

Mary Wollstonecraft, the Lilith of women's liberation, a noble, tragic woman who towards the end of her life had the misfortune to marry and be bored by Godwin, spent thirteen months, from 1787-8, as governess with the Kingsboroughs at Michelstown Castle, not far from the caves. She liked being a governess no better than any governess ever did but she was better able than most to put her feelings into words and so to get some of the poison out of her system. She wrote:

There is such a solemn kind of stupidity about this place as freezes my very blood. Lady Kingsborough is a shrewd, clever woman, a great talker, but her passion for animals fills the hours which are not spent in dressing. She rouges and is, in short, a fine lady, without fancy or sensibility, and I am almost tormented to death with her dogs. I am, however, treated like a gentlewoman by every part of the family, but the forms and parades of high life suit not my mind.

Claire Tomalin's fine life of Mary goes into the matter in detail. There in Mitchelstown she planned a novel to be called "Mary" and a fantastical piece to be called "The Cave of Fancy". It had been suggested that she might have been inspired by the proximity of Coolagarranroe.

Often, indeed, have I dined and wined and more so in Kilcoran Lodge but I have never been to the caves although nearly 50 years ago when I first read about them, as I said in the *Our Boys*, I vowed to myself that they'd be the first wonders of Munster I'd visit when I came south to the land of my father's father's people. But as you grow older the appetite for darkness in the bowels of the earth or ruins on the surface of the earth diminishes: and Ireland, surely to God, has had enough of darkness and ruins.

Now the *Our Boys*, and the sturdy Irish Christian Brothers who produced it, may, as has been often said, have over-inflated young Irish fellows with a certain sort of Irish patriotism: rush to the standard of dauntless Red Hugh, out and make way for the bold Fenian men, forget not the boys of the heather where rallied our bravest and best, who fears to speak of Easter week—and a lot more besides. And in these days we have seen done in those names, or under the influence of those ideas, deeds that would darken the sun—followed by the inevitable backlash from the backward men who think that churches are as much military objectives as restaurants and pubs and typists. And the only good Pape is a dead one.

But for young fellows going to school in the six north-eastern counties of Ulster in my time, the 1930s, the Brothers and the *Our Boys* did provide a real service in telling them what and where the other three provinces were. For myself, I had all that at home anyway, but there were others who hadn't, and the Stormont Ministry of Education, bless the mark, wasn't much interested, if it even knew. For senior certificate, the exam that then terminated secondary education, the two prescribed history textbooks were written by somebody called Southgate, one of them about Europe, the other about England. The one about England contained two or three brief chapters about Ireland. The most notable statement made in those chapters was that the Irish people were "ignorant, priest-ridden and superstitious". Well, perhaps, but we didn't want to hear it from some nobody called Southgate nor by way of the Stormont "monastery" of education.

On one occasion our history teacher when he could no longer thole the general offensiveness of myself and some of my companions threw Southgate's English history at me. It occurred to me, and to him, after-wards that that was the only good use the book could be put to. There may have been one other.

On our English course at the same time there was a history of literature by some savant called Albert who, at one stage, was magnanimous enough to say that now and again the Irish had brought something to English literature: a certain native woodnote wild perhaps. But as a general rule Irish writers were uncouth and uneducated. (Virginia Woolf wasn't much better about James Joyce: that educated workman.) The period that Albert was dealing with when he made that statement was the period made notable by the names of Berkeley, Swift, Goldsmith, Burke. When I mentioned this to a man, now a minister (governmental), he said with humour: "What they might have been had they had an education."

No, compared with Southgate and Albert, whoever they were, the *Our Boys* was a recurring manual of liberal education and even Victor O'Donovan Power's tales of Kitty the Hare, rambling woman and story-teller, was a sort of a link with a tradition that the Stormont system knew and cared little about.

We could spend a long time here with the humped back of the Galtees behind us, the glorious valley below us, the Knockmealdowns and the Comeraghs beyond and the Suir to the left flowing on towards the meadow of honey. But the purpose of this exercise or expedition is to get the four of us, the Californian, the Manhattan Islander, the red-bearded Limerick man and myself, as far as Dunboy that was once the fort of O'Sullivan Beare:

He sleeps the great O'Sullivan where thunder cannot rouse,
Then ask yourself should you be proud oh woman of three cows.

It's still a long way from Tipperary to Dunboy and everything in
Ireland reminds me of something else.

HOMAGE TO JOHN MANDEVILLE

One dark and stormy winter night when the snow lay on the ground I
came here into Mitchelstown to write a feature article for a newspaper—
about the famous Mitchelstown co-operative creamery, of course, and the
Mitchelstown cheeses which are not theological, and about the wild bulls
of Mitchelstown who, more than most love-lorn men, are led by the nose
and cruelly deceived. The snow made the visit more memorable, nor have
I ever been able to forget the bulls.

From Limerick Junction I took a car, and the driver, with a touch of
genius and seeing that the bill was being paid by a munificent newspaper,
suggested that we should take a look at the Glen of Aherlow under snow
and before the wintry light faded. Which we did.

It's always, I feel, a holy moment when you top the high ridge at
Carriglenina, on the road from Tipperary town, and look down on the
richness of the most beautiful glen in Ireland, and on a peace as yet
mercifully undisturbed. But to see it shining under new snow is a privilege
granted seldom to people who haven't the luck to live in that part of the
world. That day, too, for a few brief minutes the winter relented and
allowed the sun to write his sign with a forefinger along the Galtees,
picking out, here and there, a farmhouse, a fist of rock, the glitter of a
falling stream, the bare sculptured branches of a slanting wood. It was a
day for visions and for promising oneself to come back often to Aherlow.

That night in Mitchelstown the creamery people were having their
annual dance. On the floor the young people of the time slithered around
to string music and soft drinks, and it's doubtful if young people anywhere
do that anymore. But in what the song once popular in Larne, Co.
Antrim, before the singing stopped and the murdering began, called "the
wee room underneath the stair", a few of the non-dancing elders kept
out the snow and the frost with something warmer than soft drinks and
more stimulating than string music. The visitor was invited to join them:

All gay and merry,
Each in his chair,
Down in the wee room
Underneath the stair.

Afterwards there was some question of some agile fellow climbing up on the pedestal in the square beside John Mandeville, a man who really died for the people, and making a speech to the sleeping town, the quiet skies, the frosty night, while deep on the convent roof the snows were glistening to the moon. Not even my best friends would accuse me of such agility. My memory tells me that it was a very good speech, yet every time since then that I pass here through Mitchelstown I salute John Mandeville with a nervous respect. He might have come alive that night and routed the roisterers as, it is said, he once horse-whipped some soldiers on this very street, and he was only a young fellow at the time.

A man of nobility and self-sacrifice but somewhat awesome, and his statue, by Doyle-Jones, does get the message across. When in 1877 the body of his uncle, John O'Mahony the great Fenian, was brought back from the States for burial, Mandeville and his five brothers marched through Cork city after the coffin, and every one of the brothers well over six feet in height. No men to treat lightly or pick a quarrel with. Normans they would have been, with a long history, and married into the O'Mahonys, and even after the wars and despoliations of centuries the clans were still tough enough to hold on to wide acres by the Funcheon River. Yet Mandeville, the landowner, went out to lead the people against the evicting Kingstons and died as a result of ill-treatment received and a throat-ailment contracted in Tullamore Jail.

Old unhappy far-off things, and so on. Perhaps if we had been quietly receptive on that night of snow we might have heard the echoes of the day when the people here came to battle with 100 soldiers and 300 police, and fought up and down the street, and Lonnergan, Shinnick and Casey were shot. All on a fine day 90 years ago. Is there a corner of the world, except perhaps on the heights of Everest or in the centre of Greenland, that is not afflicted by some such echoes?

Mandeville up there now on his pedestal was noble to the end, and even in these times, or perhaps the more so in these times, his last message is impressive:

No man can say that I have ever been an inciter to mean strife; no man can say that I have been an inciter to dissension amongst my neighbours; but, knowing the sufferings of the tenantry, I sacrificed my liberty, and I am prepared to sacrifice my life, if necessary, in defending them. I have had my two months of suffering, but I forgive the majority of the English people. It was more a Tory spirit that prompted my jailers to persecute me. I come out of jail as unfettered as I went in and the principles I hold I will continue to advocate to the last moment of my life.

He would never have seen the merit in bombs in Victoria. Or in churches and orphanages.

We go on south. The gigantic nose-bound bulls in the pens attached to the creamery may be roaring behind us and wondering what life was like before artificial insemination. Araglen is over there—where Denny Lane saw Kate and wrote the lovely song and afterwards married her:

> *When first I saw thee, Kate,*
> *That summer evening late,*
> *Down at the orchard gate*
> *Of Araglen. . . .*
>
> *The swan upon the lake,*
> *The wild rose in the brake,*
> *The golden clouds that make*
> *The west their home,*
> *The wild ash by the stream,*
> *The full moon's silver beam,*
> *The evening star's soft gleam,*
> *Shining alone. . . .*

A glorious vision for a Cork man to see who was not only a great song-writer but also the manager of the gasworks in Cork city: and Kildorrery is over there and the place where Bowenscourt, now gone, was once, in the early days of the Anglo-Irish, laid down like a simple Roman colonial pattern on a conquered countryside. The great novelist who wrote so well about the house of her people saw that great house and this country-side around it as a place where she could feel relaxed, part of a pattern. On Sundays, she once wrote, she got the idea of the population by watching the country people going to mass, horses and traps (this was away back) turning out of impossibly narrow lanes, cyclists free-wheeling down from mountainy farms, dark Sundayfied figures balancing on stepping-stones, or crossing stiles, or following paths through plantations.

Her ruling class may have planted the house on the virgin anonymous countryside but since they built it from the native rock it was not unrelated to the mountain above or to the ancient ruin in what once seemed to be a land of ruins. She wrote: "Lordly or humble, military or domestic, standing up with furious gauntness like Kilcolman, or shelving weakly into the soil, ruins feature the landscape—uplands or river valleys—and make a ghostly extra quarter to towns. They give clearings in woods, reaches of mountain or sudden turns of a road, a meaning and preinhabited air." In Bowen's Court when she was there for Christmas she burned Christmas candles, the gift of a neighbour in Farrahey, and was glad to think that the fellows of the candle were alight in windows all over Farrahey and Kildorrery.

A ghostly extra quarter to towns! Well, the Tidy Towns competition organised by the Tourist Board, and more work on the restoration of ancient buildings, and the boom about which for a few years we heard so much, have taken something of the melancholy Gothic out of Irish landscape. But then the madmen in the north, IRA and UVF, are doing their heroic best to ensure that ghost towns in Ireland will never be in short supply.

All to one side, I've heard it said, like the town of Fermoy.

Was it because the bulk of the town must once have been and more-or-less still is, to one side of the Great River, properly so-called, but just now flowing shabbier and dirtier than I ever remember seeing it before. For how could even the Blackwater flow free, when the lovely sweet banks of the Suir are now regularly polluted?

All to one side like the town of Fermoy, and no harm at all to that fine town and the people in it, but the first thing I think of when I top the ridge and look down the slope to the river is some of the wilder verses of Frank O'Connor. You'll find the full poem in that precious little book, *Three Old Brothers and other Poems*, published by Nelson in 1936 and dedicated to Séan Ó Fáolain:

> Be Jasus, before ye inter me,
> I'll show you all up!
> I've everything stored in the memory,
> Facts, figures enough,
> Since I first swore me oath of allegiance
> As a patriot boy
> To avenge me maternal grandfather
> They hanged at Fermoy.

It's the comic obverse of the relentless old patriot (in the romantic story by Daniel Corkery), preserving the spark of fire to the next generation, even to the second next, an old ember seemingly extinct and grey, an Oisin dreaming of the heroic dead he has so long outlived, but still having in him enough vital heat to set the young fellows burning. Burning! An unfortunate word nowadays.

The old hero of O'Connor's poem, ranting on his death-bed, is, by God and St Patrick, a crusty sort of an Oisin. He looks back at a race of madmen, traitors and poltroons, and recalls every detail of cowardly behaviour:

> From Healy that ran for his life
> The night they murdered the peeler,
> To Leahy that married his wife.

He threatens that even the clay of the grave will not silence him, that he'll conduct his own private general judgement on all his sometime comrades, that while God may show mercy he will show none. He's no hand with the pen but before they give him his military funeral—the funeral to his grave in Glasnevin of "the one man that was true"—he will write one terrible book.

Patriotism, whatever it is, might rest a little easier on the Irish if we learned to laugh at it as O'Connor tried to teach us to do—and got little thanks for his efforts. Cruel laughter, perhaps, but cleansing and capable of ridding the bosom and brain of much perilous stuff.

By way of contrast, Fermoy reminds me of the clerical novelist, Canon Sheehan.[3] Perhaps the contrast isn't so great. What after all, if not about the one man that was true, was Sheehan writing about when in his novel, *The Graves at Kilmorna*, he wrote about the unconquerable and incorruptible Fenian, Myles Cogan. Even if the mood was different. Anyway, as a student, Sheehan stood with the other students up there above the town on the terrace of St Colman's college and watched a Fenian funeral go through one of the greatest of the British army garrison towns:

It was in March of that year (1867) about the middle of the month, while the long flank of the Galtee mountains was a mass of glistening ice, that the reports reached our college of the Fenian forces having been surrounded in Kilclooney Wood. Peter O'Neill Crowley, they said, had been killed with English bullets on the bank of the mountain stream. He had previously ordered his men to flee and save themselves.

J. J. Callanan, the nineteenth-century poet who wrote, or took out of the Irish, "The Convict of Clonmel", also wrote a poem about the odd legend connected with this West Cork Rock: "Tradition tells that the Virgin came one night to this hillock to pray and was discovered kneeling there by the crew of a vessel that was coming to anchor near the place. They laughed at her piety and made some merry and unbecoming remarks on her beauty upon which a storm arose and destroyed the ship and crew. Since that time no vessel has been known to anchor near the spot." And no wonder. A most irascible Virgin, Andromeda?

Through such wild land, with Hungry Hill in the background, Colonel Goring (Puxley)
rode in Froude's novel, *The Two Chiefs of Dunboy*.

One of the two ruins of Dunboy, the burned-out Puxley Mansion.

Below: A sylvan, well-watered corner of Donegal, but not all that far away from hard rocks and lonely moors: Rathmelton on Lough Swilly. An uncle of mine distinguished himself by backing a loaded truck into that water—a little to the right of the picture.

Coomhola: the valley of a million sheep.

They said it was only at his earnest entreaty that Captains Kelly and McClure had consented to leave him and withdraw.

Peter Crowley himself had continued to keep at bay the entire British regiment and a posse of police, by dodging from tree to tree, and firing steadily at the advancing soldiers until at last his ammunition gave out. When he had fallen, pierced with bullets, he asked one of the men for a priest. Fortunately, Father Tim O'Connell, the curate of Mitchelstown, was nearby, knowing of the fray and the danger. He ran to the dying man's aid and gave him the last sacraments. Crowley's own people came to bury him.

I remember well the evening on which that remarkable funeral took place. It was computed that at least 5,000 men took part in the procession. They shouldered the coffin of the dead patriot over mountain and valley and river, until they placed the sacred burden down by the sea and under the shadow of the church of Ballymacoda. I recall how a group of us young lads shivered in the cold March wind on the college terrace at Fermoy, and watched the dark masses of men swaying over the bridge, the yellow coffin conspicuous in their midst. We caught another glimpse of the funeral cortege as it passed the sergeant's lodge. Then we turned away with tears of sorrow and anger.

A century and eleven years ago, and here on the bridge in the town of Fermoy.

Well, it was a different sort of war from what goes on in these days of technological advancement when the heroes are prepared to fight Britain to the last shop in Belfast or the last house in the village of Belleek. In Kilclooney wood only a soldier was killed, *sed miles sed pro patria*, and not a shopfront blown in nor out in Mitchelstown or Fermoy.

It's a through-other, *eadar eathorra* class of a country to travel in if you are in any way conscious of the past; and totally incomprehensible, I feel, if you are not.

As we pull up the hill out of Fermoy the Californian suggests a detour to have afternoon tea with a lady who works with him in a college within sight of the Golden Gate Bridge. This, thank heaven, does not mean detouring all the way to the coast of Californey. No, the lady is Irish and spends her summers at home. Her husband is also Irish and also works, at science and things, in the Californian college. So we detour into a quiet valley with deep meadows, sleepy trees, a little stream, and find the lady—who is also a poet and a good one—in her own garden. Children's voices are somewhere around. Her husband has gone west a little ahead of his family, back to his Californian pestles and mortars. It is the afternoon of a day after a night in which an airliner has crashed in Boston. She says: "Guess where he was last night. Landing in Boston. It wasn't so good when the teevee told us about the crash. But he 'phoned. He should be in California by now."

We listen. The airliner goes west over mountains that would make the Galtees look as friendly as a plump laughing girl on a fair-day. There is no anger now in the mountains above Aherlow.

The tea is delicious. Tea is the best thing on a sultry afternoon.

Over the bridge in Fermoy goes the dark mass of men, the swaying yellow coffin notable in their midst; in the quiet valley images settle like homing birds.

On a low table the children have left an unfinished jigsaw. The Limerick man who has a compulsion about such things, and a certain genius, cleans it up in five minutes.

The plane flies west. Oh my America, my new-found land, as the warm poet said to the woman. She must have been a fat one.

Oh my Hibernia, my jigsaw puzzle, a thrawn neurotic bitch, never fully to be satisfied, never complete.

How Walter Scott came to Watergrasshill

It's an odd thing that a place can become real to you because of a person who never existed. Think of all the people who have patiently walked Baker Street looking for the house in which ox-like Watson listened to the cogitations of Sherlock Holmes. And recently when I said in a gathering of people, several of them Dickensians, that I had sat with Miss Havisham in the decayed room described by Dickens in *Great Expectations* there was for the fraction of a second the silence of acceptance before everybody woke up and somebody asked me had I gone astray in the head. This was what I meant.

In the year, about 1946, in which J. Arthur Rank bought or bludgeoned his way into Irish cinemas, the big millionaire and Sunday school teacher invited the then critics of the films in Dublin over to London so that, at a dinner in the Dorchester, he could give them the good tidings of great joy. The film version of *Great Expectations* was in the making at the time and we sat in the most realistic sets in Denham studios in that forlorn room with Miss Havisham (Martita Hunt) and with a bright fourteen-year-old by the name of Jean Simmons whose looks and style, indeed, were even to improve as the years went by, but who, even at fourteen, caught the eye.

That room and the lonely lady in it had so marked themselves on the minds of the Dickensians that for some sleeping seconds they were almost prepared to accept my jocose and extravagant claim.

Just as when I pass through this village in the high places of north Cork I keep an eye out for the parish priest's house and wonder if it is haunted by the ghost of a man who was never there, or anywhere else, who never existed: that amiable, learned pastor of the uplands, a man well-known in the south of Ireland, the parish priest of this village of Watergrasshill about 130 years ago. There are many people (and I exclude Mr Thackeray, the novelist) who think that the famous song, "The Bells of Shandon", was written by a clergyman by the name of Father Prout. Let me quote:

His modest parlour would not ill become the hut of one of the fishermen of Galilee. A huge net in festoons curtained his casements; a salmon-spear, sundry rods and fishing tackles, hung round the walls, and over his bookcase, which latter object was to him the perennial spring of refined enjoyment. Still he would sigh for the vast libraries of France and her well-appointed scientific halls where he had spent his youth in converse with the first literary characters and most learned divines. . . .

He was extremely fond of angling; a recreation which, while it ministered to his necessary relaxation from the toils of the mission, enabled him to observe cheaply the fish diet imperative on fast-days. For this he had established his residence at the mountain source of a considerable brook which after winding through the parish, joins the Blackwater at Fermoy; and on its banks he would be found, armed with his rod, and wrapped in his strange cassock, fit to personate the river-god or presiding genius of the stream.

To his door then in Watergrasshill came a messenger from "The most respectable civic worthy" that had in Cork worn the cocked hat and chain "since the days of John Walters who boldly proclaimed Perkin Warbeck in the reign of Henry VII": a messenger from Lord Mayor Knapp who was chiefly renowned for his zeal, during the canicule of 1825, in killing mad dogs. "So vigorously did he urge the carnage during the summer of his mayoralty that some thought he wished to eclipse the exploit of St Patrick in destroying the breed altogether as the saint did that of toads."

That mayor was celebrated by a Cork poet in a work called: "Dog-Killing: A Poem". And for all I know the poet and the mayor and the mad dogs did exist, but scarcely the messenger who came to a door that was never there to tell Father Prout that the Wizard of the North, the Great Unknown, Sir Walter Scott, was hirpling on the way and would be glad to meet with Father Prout and to walk and talk with him in the Groves of Blarney:

> *The groves of Blarney, they look so charming,*
> *Down by the purlings of sweet silent brooks,*
> *All decked by posies that spontaneous grow there*
> *Planted in order in the rocky nooks. . . .*
>
> *'Tis Lady Jeffers owns this plantation,*
> *Like Alexander or Helen fair,*
> *There's no commander in all the nation*
> *For regulation can with her compare.*
> *Such walls surround her that no nine-pounder*
> *Could ever plunder her place of strength,*
> *But Oliver Cromwell her he did pommel,*
> *And made a breach in her battlement. . . .*

Walter Scott had genuinely been to Edgeworthstown to talk to that mighty atom, Maria Edgeworth. Francis Sylvester Mahony who invented Prout had nothing against either Maria or Sir Walter as he had against Lady Morgan and Daniel O'Connell and Tom Moore. But the spectacle of pretence or solemnity of any sort was always too much for him, and Sir Walter and Maria walking and talking in Edgeworthstown had to become Prout and Sir Walter walking and talking in Watergrasshill: about Erasmus for whom Mahony always had a fancy, about the Plantagenet monarchs and how they got their name, about Lough Derg and Blarney as places of pilgrimage, about Herodotus and history, Pythagoras and Byron and the real true history of the Blarney Stone.

All ending with Prout (Mahony) upsetting Millikin's "The Groves of Blarney" back into its original Greek, which never existed, and also into French and Latin. That was a caper Mahony (Prout) was to repeat in the grand style when he turned to rend the national bard in the wicked double-edged satire of "The Rogueries of Tom Moore". Double-edged: for if Moore hadn't, as Mahony pretended to think, stolen his words from the Greek, Latin or French originals, provided in the essay then he certainly in the music department had made a considerable steal from

Edward Bunting. To be able to steal, or translate, was as Mahony (Prout) said almost as good as having a genius of your own.

> *Plumbea signa deum*
> *Nemus ornant, grande trophaeum!*
> *Stas ibi, Bacche teres!*
> *Nec sine fruge Ceres,*
> *Neptunique vago*
> *De flumine surgit imago. . . .*

> (*There are statues gracing this noble place in,*
> *All heathen gods and nymphs so fair:*
> *Bold Neptune, Caesar, and Nebuchadnezzar*
> *All standing naked in the open air.*)

Watergrasshill is behind us, the lively city of Cork below us in the hollow. Some day I must stop for a long time in Watergrasshill to search for the ghost of that man who was never there. An original for Prout may have existed, but the Prout we confuse with reality was both Mahony himself and the invention of his genius.

What an odd man Mahony was, who decided in this way to do comic honour to the name of Sir Walter Scott.

He would be a Jesuit, although the Jesuits prudently advised him against it. He kept trying until the fatal day when, as a scholastic in Clongowes Wood College, he went out walking with a group of students, stopped for lunch at the house of the parents of one of them. The wine was plentiful. The scholastic and the students got drunk. Somebody made a speech and praised the Liberator. Mahony leaped up and attacked him. Hard feelings all round.

Did he talk of the map that he was later to say was on the wall of Daniel's study at Darrynane, a map with coloured flags to indicate the copper-producing or penny-tribute resources of every parish in Ireland, a map that also never existed?

Then in the dusk, and the rain pouring, the embryo Jesuit, high as a kite, led his charges back to Clongowes, the ones who were too drunk or comatose to walk being roped to the tops of turf-carts that happened to be passing that way. After that there was nothing for it but the door. Then he would be a secular priest. Then, when he was a priest, he would be a literary man with Thackeray and the boys, writing for Frazer's, displaying a type of mind that we did not have again in Ireland until Flann O'Brien. So he brought Walter Scott to Watergrasshill and Blarney to meet a man who was never there, which when you come to think of it is the ultimate in Blarney:

> There is a stone there that whoever kisses
> Oh, he never misses to grow eloquent.
> 'Tis he can clamber to a lady's chamber
> Or become a member of parliament.

But somebody told me that like the *Odyssey* itself it sounds much more impressive in the original Greek.

SHADOWS OF THACKERAY AND SHAW

Never before have I passed through Cork city without stopping, and I hope I will never do so again. But my three companions and myself are heading westwards in haste and the day is shortening, the rain threatening. At Macroom the tempest bursts. Shadows and shapes of the mountains, monstrous in the shattered light, come and go through the rainclouds. In blinding swirling mist we stumble along by Bantry Bay and into Glengariff from whence, also in bad weather but 375 years ago, the great Domhnall Cam O'Sullivan who, according to the poet, now sleeps where thunder cannot rouse, took off to lead the remnants of his people, a thousand of them, to O'Rourke's stronghold in the north-west where Leitrim Village now is:

> Glengariff's shore could give no more
> The shelter strong we needed,
> So away we strode on our wintry road
> With danger all unheeded. . . .

In the desperation of the Irish at the end of the wars with Elizabeth Tudor, the march to Leitrim, in terrible weather and mostly through hostile country, was certainly not undertaken in the happy vacationing spirit that those lines would seem to indicate. Who wrote them, I can't remember: I quote from memory. But the lines or something like them are to be found in Joyce's yellow-backed, *Songs of the Gael*, a book that nowadays I seldom see around; nowadays some of the heroic Gaels act so oddly.

Walter Scott never was in Watergrasshill but a better novelist, William Makepeace Thackeray, boozing pal of Francis Sylvester Mahony, did get to Glengariff and wrote about it in what is still one of the best books on Ireland ever written by an Englishman: *The Irish Sketchbook: 1842*. He came to Glengariff in wet weather as we are now doing and as nearly everybody, who has come to Glengariff more than twice, has done. He fell in love with the place right away and would have preferred it, perhaps, to any other place in Ireland. My own notion about Thackeray, the traveller, is that he loved wet weather because it set him free to sit in a chair and read, and spared him the labour of rushing around looking at places and pushing his way through and genuinely pitying the hordes of poverty-stricken people. In 1842 famine had not achieved its celebrated worst, and the roads and lanes of Ireland were very crowded.

So Mr M. A. Titmarsh was allowed by Thackeray to write the celebrated praise of Glengariff: "What sends picturesque tourists to the Rhine and Saxon Switzerland? Within five miles round the pretty inn of Glengariff there is a country of the magnificence of which no pen can give an idea. I would like to be a great prince and bring a train of painters over to make if they could, and according to their capabilities, a set of pictures of the place."

Nothing of which was he able to see on the day he got there by the smart two-horse car that then carried the traveller twice a week from Bantry to Killarney by way of Glengariff and Kenmare: short of flying there was no other way it could conveniently go. But his view in the morning from the windows of the pretty inn would have given him some idea of the wonders of the place: the pretty inn being the Eccles hotel close to which (they say) Glengariff is situated and in which, long after Mr Titmarsh, Mr Shaw was to write about a French virgin who heard voices and nobody visible to account for them.

The Manhattan Islander is prepared to agree with Mr Titmarsh. Once already he has stayed in the Eccles and has never quite recovered from the vision of the sun coming up over Muntervary and Whiddy Island and setting the whole bay on fire, golden at first and then dancing silver. But now the night, the mist and the rain are all around us and Glengariff is more than ever, as it has been to me on the few occasions on which I have visited it, a dark, dank, claustrophobic place. Will the mountains move before morning and push the whole bloody lot of us into the sea? Will the semi-tropical vegetation grow and grow and eat us all up?

"Annexed to the hotel," wrote Titmarsh-Thackeray, "is a flourishing garden where the vegetation is so great that the landlord told me it was all he could do to check the trees from growing: round about the bay, in several places, they come clustering down to the water-edge nor does the salt water interfere with them."

That was 136 years ago and the mountains have not moved since then, nor has the Eccles hotel been devoured by a giant arbutus. So with minds at ease we sit where Shaw sat and where Domhnall Cam O'Sullivan, chieftain of Beare, mustered his people for the final march. We sit also where the holidaymakers, many of them still English, sit and wait for the dinner-bell.

This business of waiting to be summoned by bells (see under Betjeman) to march to the manger is something I first encountered, in Irish hotels, 30 or 40 years ago in the Lake hotel at Waterville, County Kerry. Only in the south-west in those days did you encounter large bodies of Saxons who went thus to dine in a disciplined fashion. Elsewhere in Ireland the rough rugheaded kernes moved towards the tables as soon as they felt snappish or heard the sizzle and smelled the smell of the eternal bacon and eggs.

Here in the Eccles there's a long tradition of people who wait until they're asked. The orderly English, God bless them, are still here. Shure, where else would they go? But the four ladies at the table to my left are from Denmark. The twenty or so people at the long central table are Belgians: fine, big, besweatered young men; bouncing, well-breasted, bespoke girls. Skin-divers, we are told. It's a diverting thought and an aid even to an aged digestion.

Rain or no rain, we walk out after dinner. The advantage of the dark and the downpour is that we are not likely to be kidnapped by boatmen and dragged away, whether we will or no, to the gardens of Garinish island. Unmolested we walk all the way to the village and shelter in a pub. In the inner room overheated hundreds sit on top of each other and suffer from ballads. Ah, the Irish must love music or they wouldn't endure so much for it. God be with the days when a man could talk and have a drink in peace.

Midges, though, are the main menace in modern Glengariff. They wouldn't much have worried Domhnall Cam O'Sullivan who had, I'd say, a pretty thick hide and who, when camped here for the last time 375 years ago, had other things on his mind. Leave the window open for a while, and the lights on, and myriads of Cork midges will be your pillow companions. The Manhattan Islander and myself who share a room make that mistake and, having introduced ourselves to the midges, slip into the room occupied by the Californian and the Limerickman, switch on the lights, leave the windows open. Friends should share everything.

Later when peace is restored and the midges routed by lethal spraying, the four of us sit and drink by a closed window and look across the bay at the baleful brightness from the Oilery on Whiddy Island. All the big talk of a million jobs has refined itself down to a handful of men in charge of enough oil to pollute all the waters from Bantry to Bilbao. So, after the night's last whiskey we kneel down and pray to the statue of St Brendan the Navigator, presented by Gulf Oil to the town of Bantry, that the viscous black gold be contained in the tanks and that Bantry Bay in the morning will be able to laugh back at the sun.

Footnote: We should have kept the prayers up for a long time after that, because since that wet night Bantry Bay has had the full and greasy benefit of what the trade calls major oil-spills.

THE TANKER AND THE ANGRY MOUNTAIN

The stout smiling girl in the shop in Glengariff in which I buy a pair of sunglasses tells me that on the previous night there has been fierce thunder in Croom. We discuss thunder in several of its aspects, touching lightly even on its effect on the giving of milk by cows and the laying of eggs by hens. She also tells me that she comes from Croom. Since my grandfather came from Bruff before he joined the Royal Irish Constabulary and was transferred north, and married a McGovern from Glangevlin, Co. Cavan, and settled, or was settled, in Donegal, I feel there's a certain bond between myself and the stout girl. For sweet Adare, that lovely vale, that soft retreat of sylvan splendour, and Bruff, Bruree and Croom are the cities of the Maigue valley in faraway Limerick as surely as Ballygawley, Aughnacloy, Augher, Clogher and Fivemiletown are the cities of the Clogher valley in further-away Tyrone.

I'm ready to talk to the girl about the Gaelic poets of the Maigue, about Sean O Tuama of the Merriment and the eighteenth-century Courts of Poetry, ready even to sing or at least to hum the *Slan le Maighe*, or Farewell to the Maigue, in the late Sean O Riada's splendid arrangement. But my Californian friend whispers to me that the girl hasn't said Croom. She said Macroom. It turns out that she doesn't even know where Croom is. So that my enthusiasm and eloquence have been wasted exercises. Yet there is every sign that the sunglasses will prove to have been a useful purchase, that all the tempest and rain of last night could have been on another, unsmiling planet. The waters of Bantry Bay are shining in the morning. Tiny islets, like swans, look at their own reflections. Little coloured boats at anchor awake, winking and blinking.

The beauty of the subtropical gardens of Garinish, coloured memorial to Mr Pineto who, in the last century, designed them and to Mr Bryce of Belfast who hired him to do so, is there, dew-wet in the morning, and so on. And to add the final Arcadian touch there's a big baste of an oil-tanker on the far side of the water and every lassie, slipping on the old stone quay, and to her greasy oil-slicked lad a-saying: "You're welcome back from Bahrein to Bantry Bay." Of course, it isn't like that at all. Big modern tankers are as neat as a well-kept pharmacy, and a man in New York, who worked at the business of scouring out the innards of the tankers, told me that they take them somewhere to the Gulf of Mexico to do it. God help the Gulf of Mexico. He said that it was a well-paid job, too, but you had to plan to be out of it by 30. Nobody lasted much longer. He had seen the ones who tried.

This is the road to Seal Harbour. That is the road to Zetland pier. Both names, not lying too easily with the older Gaelic names are pretty obvious reminders that the British navy and its dependants spent a fair amount of time in the land of Beara who may have been a legendary princess from Spain who married into the people of this place long long before the Normans pushed the Sullivans south-west out of Tipperary. She may also never have existed, or simply have been the King of Spain's daughter who sat in the glow of a thousand hearths, moved through a thousand folk tales from the earliest times down to my late lamented friend, Micí Pháidi, in Rann na Feirsde in the Rosses of Donegal. Gap-toothed Micí could explain in detail how the King of Spain's daughter married a boyo who set out on his travels from Burtonport to the Indiacha Thoir, or East Indies, but who, regardless, ended up in Spain where he did well for himself and where he is to this day. At least he was there in the 1940s when Micí was alive.

> Then the wet winding roads,
> Brown bogs with black water,
> And my thoughts on white ships
> And the King of Spain's daughter.

The great tanker across the water is moving seawards—not homing. Does a tanker have a home or just a belly to fill? Whither away, oh splendid ship? Bantry to Bahrein and back again if the Arabs and Israelis don't get in my way. A big belly to be filled and then off sometime to be flushed out, or physicked, in the Gulf of Mexico by men who have to make enough money to be out of the business by the age of 30.

It's a dull thought on a sunny morning by the beauty of Bantry Bay: here, where the Spanish were with guns and gold for O'Sullivan, and the French, "the tall mast tapering on each gallant ship", and the English, and ourselves, God help us, and whoever came before us.

There between the shore and Beare Island was it that the British fleet mustered before Jutland, a sight to see surely as it set out on that doubtful voyage? Once I talked about that to an American friend of mine and he capped the tale by reminding me that he had been a ship's commander in Nimitz's fleet when it spread out across the Pacific. Which, to judge from what he said, was a real circus: his talk had the last cracked echo of the trumpet men heard when they talked of glory. Now, big bellies are filled with black oil to make the world go round and round and round until the wells run dry.

This must—by the great Donal Cam himself—be the hardest land in Ireland. Nor am I forgetting the Rosses nor portions of Connemara. There are razor edges to the slanting buttresses of Hungry hill which is an angry crouching animal of a mountain even in the morning sunlight. This description of the landscape I take from one of the two novels written about this peninsula. It's the better of the two even if, as Peter Somerville-Large points out in his fine book *The Coast of West Cork*, it is historically inaccurate, and the author was one of the most consistent anti-Irish bigots who ever masqueraded as an historian. But the man, while he wasn't much of a novelist, had an eye for landscape and a pen to follow his eye:

> Leaving Hungry Hill on his right Colonel Goring ascended the brook which fell into the sea behind his house—at Dunboy. After climbing sharply for a couple of miles he reached the cradle of the stream in a wide morass. The peat was dry in the clear autumn weather. The air was fresh and delicious and perfumed with heather. On the banks, between which the tiny rivulet trickled along, were patches of rich, green grass where sheep and cattle ought to have been feeding, but there were no signs of either nor of any human creature. Nature was left alone in her wasteful beauty and, as there was no wind, the silence was unbroken save by the croak of a passing raven, the sharp bark of an eagle, the whirr of some old cock grouse whom the dogs had scented at among the moss hags. . . .

That does get something of the great loneliness of the mountain. And here he is, watching the winter morning at Dunboy:

> A warm south-westerly was blowing in from the Atlantic; a swell was breaking on the west end of Beare Island and the clouds hung low on

Hungry hill. But the sky was open in the east and the crests of the waves in the bay were sparkling in the sunshine; while mountains and woods were steeped in the soft purple green which makes the winter landscape in the south of Ireland so peculiarly beautiful.

The Colonel Goring that James Anthony Froude put into that novel, *The Two Chiefs of Dunboy*, was (in reality) one of the landed family, the Puxleys of Dunboy. Long after Froude, Daphne du Maurier was to write about them in *Hungry Hill*, a novel that, as Somerville-Large wryly points out, was somewhat unrealistic in that, being about nineteenth-century Ireland, it didn't mention the famine. Although he does add that there is evidence to show that the famine may not have been as bad just here as in other parts of west Cork. But now, looking at those hard rocks, we wonder: and anyway in such matters comparisons may not mean a great deal.

J. A. Froude who, to put it mildly, didn't think much of the Irish except when they were British soldiers, contracted, down in these mountainy places, some sort of half-assed affection for the shadow or memory of the historic Morty Óg O'Sullivan, the other chief of his novel: wandering soldier and privateer whose dead body was hauled at the stern of an English ship all the way from here to Cork harbour. The tanker would now be ploughing across the path followed by that eighteenth-century ship and the corpse of one of the last of the great O'Sullivans.

The tanker is still very big in the bay as we come down the road into Castletownberehaven. Nearly 35 years ago, and in the middle of a tempest I came here for the first time and a young woman who had been talking to one of the Puxleys told me, among other things, the story of the four wild brothers from Adrigole.

What I remember most about that visit is (i) that it rained for three days and three nights (ii) that I was reading Maxim Gorki and (iii) that one of the two girls in the post-office had worn her way with her toenail through the toe of her right shoe. It was that girl or, perhaps, the other one who told me about the four wild brothers from Adrigole and this was how I afterwards used what she told me in a short story:

Once upon a time there lived four brothers in a rocky corner of Adrigole in west Cork, under the mountain called Hungry hill. Daphne Du Maurier wrote a book called after the mountain but divil a word in it about the four brothers of Adrigole. They lived, I heard tell, according to instinct and never laced their boots and came out

only once a year, to visit the nearest town which was Castletownberehaven on the side of Bantry Bay.

They'd stand there backs to the wall smoking, saying nothing,
contemplating the giddy market-day throng.

One day they ran out of tobacco and went into the local branch of
a certain bank to buy it, and raised havoc because the teller refused to
satisfy their needs. To pacify them the manager and the teller had to
disgorge their own supplies. So they went back to Adrigole to live
happily without lacing their boots, and ever after they thought that
in towns and cities the bank was the place where you bought tobacco.

It rained, as I've said, for three days and three nights and the dark sky,
driven like mad by a gale that came up and down the mountains from
Kerry and Kenmare Bay, was so low you could have touched it if you
cared to take the risk of bringing down worse on your head. Nor could
my companion on that journey nor myself move out of the place until
the rain stopped and the sky cleared. This was why.

He was a photographer and a very good one. The late Aodh de Blacam
had just written for the late Fr Senan Moynihan a study of that marathon
march of O'Sullivan Beare from Glengariff to Leitrim.

The photographer was there to begin the photographs to illustrate the
article. The skies did not favour photography. As for myself I was there
because I was doing an article on Daniel O'Connell's Darrynane House
then about to be converted into a museum and a monument. The photographer had just finished the Darrynane pictures and I was going the rest
of the way for the fun and the curiosity.

Howandever there we were in Castletown and in the downpours of
rain. Thirteen trawlers from Bilbao were blown in out of the storm.
The streets were crowded with little brown men, holy medals around
their necks, deeply religious oaths on their lips, merriment and good
nature in their eyes, bundles of silk stockings and bottles of quite lethal
Iberian brandy under their oxters. The stockings and the brandy they
would barter for anything available. The dances in the hall beside the
hotel were a sight to see. You wouldn't know under God what country
you were in. And the rain rained and the wind blew and the sky licked
the roofs of the houses: and I was reading Maxim Gorki.

It's quite simple how I remember that I was reading Gorki. It was
that bit in his memoirs where he describes how the wooden houses went
on fire in Osharsk Square in Nijni Novgorod now known as Gorkigrad.
The fire crackled like an animal chewing bones. It made real comic

reading when there you were and the heavens urinating on you at the far end of west Cork. The one thing Castletownberehaven was not going to do that season was bloody well go on fire.

One evening when the rain was drawing its breath a bit I walked up and up the slope behind the church, up and up until I was out there on my own and the town well below me. The clouds came at me like buffaloes. To my right hand what would normally have been a simple mountain stream went down like Niagara towards the bay. It was a wonder all out that it didn't take the town with it. Oh far away was that animal of a fire in Osharsk Square, and I thought of Standish O'Grady and a little poem he had written about a mountain stream. After all, that was O'Grady's town, so I quoted him out loud to the torrent to remind it and the weather how they should behave themselves:

> Cloud-begot, mountain-bred,
> Heather-nursed child,
> Innocent, beautiful,
> Winsome and wild:
> Here she comes dancing
> O'er boulder and rock,
> And in many a waterfall
> Shakes her white frock.

A day and a half later the rain eased off: poetry is a slow-working charm.

And one of the two girls who worked in the post-office had worn her way with her toenail through the toe of her right shoe.

She told me about this when she told me how she had been honoured to talk to one of the Puxleys of Dunboy when Brian Desmond Hurst and the actors and cameramen were there, briefly before, working on the movie based on the Du Maurier novel. There she was, she said, ashamed of her life, talking to Miss Puxley and her toe peeping out like a rabbit. So she put her left foot over the toes of her right foot and stood like that, balancing as well as she could until she noticed that the lady was balancing in the same way, except that her right foot was hiding the toes of her left foot: and the girl didn't know and never would whether there was or was not a hole also in the lady's shoe, or whether that was just the way the gentry stood, like herons, you know, or storks or flamingoes.

She was a lively west Cork brunette and I'll never know now whether or not she was making it all up. The other girl was blonde. It was a long time ago and, as I've said, you wouldn't have known, what with the rain and the men from Bilbao, what country you were in. Nor can I recall for certain which of the girls told me about the four wild brothers who lived according to instinct in the rocky wilderness of Adrigole.

A MEMORY OF DARRYNANE

That photographer was a tall man, he dressed very well, smoothed his hair all to one side. He was a reserved class of a man, spoke little, but he sang, on suitable occasions and when asked, in a good light tenor. He walked before me to the door of Darrynane House and knocked the knocker. Since the housekeeper, an elderly lady, was very deaf we were never to know how she heard the knocker, but she did, and the door opened. Perhaps the knocker made some special vibe (as the kids say) and so got to places to which the human voice could not reach. For when we told her that we were two men from a magazine in Dublin she said graciously that we were welcome and more than welcome, but that she wouldn't have much time to show us the house and the historic things in it because at any minute she was expecting two men from a magazine in Dublin.

We followed her. We meditated on a swallow's flight and on an aged woman and her house, and on the hoary joke about the pathetic plight of the two deaf motorists. The first motorist is parked on the side of the road and the second pulls up beside him and asks him is he short of petrol, and the first says he isn't, that he's short of petrol, and the second says okay so, I thought you were short of petrol—and drives on.

Several times we said again who we were but fifteen minutes later she said she must leave us, that she thought there was somebody at the door and that, as easily as not, it might be the two men from the magazine in Dublin. By that time we had inspected the pair of duelling pistols—had one of them killed that foolish man, D'Esterre?—and I had posed for a picture holding the brutal blunderbuss that was said to have belonged to Robert Emmet; and had stood at the dainty standing-writing-desk at which the great man used to stand and write, and I had written his name on a sheet of paper to see what it would feel like. And the photographer made his record; the bust of the great man silhouetted in a window as if he were looking from the sunshine into his own house; on the wall a portrait of a continental Count O'Connell, who was also a member of the family; the multi-gabled old house from the outside and from several angles; the interior of the chapel; drooping semi-tropical plants and shrubs, the shore, the mountains, the islands, the slumbrous seclusion of the place.

Later we were rejoined by the housekeeper who told us that that sudden noise had not been the two men from the magazine in Dublin, that they had not been standing on the threshold, and that perhaps their car had broken down on the way. Then we were joined by two members of the family who got through to her that we were the reely-reely two men from the magazine in Dublin. We all laughed at the joke, the lovely old lady wiping the tears from her eyes and saying that, honest to God, it hadn't occurred to her that men from magazines would look just like ordinary people. There wasn't so much media moving about in rural places in those days.

We sat in a drawing-room that was crammed with the past but was still a pleasant and cheerful room. We sipped tea and talked at our ease and felt very content. We looked out the wide windows at the trees bending in the autumn wind and the flung spray white against the rocks that rimmed the bay. We remembered that Daniel O'Connell had had his own poet, an O'Sullivan, who was also a postman, and who on the high ridge of Coomakesta used to sing welcome to the Liberator. From which O'Connell would go down to the place where his people had lived for so long in ancient secretive peace. His grandfather had entertained a man called Smith who wrote a history of Kerry and had given him valuable information for that history. But that was well back in the eighteenth century at a time when visitors were not all that welcome at Darrynane, and that particular O'Connell had written to Smith:

We have peace and comfort here, Mr Smith. We love the faith of our fathers and, amidst the seclusion of these glens, enjoy a respite from persecution. If man is against us, God is for us. He gives us wherewithal to pay for the education of our children and enough to assist their advancement in the Irish brigade; but if you mention me or mine, the solitude of the seashore will no longer be our security. The Sassenach will scale the mountains of Derrynane, and we shall be driven upon the world without house or home.

By the time of the power of the great Daniel that secretiveness was no longer necessary and in 1833, very much in the style of a man who had read MacPherson's "Ossian", he was writing to William Fagan in Cork about the sanative effects a return to Darrynane had on him: the calm and quiet of his loved native hills, the bracing air purified as it comes over the world of waters:

. . . the majestic scenery of these awful mountains whose wildest and most romantic glens are awakened by the cries of my merry beagles, whose deep notes, multiplied one million times by the echoes, speak to my senses as if it were the voice of magic powers commingling, as it does, with the eternal roar of the mighty Atlantic that breaks and foams with impotent rage at the foot of our stupendous cliffs. Oh! these scenes do revive all the forces of natural strength. . . .

And visitors followed him there to see the great tribune at home. Puckler-Muskau, the German prince, in the autumn of 1828, lost his way on the uncertain road from Kenmare, arrived miserably late at night, expecting to find everyone in bed, but instead heard sounds in the house and a handsomely-dressed servant appeared, bearing silver candlesticks, and opened the door of a room in which at a long table, at wine and dessert, sat fifteen or twenty persons. No deaf old lady told him that she hadn't time to show him around because she was expecting a prince from Germany. But a tall handsome man, "of cheerful and agreeable aspect rose to receive me, apologising for having given me up in consequence of the lateness of the hour, regretted that I had made such a journey in such terrible weather, presented me in a cursory manner to his family who formed the majority of the company, and then conducted me to my bedroom. This was the great O'Connell."

Puckler-Muskau was only one of the many who had a prince's welcome at the end of a wearying journey: and the only person to resent and regret the hospitality of the place was possibly the first representative of the media to cross these mountains. Mr Foster of the London *Times* came, smarting from the attacks of O'Connell's terrible tongue, to prove— mostly on the argument that windowpanes were then uncommon in Kerry cabins—that O'Connell's wickedness as a landlord made a mockery of all his talk of liberty. He refused the offer of hospitality because he suspected that Dan would later say: "This man broke bread with me and now he vilifies me." Indeed, and Dan might have. Yet Foster was a begrudger: nor was it all that usual for a media man to turn down the offer of a decent kip. The two men from the Dublin magazine didn't act like that and, although Dan himself was no longer there, they enjoyed and long remembered the hospitality of his house.

But that visit of the photographer and myself to Darrynane over the mountains in Kerry was exactly 36 years ago: and, here and now, there are four of us finally arrived at the ruins of Dunboy in west Cork, and between Dunboy and Darrynane we have much matter for meditation on the ancient homes of the ultimate south-west.

G

BIRDS AND BENWEEDS AT DUNBOY

Was it the Cornish miners that the Puxleys brought in to dig the copper in the coves of west Cork who brought with them also the Japanese fuchsia, Deora De, the tears of God? Cornwall, I've heard, was the first place it was ever seen in these islands. It blooms well along this Bantry shore as it does all along the north-west and west and south-west, achieving a particular glory in the Dingle peninsula. A good friend of mine feels that the fuchsia has some sort of almost mystical connection with the Gaeltacht and the Irish language. This could scarcely be so, considering its faraway origins, and that story that the planters and their workmen brought it in. The mystical thing is only in seawind and weather and in my friend's coloured imagination: although if I wanted to be facetious about it I could remember that I did meet in Seattle, USA, a Japanese girl who was learning Irish on her own out of O'Growney's book[4] and doing very well at it—and fuchsia grows well in and around Seattle.

The miners have gone from the Beare peninsula and the oil-tankers have come to Bantry Bay, and the Puxleys have gone from Dunboy. The birds and the benweeds here proclaim impermanence as distinctly as the two vast and trunkless legs of stone that Ozymandias left behind him in the desert. Even in decay there is something slightly vulgar about the gaunt eyeless ruin of the Puxley mansion when compared with the desolate, tragic, quietude where O'Sullivan's fort of Dunboy had its bloody and heroic end.

There are campers and a few trailers irrelevantly by the edge of the water.

The Manhattan Islander is a Sullivan. He is very quiet as we go under the great trees to the knoll on the point, and the scant ruins of the fort. For a man of the name the place must have something more than mystical. Or for a Geoghegan of the clan of Richard, the wild captain, who in an effort to blow the whole place to the moon, and the invading English and the Queen's Irish and himself with it, died here 377 years ago where the great hall of the fort then was!

"An immense piece of the works tumbled in ruins, carrying with it the men and burying the soldiers under the fallen stones. The royalists rushed in through the breach; the besieged overwhelmed them with shot and stones, ran them through with pikes, slew them with swords, advanced barriers, rolled up stones, and drove them headlong out again. . . ."

There isn't a sound to be heard here and now but the wind in the trees, the birds, the sucking of the water about the rocks. . . .

There lay a great heap of bodies and arms, the whole hall ran streams of blood. For the greatest part of the defenders (120 in all) fell, especially the captain, Richard Geoghegan, whose high spirit was defending the chieftaincy (of O'Sullivan) with the valour of his race. Fighting with the utmost vigour he fell amongst the corpses, covered with many deadly wounds and half dead.

The man from Manhattan stands on a mound and surveys his inheritance through a polaroid camera. There is one tall white yacht on the sunny water over which Carew came and through which 200 years later the body of Morty Óg O'Sullivan, the privateer, was dragged at the stern of an English ship . . .

Richard who was still alive, when he heard the voice of the English, recalled his fading spirit and tried to set fire to the gunpowder of which there was no mean store in the fort. And undoubtedly he would have blown up the enemy were it not that, before he had accomplished his object, life had failed him. . . .

Are the bones, or is the dust, of Captain Richard, still somewhere under these mounds on this quiet morning? That Geoghegan, the nineteenth-century poet, who wrote, "The Monks of Kilcrea", and "The Ballad of Tyrellspass", must often have come to this place. Kilcrea is not so far away, over there beyond the Pass of Kimaneigh and Gougane Barra and Aghris (Eachros), that saucer in the Muskerry mountains where his favourite horse died under the great O'Sullivan, and gave the place its name. . . .
"The treaty and compact was kept with English scrupulosity, for men and women were hanged. All are not agreed as to the number of assailants who perished, some say 600, others less, others more. . . ."
Fifty-eight plus twelve of the Irish were hanged in Castletown, and Thomas Taylor, an Englishman, was hanged in Cork; and there was slaughter on Dursey Island, and Dominic Collins, a Jesuit lay-brother, was taken back to his native Youghal and being "dragged at the tails of horses, hanged with a halter, and his breast being cut open with sharp knives he rendered his soul to God in the year 1602, on the last day of October".
All quiet now, not a sound on the air, not a ghostly voice except that voice I have just quoted: of Don Philip O'Sullivan, nephew of Domhnall

Cam, speaking bitterly out of Spain about the last bloody battle in a terrible war. For extra effect the Californian in our company reads the words out loud. California in a way is as close to Spain as is Castletownberehaven.

Yet to be reasonable about it all—as even in Ireland one may try to be almost four centuries later—this place must also have its significance for a Carew. Because long before George, the greatest and toughest of that clan, and president of Munster for the English queen, came by Bantry and Beare Island to destroy O'Sullivan, there was another Carew who thought he had some ancient right to this part of the world. As well as which, it was a pretty considerable achievement to storm the last stronghold of the man who held out after the great O'Neill had submitted and who marched, before he crossed the seas, to seek his master in the mountains of Tyrone.

And to be more reasonable still the place must also have its significance for a Puxley. They lived here for a long time in this land of green beauty and iron rock and wide water, and had their own ambitions and good intentions, and left it also in flames and ruin. None of which arguments neither a Flanagan from California nor a Hanley from Limerick nor a Kiely from Tyrone would care to advance to a Sullivan from Manhattan who has come a long way to walk his native heath, nor indeed to any Sullivan still resident anywhere along that hard peninsula.

For Peter Somerville-Large records that though the IRA of the 1920s said the mansion was burned because the British might have used it as a billet, it could also be true that it might have met its doom simply because it belonged to the unpopular Puxleys, tough landlords who liked neither tenants nor trespassers. Yet shall some tribute of regret be paid and Somerville-Large quotes the English butler, Albert Thomas, on the last ruin of Dunboy:

> One night I was called up (in the British garrison on the island where he was in refuge) and was shown a very large glow in the sky overlooking the castle about a mile away. The rebels had burned the castle down as they said they would. I was very sorry, sorry for all the lovely old silver, the beautiful glass and splendid linen all being burnt, all those gorgeous statues and pictures, the wonderful drawing-room all burning for what? One can sometimes understand war with all its horrors, but this seemed to me a very wanton thing to do.

Indeed and indeed, Albert, and you were a very understanding man. As for myself I make no pretence to understanding the craziness, the infamy, the destructive lust of my species—including myself. Or the greed and the robbery. In this place there has been an awful lot of blood and burning.

The tall white yacht moves like a queen over the water that Beatty's battleships traversed on the way to the blood and burning of Jutland. It nods with hauteur, you might say, towards the white lighthouse on the tip of the island. It stands out over the swell of the open sea.

The Valley of a Million Sheep

The Pass of Keimaneigh, I maintain, was never the same since they widened the road. The machines and the men that did the dirty work took away with them the sense of Gothic gloom, of precipice and over-hanging crag, of clansmen lurking behind rocks and ready to leap out with what used to be called an earsplitting yell. That was in the days when the world was quiet enough to allow you to hear a yell!

> *Come one, come all, this rock shall fly*
> *From its firm base as soon as I.*

At least that was the way Keimaneigh was when I first saw it, not unlike a moment in the verse of Sir Walter Scott whom, possibly for good reasons, nobody reads any more.

And I was the more impressed by the place when I thought how O'Sullivan Beare had led his people over the pass when there was no road there but only a mountain track: and headed north on the long wintry march towards the country of O'Rourke.

"But," says Sullivan from Manhattan, "it's unlikely that on the march Donal Cam O'Sullivan crossed Keimaneigh at all. Wilmot and his tough Elizabethans and renegade Irish were just over here, and O'Sullivan may have been forced further west up the wild valley of Coomhola and then over the ridge, and a rocky one it is, and so into Gougane Barra—where we know he was."

The argument begins. Not that either of us were there to see what mountain path O'Sullivan and his people crossed to St Finbarr's holy place by the quiet lake in the silence of the valley. But to keep the Manhattan man happy and since he has taken a fancy not only to his theory but to the valley it involves, we swing sharp left from Bantry Bay, by the Coomhola river and the Borlin valley, and face ourselves in the general direction of Kilgarvan and the mountains of Kerry.

Aodh de Blacam when he was writing about O'Sullivan's march⁵ did, though, take cognisance of the variant Coomhola–Keimaneigh routes. In favour of Keimaneigh he cited A. M. Sullivan, not perhaps the world's most exact scientific historian, but he did know the place he was talking about and in such matters that knowledge can be of more importance than all the State papers ever concocted by salaried and certified liars. But against A. M. Sullivan, De Blacam did in 1946 find some local shanachies to say that Domhnall the Crooked turned inland at a place called Snave and marched up Coomhola, "on a road which rises steep and fearsome to twist over the mountain tops northward to Kilgarvan". It does indeed, just that.

At a height of about 1,000 feet the column would leave the road and face a great wall of crags that seems to hang against the western sky. The merest sheep-paths cross between the summits of Bealick (1,764 feet) and Foilastookee (1,698 feet)—yet O'Sullivan's men and horses and the womenfolk and the baggage, would have to be got over: and behold, beneath their feet, 1,200 feet below, the holy valley of Gougane Barra (Gabhagan Barra, St Finbarr's mountain hollow). The column has marched some twenty odd miles at this point.

Very odd miles they were indeed, and that rugged passage is a fair description of a rugged terrain and my sympathy goes out to anybody who would have to go walking there on a winter's day. But this morning the sun is shining on wild Coomhola and we go up and up until we come to that place where the crags seem to hang against the eastern sky. They don't even seem to—they do hang.

Below us is the sweep of the valley, widening from nothing in the grey-brown mountains down to deep-green pasture-land. The river winds in the most approved style. The farmhouses are square and white and solid. No poverty, by God, in this part of the world. Never in my life nor in my nightmares have I heard so many sheep—heard rather than seen. Thousands of them. Say a million for the sake of easy accountancy. Their mouth-noises after a while seem to disturb the primeval peace even more than the noise of engines. Bleats and meh-meh-mehs by the million, and nonstop, while in the sky the larks still gaily singing fly, scarce heard amid the sheep below.

We sit on the roadside and forget about the great O'Sullivan and his marathon march and meditate instead on the price and succulence of mutton and on the obvious advantages of being a sheep-farmer in a wild and beautiful valley in west Cork. Think of what you'd pay for a plate of that in the Hibernian or the Gresham or the Shelbourne in Dublin or in Simpson's on London's Strand. Not to talk of the wool. We wonder how you get into the business: two professors, a public official and myself. Listening to the bleats might be the hardest part of it. Peter Somerville-Large's book on these places reminds us that the pockets of fields north of the Miskish range over there, which seem exquisitely rich and green, were once known as the fields of a Thousand Cattle. So this is the Valley of a Million Sheep.

The Californian, who is a sound Spenserian, reminds us that the Elizabethan poet, before the Doneraile people burned him out and mercifully stopped him writing "The Faerie Queene", had observed that we, the Irish, possibly inherited our custom of booleying from the Scythians. Booleying, or moving out cattle to fresh and wild pastures and "feeding only on their milk and white meats". The English objected to us doing that. Always a sore-assed crowd of begrudgers.

Since we have fine weather and time to spare and a motor-car, advantages that the great O'Sullivan did not have, we go on at our ease towards the Kingdom of Kerry. Another story. Another time.

NOTES

1. *To the Lake of the Salmon*

1. The cottage in which the Carletons lived still stands at Springtown in south Tyrone. A family called McKenna have lived in it since Carleton's father died. In the present "troubles" the cottage was raided again, this time by the Provisional IRA who stole (hijacked) the car belonging to Mrs McKenna's grandson and used it to plant a bomb in the village of Augher. The car went up with the bomb. All for Ireland.

2. *The Elk and the Ponderosa*

1. An anachronism. As a political title, Fenian was not in use until much later.
2. The River Bann and Seamus Heaney.
3. Patriotic poetess (Anna Johnston MacManus) who died in 1902.
4. This is Thomas MacDonagh's English version of "The Yellow Bittern" or, rather, of "An Bunan Buidhe":

> *The yellow bittern that never broke out*
> *In a drinking-bout, might well have drunk;*
> *His bones are thrown on a naked stone*
> *Where he lived alone like a hermit monk.*
> *O yellow bittern! I pity your lot,*
> *Though they say that a sot like myself is curst—*
> *I was sober a while, but I'll drink and be wise*
> *For fear I should die in the end of thirst.*
>
> *It's not for the common birds that I'd mourn,*
> *The blackbird, the corncrake or the crane,*
> *But for the bittern that's shy and apart*
> *And drinks in the marsh from the lone bog-drain.*
> *Oh! if I had known you were near your death,*
> *While my breath held out I'd have run to you,*
> *Till a splash from the lake of the Son of the Bird*
> *Your soul would have stirred and waked anew.*
>
> *My darling told me to drink no more*
> *Or my life would be o'er in a little short while;*
> *But I told her 'tis drink gives me health and strength,*
> *And will lengthen my road by many a mile.*
> *You see how the bird of the long smooth neck*

Could get his death from the thirst at last—
Come, son of my soul, and drain your cup,
You'll get no sup when your life is past.

In a wintering island by Constantine's halls
A bittern calls from a wineless place,
And tells me that hither he cannot come
Till the summer is here and the sunny days.
When he crosses the stream there and wings o'er the sea,
Then a fear comes to me he may fail in his flight—
Well the milk and the ale are drunk every drop,
And a dram won't stop our thirst this night.

5. This, on Brian Merriman, is from Douglas Hyde's *Literary History of Ireland:*

Brian MacGiolla Meidhre or Merriman, whose poem of the "Midnight Court" contains about a thousand lines with four rhymes in each line was [a] native of County Clare. This amusing and witty poem, one certainly not intended "virginibus puerisque", is a vision of Aoibhill [Eevil] queen of the Fairies of Munster, holding a court, where, when the poet sees it, a handsome girl is in the act of complaining to the queen that in spite of her beauty, and fine figure and accomplishments she is in danger of dying unwed and asking for relief. She is opposed by an old man, who argues against her. She answers him again, and the court finally pronounces judgment. Standish Hayes O'Grady once characterised this poem as being "with all its defects, perhaps the most tasteful piece in the language", and it is certainly a wonderful example of sustained rhythm and vowel rhyme. It was written in 1781.

Other authorities say 1780 and dispute the spelling of the Irish version of his name. There are several translations of "Cuirt an Mheadhon Oidhche" (The Midnight Court) by Frank O'Connor, David Marcus, Arland Ussher, the late Earl of Longford (Edward Pakenham), and Patrick C. Power.

When in the late '40s or early '50s the then ludicrous book-censorship banned O'Connor's version as being "in general tendency indecent or obscene" Frank O'Connor said that the only compliment his countrymen had ever paid him was to think that he had written "The Midnight Court". It is possible that the censors, bless them, knew no Irish and that the naked English lifted them. At that time a proposal to erect a memorial to Merriman in the graveyard where he was buried was violently opposed by some members of Clare County Council. *Tempora mutantur*, etc. Today, under enlightened scholars, a Merriman Summer School and Winter School are held annually in Clare: studying various aspects of Irish life.

3. The Star Over Cassidy's Hill

1. In a biographical-critical study of Carleton, *Poor Scholar*, published by Sheed and Ward (London and New York) in the 1940s and recently reprinted by the Talbot Press, Dublin. And in a series of articles commencing in the *Irish Times* on 12 July 1972, in which I pay tribute to T. G. F. Paterson's "The Burning of Wildgoose Lodge" published (from the County Louth Archaeological Journal) by the Dundealgan Press (W. Tempest) Ltd., Dundalk, at the modest price of 20p.

   Carleton wrote about it long after the event and his memory may have been faulty—and he was a creative writer.

   At the moment notable research is being done on the matter and on other aspects of Carleton by Professor Daniel Casey of the University of New York State at Oneonta, from which research, I feel sure, a major work on Carleton will emerge. Professor Casey has the advantage of knowing the land and the people as well as he knows the Catskill Mountains.

4. A Gift of Donegal

1. Ardee, as I've said earlier in "The Star Over Cassidy's Hill", is Baile Atha Fhirdiaidh or the Town of the Ford of Ferdiad: and Ferdiad was the hero, friend of Cuchullain and slain by him in the combat at the ford in our ancestral head-hunting epic, "Táin Bó Cuailgne", or the Cattle Raid of Cooley. The poet Thomas Kinsella has made a most distinguished translation of the Táin.

   The country ballad about the Turfman from Ardee celebrates one of those men who used to cart cut peat to the towns for sale as fuel: nothing at all to do with the other turf on which horses are raced. In my time the ballad has been best sung by my friend Margaret Barry, a singer of the travelling people who has travelled as far west as Boston and as far east as the Albert Hall.

2. Father Tom Finlay was one of two famous brothers, both Jesuits, who flourished in the early years of this century. Father Tom's chief concern, apart from the salvation of his soul, was the advancement of the co-operative movement under the leadership of Sir Horace Plunkett. In his final days in 1939 I had the privilege of meeting him in Linden Convalescent Home in Blackrock, South Dublin, where he talked of the strangest people in words something like this: "Hopkins used to complain to Darlington about nervous headaches and Darlington would say: 'What else can you expect, sitting in your room all day writing rubbish.'" Darlington was the original of the Prefect of Studies in *A Portrait of the Artist as a Young Man*, and Hopkins was, well, Hopkins.

   My memories of Father Tom found their way into a short story called, "A Room in Linden", in the collection, *A Ball of Malt and Madame Butterfly* (Gollancz and Penguin Books).

3. The gentle poet, Sean Gallen, lives in the memories of his friends and in one poem to be found in an anthology compiled by the poets, Valentine Iremonger and Robert Greacen, *Contemporary Irish Poetry*, (Faber 1949)

> "Lines on the Death of a Cat"
> *It is so important that my grief be not absurd.*
> *Some part of me is under earth with the cat:*
> *The black-and-white, the woman-looking cat—*
> *(Children sob for dogs, dead aunts only frighten them)*
> *This is the stammering sincerity of the humbled.*
>
> *It is so important that you should not laugh—*
> *Some life that loved me is sordidly ceased.*
> *Me out of a world of betters this free warm thing*
> *Sought me and me at every instant. Who now*
> *Seeks so? None. I pray you do not smile:*
> *For o it is so important my grief be not absurd.*

5. *To Sligo Town*

1. Edgeworthstown in County Longford has the house (now a hospital run by nuns) that was once the home of the Edgeworth family and in which the mighty atom, Maria, who wrote her novels there was visited by Sir Walter Scott. Gaelic enthusiasts have endeavoured not too successfully to persuade people to call the place by an earlier Gaelic name: Meas Truim, half-Englished as Mostrim. Since the Edgeworth name, and not only for Maria's sake, is to be held in honour, my hyphenated compromise would seem to be both musical and meaningful.
2. "The Pursuit of Diarmuid and Gráinne" is, for my taste, the most colourful and exciting tale of all the tales in our ancient sagas. See *Ancient Irish Tales* by Cross and Slover (Harrap).
3. This poet is Patrick J. O'Rourke of Kiltyclogher, Co. Leitrim.
4. That most valuable book, *The Festival of Lughnasa*, by Maire MacNeill (Oxford University Press) now, alas, out of print and only to be found in libraries. Lughnasa equals the games or festivities in honour of the bright god, Lugh, as opposed to the dark god, Crom Dubh, or for that matter, Balor of the Evil Eye, and the book deals with the sites where the Celtic festival of the first fruits was celebrated by our remote ancestors, memories of the rituals lingering on right into our own times.
5. A lady of ancient lineage, who lives in that area, has a slight quarrel with me about that matter of Red Hugh and the Curlew Mountains. She writes:

> The body of Sir Conyers Clifford, Governor of Connacht, who fell nobly in the battle, protesting to his last breath against the vileness and baseness of his troops, was beheaded when it was found, not in savagery, but in

order that Red Hugh might send the head to O'Conor Sligo who was holding his castle of Collooney in the English interest: to induce him to surrender without further bloodshed. This was achieved.

The following letter was sent to the Constable of Boyle by Conor MacDermot, leading his people during the minority of his nephew, Brian Óg:

"Be it known to you that I have sent the body of the Governor to the monastery of the Holy Trinity (his own family burial place and the object of much pilgrimage where it was an honour to be buried) out of my regard for him as well as for other reasons. If you are willing to exchange some of our people for the aforesaid body, I shall be glad to treat with you on the subject. In any case the body was buried honourably in the aforesaid monastery and so farewell.
Written at Gaywash, 15 August 1599.
Take care however to wrap the body in a good linen winding sheet; and should you wish to bring all the other nobles that have fallen, I shall not prevent you from rendering them that service.

MacDermod.'

I do not think these transactions reveal anything of the savage or the killer ape, and we have *not* improved in four hundred years, whatever the weapons.

6. William Bulfin so writes of O'Rourke's Table in *Rambles in Erin*. Bulfin, a midland man who emigrated as so many midland men used to do, to the Argentine, became editor of the newspaper, *The Southern Cross*. Revisiting Ireland about the turn of the century he cycled here, there and everywhere and wrote articles for his newspaper and developed them into a fine book. A footnote in the book mentions how he visited a Martello tower near Dublin and talked there to a young Englishman and a young poet.

6. Return to Coolbanagher

1. In a novel, *There Was an Ancient House*, published by Methuen in the 1950s.

8. Honeymeadow Revisited

1. Richard Lalor Sheil (1791–1851). Orator, very much in the style of the period, politician and author, and even playwright. As an Irish lawyer of the time he naturally gravitated to politics, first as an anti-O'Connellite but, after a meeting in 1822, Sheil and Daniel O'Connell, the Liberator, became friends, and co-workers in the agitation for Catholic Emancipation. He was born Sheil but in 1830 took also the name of Lalor because he had married his second wife, the widow of Mr Power of Gurteen, who inherited large property in the County Tipperary from her father Mr Lalor of Crenagh.

His first speech in parliament was made, on the Reform Bill, in March 1831. He rose to high eminence in law and politics, was in Florence as ambassador to the court of Tuscany where he died of gout. His speeches are still readable. Gladstone said that, although he had a voice like a tin kettle being battered from place to place, he was a great orator.

2. Charles Joseph Kickham (1826–1882). Born at Mullinahone, County Tipperary. As a member of the Fenians he was imprisoned in 1865, and released, broken down in health, after four years. A man of gentleness and indomitable spirit, his great work, the novel *Knocknagow or The Homes of Tipperary*, was deservedly and for long a national piety. James Maher of Mullinahone, a good friend of mine, a teacher and scholar, devoted himself in many books to keeping the memory of Kickham alive.

3. The rousing drinking ballad about the Bold Thady Quill of Ballinagree in west Cork celebrated, in mock-heroic fashion, the imaginary exploits of a local "character" in athletics, love, politics. His period, according to the internal evidence of the ballad, would have been the 1880s to 1890s. The ballad has been sung, well or ill, by so many ballad groups that quotation would be an insult.

4. Edel Quinn: a devoted member of the religious organisation, the Legion of Mary, went, in spite of frail health, around the third world on missionary work—and died at her task.

9. *All the Way to Bantry Bay*

1. That tall cross was not long ago blown down, not by a bomb but by the wind. *Vanitas vanitatum!*

2. John O'Mahony, the noblest of the Fenian (Irish Republican Brotherhood) revolutionaries, was out in the abortive attempt at revolution made by the Young Irelanders in 1848. He was a pretty well-to-do landowner and a scholar: having even, in Trinity College, Dublin, studied Greek and Latin, of course, but also Hebrew and Sanscrit: he wrote good French, and from the Gaelic did a fine translation of Geoffrey Keating's seventeenth-century history of Ireland.

With James Stephens and Michael Doheny he founded the Brotherhood which, through him, took its poetic title from Fionn Mac Cumhaill and his companions, the heroes of the ancient saga *An Fhiannuidheacht*.

After a long political exile in New York he died in poverty in a garret on 6th Avenue in 1877. His body was brought back to Ireland for one of those great Irish nineteenth-century political funerals: in Ireland everything begins at a funeral. Cardinal Cullen, the head of the Irish Church at the time, refused to allow the remains to lie in any Catholic Church in the archdiocese of Dublin. O'Mahony is buried in Glasnevin cemetery.

From information and insight Douglas Hyde wrote about him a remarkable poem that should be learned by heart by some of the odd fellows of the present who may think that they are walking in the footsteps of the Fenians:

In a foreign land, in a lonesome city,
With few to pity or know or care,
I sleep each night while my heart is burning
And wake each morning to new despair.

Let no one venture to ask my story
Who believes in glory or trusts to fame;
Yes! I have within me such demons in keeping
As are better sleeping without a name.

From many a day of blood and horror,
And night of terror and work of dread,
I have rescued nought but my honour only,
And this aged, lonely, and whitening head.

Not a single hope have I seen fulfilled
For the blood we spilled when we cast the die;
And the future I painted in brightness and pride
Has the present belied and shall still belie.

In this far-off country, this city dreary,
I languished weary, and sad, and sore,
Till the flower of youth in glooms o'er shaded
Grew seared, and faded for evermore.

Oh my land! from thee driven—our old flag furled—
I renounced the world when I went from thee;
My heart lingers still on its native strand
And American land holds nought for me.

Through a long life contriving, hoping, striving,
Driven and driving, leading and led;
I have rescued nought but my honour only
And this aged, lonely and whitening head.

3. Canon (Patrick Augustine) Sheehan, 1852–1913. Born in Mallow, Co. Cork, became a Catholic priest and pastor of Doneraile, in the same county and close to Spenser's Kilcolman. As a young priest he spent some years in Britain or, as we used to, and may still say, "On the English mission". A scholar and very considerable novelist. In the time of George Moore and others, it was *de more* for the Irish literati to pass him by because it seemed impossible to them that in Ireland a man could be both an Irish parish priest and a novelist of note.

Contemporary Irish writers have thought otherwise, to mention only the late Francis MacManus, John Jordan, Con Houlihan and, in all modesty, myself. There is still a tendency to make out of him a national piety but a reading of his novels, beginning with *Luke Delmege*, *The Blindness of Dr Gray*, *The Graves at Kilmorna*, should preserve him from that fate. One of the most interesting things about him is the struggle and the reconciliation in him between his pastoral duties and his part as a recorder of the lives of the people to whose welfare he was devoted.

4. "In October 1899 (Fr) Eugene O'Growney died in San Francisco where he had gone in ill-health. Four years later, in September 1903, he was exhumed. The Gaelic League treated it as a military occasion: they organised a national day of mourning, bringing back his corpse [to Ireland] like that of an exiled revolutionary and strengthening their movement by the very massiveness of the assembled multitude." See *passim, The Scholar Revolutionary: Eoin MacNeill, 1867–1945 and the Making of the New Ireland*, ed. F. X. Martin and F. J. Byrne (Irish University Press, 1973).

   O'Growney's statue is to be seen outside the Catholic Church in Athboy, Co. Meath. For twenty or more years his famous "Book" was the *vade mecum* of teachers and learners of Irish.

5. Aodh de Blacam's article on the marathon march of O'Sullivan Beare appeared in *The Capuchin Annual* in 1947. It has not, alas, been reprinted as a separate book and the *Annual*, again alas, is now defunct.